MIGHTY EIGHTH
WARPAINT & HERALDRY

The 491st Bomb Group's 852nd Bomb Squadron chose to give its Liberators red engine cowling rings as an additional recognition marking. The yellow propeller bosses on B-24J serial 44-40117 3Q:J Hare Power were purely ornamental. The code 3Q is painted in grey, as it was on several other aircraft of this squadron. (USAAF)

MIGHTY EIGHTH
WARPAINT & HERALDRY

ROGER A. FREEMAN

ARMS AND

ARMS & ARMOUR PRESS
An imprint of the Cassell Group
Wellington House, 125 Strand, London WC2R 0BB

Distributed in the USA by Sterling Publishing Co. Inc.,
387 Park Avenue South, New York, NY10016-8810

British Library Cataloguing-in-Publication data:
A catalogue record for this book is available from the
British Library.

ISBN 1 85409 373 8

Edited and designed by Roger Chesneau/DAG
Publications Ltd

Printed and bound in Hong Kong

CONTENTS

INTRODUCTION

A production aircraft bereft of markings is a nonentity, but a warplane, serving with a combat unit in a theatre of operations, displays markings that are all indicative. First, it has nationality by means of national insignia: for the United States Army Air Forces (USAAF) during the Second World War, this varied in colours, composition and form, at set periods, giving an indication of period in the dating of photographs.

Secondly, overall finishes show military requirements: shades are suited to concealment at bases and give some indication of function, with undersurfaces designed to merge into day or night skies. An abandonment of camouflage, such as occurred, reflected air supremacy, and its reintroduction portended a projected move from Britain to Continental bases.

Thirdly, and most important of all, when visible, are identity numbers that set a particular aircraft apart from any other in its Service or, indeed, the world. Linked to existing documentation, it can tell of the units in which it served, missions participated in, damage sustained, modifications incorporated and subsequent fate.

Fourthly, matching the guidons and colours of military units throughout history are the colours and symbols of the large aerial formations down to the badges and colours of individual squadrons. Communication by wireless telegraphy and radio telephony led to the marking of call-signs used in air-to-air and ground-to-air control.

Finally, and most personal and picturesque, are the markings of air and ground crews, giving further identity to their charges by names and associated artwork that reflect the tenor of their times.

These markings are the keys by which aviation historians have over the years given meaning and detail to the photographs that abound of USAAF aircraft. In the same way, from this book, the reader or researcher can similarly find the origins, introductory dates, colours and form of the many and varied markings borne by aircraft of the US 8th Air Force during its wartime service in the United Kingdom.

Scant official records exist that refer to these markings, and where they do it is sometimes the case that the instructions detailed were not in fact effected. Often markings were devised at unit level and simply endorsed by higher command. Brief coverage of 8th Air Force markings is given in the author's *The Mighty Eighth*, first published in 1970. This new compilation greatly enlarges on those details and adds much information that has subsequently come to light.

Markings as decreed in orders could vary in application. The implementation of markings, specified by command, could vary between squadrons of the same Group. Uniformity in marking style was best achieved on stations where a servicing section did the spray application for all its based squadrons, for they were more likely to use the same shade of paint, stencils and other aids. Inevitably, where there was much freehand work, left to the whims and fancies of those in charge of the painters, uniformity was not achieved except when by firm direction from higher command. There was certainly no lack of variety in the adornment of the 8th's aircraft.

For airmen flying these warplanes in combat there was no distinguishing insignia on their uniforms other than rank and medal ribbons where appropriate. At bases it was permissible, and the fashion, to wear a leather flight jacket, the A-2 or similar issue, with the unit 'patch' on the left breast pocket from a pre-war tradition. In general the patch was the representative insignia of the Group or squadron. Because many of these emblems were unofficial they are not recorded in USAF archives. Their representation in this book is of all known insignia of Second World War 8th Air Force Groups and squadrons, to preserve a record of these colourful emblems in the absence of any other source.

Author's Note

Although the full term is 'Bombardment' for Group and squadron designations, the abbreviated forms Bomb Group and Bomb Squadron were commonly used by the USAAF during the Second World War, so these terms are used in this book. Other forms of wartime terminology and designation are also employed, their being in keeping with the period under review.

To distinguish between references to colours and the Official British or United States terms for a particular shade, the former are given in lower case while the latter are given initial capital letters. For example, the British Dark Green was a specific shade from an official colour guide, whereas dark green is any shade coming within that description.

The tailplane and fin of an aircraft in American parlance are known as the horizontal and vertical stabiliser respectively. While it is usual to use British terms in a book published in the United Kingdom, the American terms have been used here since these match more closely the precise instructions issued on markings, some of which are quoted verbatim. For this same reason, the port and starboard sides of an aircraft are given in the American way of left and right respectively.

Imperial measurements for dimensions have been used as these were general for the period and given that way in official USAAF instructions.

Acknowledgements

The collection of material and information for this compilation necessiated approaches to several individuals who were most generous with assistance. They are: John Archer, Richard Atkins, Dana Bell, Quenten Bland, Tom Brittan, Pat Carty, Oliver Daugherty, Jeffrey L. Ethell, Ken Everett, Garry Fry, Mike Gibson, Harry Gobrecht, Ken Godfrey, Rocky Gooch, Steve Gotts, Alan Haig, Ken Harbour, Hjatmar Hellberg, Mrs E. J. Huntzinger, David E. Hubler, Martin Jeffrey, Assy B. Johnson, Ralph A. Johnson, Albert T. Keeler, Patricia Keen, Albert Krassman, Robert E. Kuhnert, Molly and Louis Loevsky, Floyd H. Mabee, Ian McLachlan, Hank North, Merle Olmsted, David Osborne, Orlando Petrillo, Robert Pinson, Pat Ramm, Gordon Richards, Morton Ronson, Robert Sand, Sam Sox, James R. Starnes, George Stebbings, Donald J. Strait, R. C. Sturtivant, Russell A. Strong, Geoffrey Ward, Earl Wassom, Edwin C. Watson, James G. Young and Earl L. Zimmerman. Special acknowledgement is due to Michael Bailey for artistic aid and to Ian Mactaggart who was resonsible for almost all the photographic work required. Bruce Robertson cast a critical eye upon the text and gave valuable editorial guidance. To all these good people I offer my sincere appreciation for their help with this exacting project.

The line drawings are the work of the late Norman Ottaway, avid aviation enthusiast and superb draughtsman.

Roger A. Freeman
January 1997

AIRCRAFT WARPAINT

Aircraft Finishes

The basic colours used on aircraft of the United States Army Air Forces during the Second World War were established in September 1940 as No 41 Dark Olive Drab, No 42 Medium Green, No 43 Neutral Gray, No 44 Black, No 45 Insignia Red, No 46 Insignia White, No 47 Insignia Blue and No 48 Identification Yellow.

At the time of the arrival in the United Kingdom of the first B-17s and C-47s for the 8th Air Force, in July 1942, the finish for USAAF combat aircraft applied at their manufacturing sources was Dark Olive Drab upper surfaces and Neutral Gray lower surfaces. These shades were a matt dark green with a brown element and a matt medium grey.

The early Dark Olive Drab, with a high pigment content, was subject to fading, particularly the finish used by Boeing evident on the B-17E models brought to the UK by the 97th Bomb Group and later passed to training units: by 1945 the olive drab had taken on a brownish-purple hue. The diversity of paint composition and manufacturers meant that there were varying degrees of fade, most pronounced on early B-17Fs but less so on B-17Gs. An idea of the measure of fade can be seen in photographs showing the contrast between old and new paints after skin repairs have been painted with olive drab.

The USAAF agency responsible for paint supply was Materiel Command. Despite their issue of a specification and paint 'chips', Dark Olive Drab appeared in slightly varying shades from manufacturing sources. In the spring of 1943 a combined Army-Navy specification for camouflage colours was adopted and Dark Olive Drab 41 was replaced by a slightly greener shade eventually identified as ANA Olive Drab No 613. However, considerable quantities of No 41 were in stock and it was still in use well into 1944.

The USAAF Technical Order covering aircraft paintwork was T/O 07-1-1 and the issue dated April 1941 recommended that Medium Green shade No 42 be used to break up the outline of the upper surfaces of wings and empennage. This was effected on many of the early B-17F and B-24D models that the 44th, 91st, 93rd, 303rd, 305th and 306th Bomb Groups brought to the UK in the autumn of 1942. This suggests that the application was carried out at modification centres after manufacture, and it is known that some of the work was done in the UK. Medium Green, being a darker, greener shade, than Dark Olive Drab, contrasted more so as the latter

Right: Dark Earth equivalent applied over Dark Olive Drab in a disruptive pattern to B-17E 41-9023, which also has the undersurfaces oversprayed with the US shade equivalent to the British Sky. This aircraft came to the UK with the 97th Bomb Group and carried General Ira Eaker on VIII Bomber Command's first heavy bomber mission, 17 August 1942. Photographed at Bodney in the summer of 1944, *Yankee Doodle* was serving the 322nd Bomb Squadron in a communications role and carried the letters LG:X. The motif was derived from that unit's official emblem. (Via Sam Sox)

Left, upper: Medium Green blotching along the edges of flight surfaces show clearly on B-17F 41-24453 LG:O of the 322nd Bomb Squadron, 91st Bomb Group (nearest camera), photographed early in 1943. The stars of the cocardes on wing and fuselage have been dulled to a pale grey. The dark green patch below the tail number is where the call-letter O was painted out at the time fuselage letters were applied. An original combat machine of the squadron, this aircraft was lost on the first Schweinfurt mission, 17 August 1943. (USAF)

Left, lower: A good example of Dark Olive Drab fade is seen on this 92nd Bomb Group B-17G abandoned on Asch airfield after extensive battle damage during a November 1944 mission. Radar-equipped, it had served with the 422nd Bomb Squadron, 305th Bomb Group, until transferred to the 92nd in August 1944. The dark green used to paint out the code letters JJ shows under the code UX. The contrast between the faded olive drab and Medium Green of the centre fin and the rudder is equally pronounced. (John Quincey)

Below: Goodbye to camouflage. An early 'silver' Fortress rides high over Germany, spring 1944. This B-17G, 42-107175 FR:Z of the 525th Bomb Squadron, 379th Bomb Group, displays the olive drab panel in front of the pilots' windshield and similar anti-glare paintwork on the upper, inner sides of engine nacelles. Discoloration of the nacelles caused by fumes and heat also shows in this photograph. The letter K of the 379th Bomb Group's marking is bare metal and achieved by masking. (Edmund Lutz)

faded, which was noticeable after only a few months' exposure to bright sunlight.

The 97th Bomb Group's B-17Es had three distinct camouflage finishes: the standard Dark Olive Drab uppersurfaces and Neutral Gray undersurfaces; Dark Olive Drab and Dark Earth in a disruptive pattern on upper and Sky (a light blue-grey), on undersurfaces; and a British scheme of Dark Earth and Medium Green shadow-shading with Deep Sky undersides. Shadow-shading, originally the British Air Ministry term for a disruptive pattern of two camouflage colours, was also used in some early US references to camouflage. The purpose of the disruptive pattern was to break up the outline of an aircraft when viewed against an airfield background. A few Fortresses in production for the RAF when the United States came into the war were diverted for USAAF use, retaining the camouflage paintwork specified by the British. Dark Earth was a medium brown, and Medium Green was substituted for the RAF Dark Green shade, although manufacturers were informed that Dark Olive Drab could be used in lieu of Dark Green. For high-altitude operations the RAF had requested Deep Sky, a dark azure blue, and some Fortresses were painted with the US-manufactured product of this shade known as Deep Sky. Only one or two of the Fortresses originally intended for the RAF in this scheme reached the 8th Air Force. However, several of the

97th's B-17Es were shadow-shaded with Dark Earth over the Dark Olive Drab while undersurfaces were Sky, a very pale blue-grey shade often referred to as 'duck-egg blue'. This last-named was a mixture originally prepared for RAF requirements. While existing records are ambiguous on this matter, it appears that an order was issued that USAAF aircraft destined for operations from the UK should be painted in what were described as UK colours, akin to the disruptive pattern applied to B-17s originally destined for the RAF. Approximately 35 B-17Es that were to equip the 97th Bomb Group for its overseas movement were thus painted at a depot or modification centre before this work was stopped in May 1942 as a result of protests about the 60lb of added weight, as quoted in official correspondence, by overspraying the existing olive drab and grey finishes.

A feature of most camouflaged B-17F/G models from the Boeing factory was the darker green of the main fin section. This resulted from the sub-contractor manufacturing this part using what is believed to have been Medium Green 42 instead of Dark Olive Drab 41 prior to delivery. To avoid adding extra weight this section was not oversprayed on the B-17 production line. When camouflage was discontinued several early production B-17Gs in natural metal finish received these painted fin sections until supplies were brought into line.

The Dark Olive Drab used by fighter aircraft manufacturers was far more durable and less given to fade. In combat service it became common practice for ground crews to polish the leading edges of a fighter's wings and empennage with beeswax, or a similar product, to provide greater speed. Despite this compromising the matt finish of the paintwork, authority does not appear to have objected to such enterprise. This polishing accounts for the sheen often seen in photographs of camouflaged P-47s and P-51s.

Most direct-purchase aircraft ordered by the British and later supplied under Lend-Lease from US manufacturers, prior to America's involvement in the war, were finished in US paint matches of the RAF camouflage colours Dark Earth, Dark Green and Sky. The first was a medium brown, the Dark Green a shade somewhere between the USAAF Medium Green and Dark Olive Drab, and Sky as described above, although the US match was inclined to be more greyish than blue. In March 1942 the Joint Aircraft Committee, set up to rationalise various aspects of production having USAAF, USN and British representation, issued a recommendation on aircraft colours in which Dark Olive Drab could be substituted for Dark Green on British deliveries. However, Douglas Bostons, Bell Airacobras and other US-built types originally destined for the RAF but diverted to the 8th Air Force in the UK had the earlier factory paintwork. Exceptions were those aircraft which had been repainted by the RAF when first used for some special purpose. Mostly these aircraft had no change of basic camouflage with the new operators. A few were repainted with the standard USAAF scheme of Dark Olive Drab and Neutral Gray, as also were a few British types used for communications, target-towing and training by 8th Air Force units.

During 1942–43 experiments in the USA on speed gains with various aircraft finishes and endeavours to increase the rate of production of combat models brought proposals for the discontinuation of camouflage finish on many types of aircraft. This was partly influenced by the promise of speed gains ranging from 5 to 25mph and weight savings of between 70 and 80lb on heavy bombers and 15–20lb on fighters which, together with savings in cost and man-hours in application, made the proposal attractive to Materiel Command. War theatre commanders were approached for their views, and in the 8th Air Force some experiments were run by removing the paint from a non-combat B-17 and B-26. The B-17F, serial number 42-29780, had been modified as a transport for use by Headquarters, 3rd Bomb Division; the Marauder was B-26B 41-18014. Both

Right, upper: The first Ford-built B-24H in natural metal finish received by the 389th Bomb Group shines in April sunshine on its Hethel hardstanding. The Base Air Depot applied the 2nd Division 'circle' markings and on this and a few other early deliveries used Insignia Blue until the use of black was notified. Liberator 42-95063 survived the war. (John Driscoll)

Right, lower: A stained and worn Dark Olive Drab and Neutral Gray-finished B-24H of the 707th Bomb Squadron, 446th Bomb Group, shows the typical variation in shades on engine cowlings where a mixture of grey, olive drab and bare metal panels were common on a long-serving veteran. *El Toro—Bull of the Woods* 41-29136 JU:Q was one of the few original 446th combat aircraft to return to the United States in May 1945. (Albert Krassman)

these aircraft appeared in bare metal finish in August 1943.

The advantages were inconclusive, but, in the United States, Materiel Command, insisting that the advantages outweighed the objections, pressed ahead and in October announced plans for discontinuing camouflage paint on most types of combat aircraft. This change came into effect at factories at various dates. The first bare B-17s were accepted from the Vega factory in mid-December 1943 but it was mid-February 1944 before they reached 8th Air Force squadrons. Because these 'silver' aircraft would be conspicuous among their camouflaged brethren they were first concentrated in selected units who did not use them on operations until there were sufficient to compose a Flight or squadron formation. The 457th Bomb Group at Glatton was the first to use bare metal-finished B-17s in strength. Unpainted B-24s did not leave the production lines until February 1944 and the first assigned to an 8th Air Force combat group was B-24J 44-40052, which joined the 389th Bomb Group at Hethel on 6 April 1944. The first natural metal-finish fighters to be seen in combat units were P-38 Lightnings during February 1944. P-47 Thunderbolts and P-51 Mustangs devoid of paint were reaching squadrons in late March. Due to delays, through modifications and repairs, camouflage-finished aircraft of all types were still being despatched from depots to operational units as late as June 1944.

The main benefit derived from discontinuing camouflage painting was the saving in production cost and time. Comparison tests had shown a gain of between 4 and 7mph, with weight-saving dependent on the aircraft size and model. More advantageous figures were claimed in some quarters but, in combat service, there was no appreciable difference in performance between painted and unpainted aircraft. Indeed, some fighter pilots claimed that polished and beeswaxed camouflage finishes gave greater speed than a bare metal finish. In bomber formations operational speed requirements highlighted no speed advantages between the naked and the clad.

With preparations for the cross-Channel invasion well advanced, 8th Air Force HQ anticipated that, once sufficient airfields became available in captured territory, its Fighter Groups could be moved to the Continent, thus reducing combat ranges. As there would then be greater probability of *Luftwaffe* at-

Above: A typical 'in the field' application of dark green to a natural metal finish is worn by P-51B 42-106950 WR:P of the 354th Fighter Squadron, 355th Fighter Group, in July 1944. Only the inner half of the wing surface was painted green, the outer parts remaining bare metal, as did the vertical tail. This was considered sufficient to break up the outline of the aircraft on the ground when viewed from above. However, the reinstatement of the P-51 type identity bands in white can hardly have enhanced concealment. The coloured trim tab was an unofficial maintenance flight identification. (USAF)

tacks on Allied Continental bases, there was some concern as to the vulnerability of bare metal-finished aircraft. In May 1944 VIII Fighter Command advised its Groups, as time permitted, to apply camouflage paint to the upper surfaces of their aircraft. There does not appear to have been a firm instruction on this subject, individual Groups being left to their own devices as to the colours used and the extent of the camouflage applied. In some Groups it was no more than sporadic olive drab or dark green blotching on the upper surfaces of wings and tailplane, whereas, at the other extreme, the entire upper and lower surfaces might be sprayed over. The most prevalent scheme was dark green upper surfaces to more or less the same limitations as laid down in T/O 7-1-1 when camouflage was factory-applied, while undersurfaces remained unpainted. The 78th and 357th were the two Groups that painted upper surfaces dark green and lower surfaces pale blue-grey. The 56th Fighter Group, always individual, used a wide variety of schemes, including many of shadow-shading verging on the exotic. The paints used by the Fighter Groups were largely from RAF camouflage shades, as paint was an item supplied by the British under reciprocal Lend-Lease arrangements.

Escort fighter leaders complained of the difficulty of identifying the other 3rd Division Groups and in October 1944 the Division's Headquarters put forward a plan whereby each Combat Wing would have the vertical tail surfaces painted a different colour—red, green and yellow were suggested—with a coloured diagonal band thereon to distinguish each Group. This idea was not acted upon and an alternative suggestion featured markings on the upper right and lower left wing surfaces. As proposed in a memorandum of 3 November, each Combat Wing would be identified by a device made up of 4ft wide bands in a different colour for each Group of the Combat Wing, red, yellow and black. The 4th Combat Bomb Wing was to use a chevron, the 13th a diagonal band, the 45th a T shape, the 92nd two parallel bands and the 93rd a single band. During November the two Groups of the 92nd Combat Bomb Wing were taken under the operational control of the 4th Combat Bomb Wing and on 1 December this organisation instigated a trial of the proposed new wing markings, now expanded with chevron devices for the added Groups. The 94th Bomb Group used red, the 385th yellow and the 447th dark blue. The additional Groups had one arm of the chevron one colour and the other arm another colour, the 486th Bomb Group using red and blue and the 487th red and yellow. The chevron was to be centred on the wing leading edge opposite the aileron with $10^1/2$ft arms of 4ft width. In practice, when adopted, the positioning, length and width varied, and in most cases the width was reduced to 3ft. Each device was reckoned to consume a quarter of a US gallon of paint and the same amount of turpentine, and cover 75 square feet.

A survey from the Division's Fighter Groups during the first week of January 1945 found the coloured wing devices wanting in visibility and a general request for better tail markings was made. On 7 January the 3rd Division issued revised markings for both wings and tails. The 4th Bomb Wing Groups were to have the chevron device on the vertical tail surfaces, with the apex towards the top of the fin and the same colours as used for the already applied wing markings. The 13th Combat Bomb Wing Groups were to have the diagonal wing stripe, as previously advised, plus a stripe of the same colour adjacent to the trailing edge of the fin and rudder. The T-shaped device originally proposed for the 45th Combat Bomb Wing Groups was replaced by two parallel stripes on both wings and vertical tail surfaces, while the 93rd Combat Bomb Wing markings would remain unchanged. However, the 4th Bomb Wing had already proposed that its B-17s should have their fins and rudders painted yellow and bands of different colours painted round the fuselages for Group identification—red for the 94th, yellow for the 385th, green for the 447th, black or brown for the 486th and no bands for the 487th. Further dialogue with Division HQ saw this idea approved, the tail chevron being considered less effective.

The 4th Bomb Wing was instructed to run a trial with these markings. This met with satisfaction from the fighter leaders, so on 4 February notification was given that yellow markings were to be applied to all B-17s of its Groups. In the meantime the 3rd

Below: The 56th Fighter Group was the first 8th Air Force organisation to introduce coloured nose markings as a form of unit identification. These are 63rd Fighter Squadron Thunderbolts marshalled for take-off at Boxted in August 1944. The aircraft on the extreme left has a field-applied coat of medium green on the upper surfaces. (Mark Brown/AF Academy)

and 25th Reconnaissance Groups, respectively, retained the PRU Blue finish common to these types.

The first 8th Air Force operations under cover of darkness involved experimental bombing and leaflet-dropping activities. B-17s used for these purposes retained their normal daytime camouflage, the leaflet-dispensing aircraft eventually having their undersurfaces sprayed black. Experiments both in Britain and the United States showed that a very high gloss black paint had advantages in reflecting bright light, instead of silhouetting, so making aircraft less visible when caught in searchlights. The US product, known as Jet 622, was first applied to the undersides of Leaflet Squadron B-17s and in a few cases an overall coat was given. B-24s received by this unit were eventually given overall coats of black, as were the Carpetbagger B-24s. Many, however, were painted with British-supplied paint, mostly the standard black used on night bombers for only in later months was sufficient Jet 622 avail-

able. It appears that these aircraft which received a coat of dull black from British sources were rarely, if ever, repainted with the gloss black material.

In January 1945 a small number of OA-10 Catalina amphibians were received by the 8th Air Force for use by the 5th Emergency Rescue Squadron. Canadian-built, the OA-10s had an overall white finish that RAF Coastal Command found gave the most effective camouflage from sea level on anti-submarine patrol flights. The white was matt finish except for the special hard-wearing under-hull paint, which had a high gloss.

National Insignia

The national insignia for military aircraft at the time of the United States' entry in to the Second World War was a device known as a cocarde, composed of a red disc centred in a white five-pointed star, contained in a blue disc. The standard placement of the national insignia on service aircraft was then on the

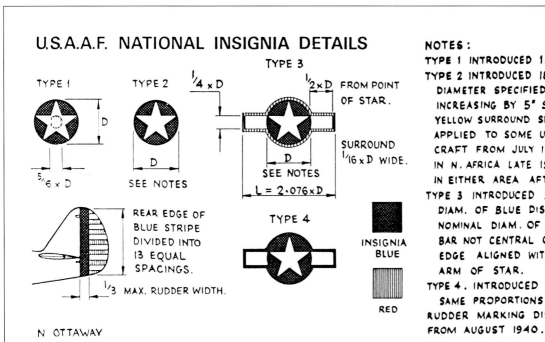

U.S.A.A.F. NATIONAL INSIGNIA DETAILS

TYPE 3

TYPE 1   TYPE 2   ¼ x D   ½ x D FROM POINT
OF STAR.

D

⁵⁄₆ x D   SEE NOTES   SURROUND
¹⁄₁₆ x D WIDE.

D
SEE NOTES
L = 2·076 x D

REAR EDGE OF
BLUE STRIPE
DIVIDED INTO
13 EQUAL
SPACINGS.

TYPE 4

INSIGNIA
BLUE

⅓ MAX. RUDDER WIDTH.

RED

N OTTAWAY

NOTES :
TYPE 1 INTRODUCED 1. JAN. 1921
TYPE 2 INTRODUCED 18. AUG. 1942
   DIAMETER SPECIFIED 20" MINIMUM
   INCREASING BY 5" STEPS.
   YELLOW SURROUND SPECIFIED 2" WIDE
   APPLIED TO SOME U.K. BASED AIR-
   CRAFT FROM JULY 1942. ALSO USED
   IN N. AFRICA LATE 1942. NOT USED
   IN EITHER AREA AFTER APRIL 1943.
TYPE 3 INTRODUCED 29. JUNE 1943
   DIAM. OF BLUE DISC TAKEN AS
   NOMINAL DIAM. OF MARKING.
   BAR NOT CENTRAL ON DISC - UPPER
   EDGE ALIGNED WITH HORIZONTAL
   ARM OF STAR.
TYPE 4. INTRODUCED 17. SEPT. 1943
   SAME PROPORTIONS AS TYPE 3.
RUDDER MARKING DISCONTINUED
FROM AUGUST 1940.

upper surface of the left wing, the lower surface of the right wing, and both sides of the fuselage between trailing edge of wing and leading edge of the tailplane, preferably mid-way. Officially the wing cocardes were to fit at nine-tenths of the chord less the ailerons and to be of seven sizes only: 30, 35, 40, 45, 50, 55 and 60in. Fuselage insignia were to

Below: A War Weary P-47D 42-7938 serving the 306th Bomb Group for formation monitoring in the spring of 1945 still had the old cocarde marking on the underside of the wing, indicative of the lack of concern about the type of national insignia displayed on USAAF aircraft in the ETO. This Thunderbolt had once been the personal aircraft of 56th Fighter Group ace David Schilling. (USAAF)

NATIONAL MARKING – TYPES AND PROPORTIONS

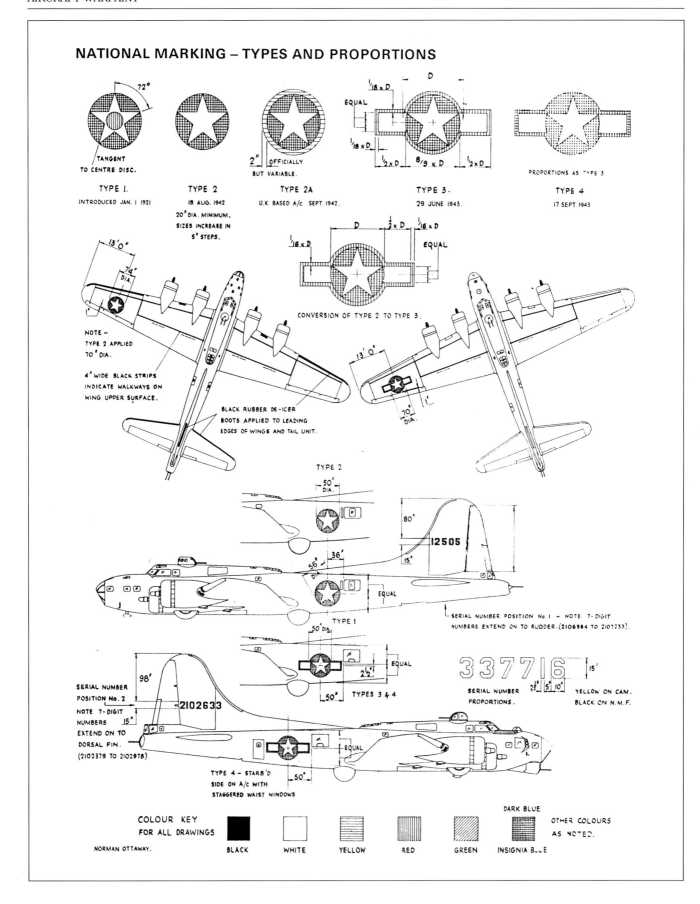

72°

TANGENT TO CENTRE DISC.

TYPE I.
INTRODUCED JAN. 1 1921

TYPE 2
18 AUG. 1942
20" DIA. MINIMUM.
SIZES INCREASE IN
5" STEPS.

2" OFFICIALLY BUT VARIABLE.

TYPE 2A
U.K. BASED A/c SEPT. 1942.

D
⅛ x D
EQUAL
⅛ x D
½ x D
8/9 x D
½ x D

TYPE 3.
29 JUNE 1943.

PROPORTIONS AS TYPE 3

TYPE 4
17 SEPT. 1943

13' 0"
74" DIA.

NOTE –
TYPE 2 APPLIED
70" DIA.

4" WIDE BLACK STRIPS
INDICATE WALKWAYS ON
WING UPPER SURFACE.

BLACK RUBBER DE-ICER
BOOTS APPLIED TO LEADING
EDGES OF WINGS AND TAIL UNIT.

D
2 x D
⅛ x D
⅛ x D
EQUAL

CONVERSION OF TYPE 2 TO TYPE 3.

13' 0"
70" DIA.

TYPE 2

50" DIA.

80"
12505
15"

56" DIA.
36"

EQUAL

SERIAL NUMBER POSITION No.1 – NOTE 7-DIGIT
NUMBERS EXTEND ON TO RUDDER. (2106984 TO 2107233).

TYPE 1.

50" DIA.

EQUAL
2½"

TYPES 3 & 4

50"

337716
15"
2" 5" 10"
SERIAL NUMBER PROPORTIONS.
YELLOW ON CAM.
BLACK ON N.M.F.

98"
SERIAL NUMBER
POSITION No. 2
NOTE 7-DIGIT
NUMBERS
EXTEND ON TO
DORSAL FIN.
(2102379 TO 2102978).

2102633
15"

EQUAL

TYPE 4 – STARB'D
SIDE ON A/C WITH
STAGGERED WAIST WINDOWS

50"

**COLOUR KEY
FOR ALL DRAWINGS**

NORMAN OTTAWAY.

| BLACK | WHITE | YELLOW | RED | GREEN | INSIGNIA BLUE | DARK BLUE / OTHER COLOURS AS NOTED. |

Above: Detail of a dirt-bespattered 446th Bomb Group B-24H national insignia, showing where a lighter blue has been used in place of the original red outline. (Albert Krassman)

be three-quarters of the depth, also in seven sizes: 20, 25, 30, 35, 40, 45 and 50in outside diameter. However, in practice the diameter of insignia tended to be rounded out to feet and half-foot divisions.

Early actions in the Far East led to confusion in combat between the Japanese red national marking and the red-centred US insignia. To avoid this the US device was modified by the deletion of the central red disc. This instruction, notified to take effect from 15 May 1942, was endorsed by Technical Order T/O 07-1-1 of 1 June. Under this order the red centre was to be removed from the national insignia on all USAAF aircraft, combat or otherwise. Thus the first aircraft for the 8th Air Force to arrive in the UK in July 1942, B-17Es of the 97th Bomb Group, had the revised marking. USAAF transport and special assignment aircraft had earlier visited the UK sporting national insignia with the red 'meatball', as this device was commonly called by USAAF personnel, but these were not assigned to the 8th Air Force. Many of the 97th's B-17Es did, however, still carry the wording 'U. S. ARMY' in bold black characters on the undersurface of the wings, although this marking was eliminated on production combat aircraft in the early spring of 1942. The lettering on B-17Es was in 48in high block capitals, with 'U. S.' under the right wing and 'ARMY' under the left, the tops of the letters towards the wing leading edges.

Spitfire Vs, used to equip the 31st and 52nd Fighter Groups when their personnel arrived in the UK during the summer of 1942, simply had the US national insignia superimposed on the British roundel. On the fuselage this was sometimes within the yellow surround of the British roundel, and later that summer the 8th Air Force accepted the Air Ministry's recommendation that the yellow surround would enhance recognition of the US marking. On 1 October 1942 the 8th Air Force issued a requirement that a 2in yellow ring be painted round the fuselage insignia. Although applied extensively to fighters and on most aircraft destined to be transferred to the 12th Air Force and despatched to North Africa late in the year, its application to the B-17Fs and B-24Ds of the remaining VIII Bomber Command Groups was fairly limited. The ring appears to have been discontinued by December 1942 and painted out on those bombers so marked, although no instruction rescinding that of 1 October is known. The width of the yellow surround on many Fortresses and Liberators was as much as 6in.

While the yellow surround was intended to enhance the circular form of the national insignia, the Air Ministry advised that the white star was too bold and likely to compromise camouflage on airfields and security in the air. As a result of this, on the same date (1 October 1942), VIII Bomber Command ordered the dulling of the star, to be effected before the next mission. This was to be done by painting over with grey paint, although some units are known to have used a grey/white mix to achieve the desired effect. Initially carried out by combat units, the dulling of insignia became one of the many tasks allocated to base air depots in preparing bombers newly arrived from the United States. It appears to have been considered one of the less vital tasks and was not always performed when time was at a premium. Eventually, in late 1943, it was discontinued simply by disappearing from the lengthy list of theatre modifications required for B-17s and B-24s.

The white star of fighter aircraft insignia was not subject to the dulling requirement. When the P-47 Thunderbolt arrived on the scene in January 1943 there existed an almost ingrained belief among the less practised in aircraft recognition that any single-engine fighter with a radial engine must be a German FW 190. Aware of the situation, the British Air Ministry advised USAAF VIII Fighter Command that special type identity markings were necessary

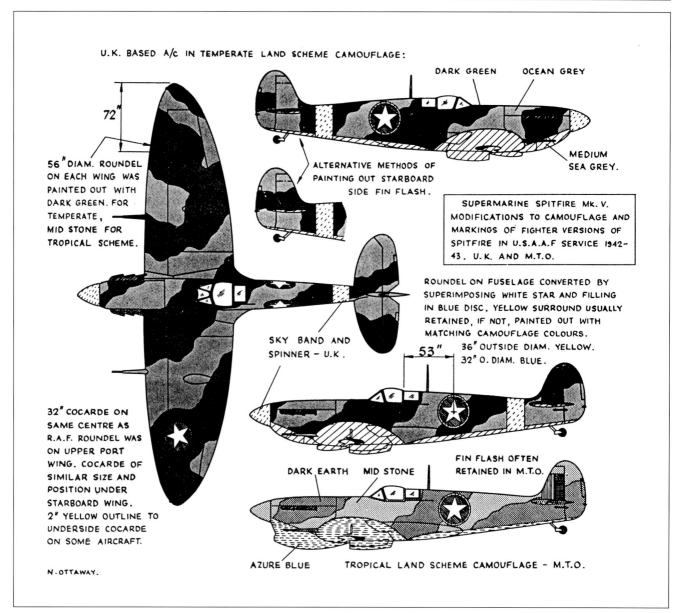

U.K. BASED A/c IN TEMPERATE LAND SCHEME CAMOUFLAGE:

DARK GREEN   OCEAN GREY

72"

56" DIAM. ROUNDEL ON EACH WING WAS PAINTED OUT WITH DARK GREEN. FOR TEMPERATE, MID STONE FOR TROPICAL SCHEME.

MEDIUM SEA GREY.

ALTERNATIVE METHODS OF PAINTING OUT STARBOARD SIDE FIN FLASH.

SUPERMARINE SPITFIRE MK. V. MODIFICATIONS TO CAMOUFLAGE AND MARKINGS OF FIGHTER VERSIONS OF SPITFIRE IN U.S.A.A.F SERVICE 1942–43. U.K. AND M.T.O.

ROUNDEL ON FUSELAGE CONVERTED BY SUPERIMPOSING WHITE STAR AND FILLING IN BLUE DISC. YELLOW SURROUND USUALLY RETAINED, IF NOT, PAINTED OUT WITH MATCHING CAMOUFLAGE COLOURS.

SKY BAND AND SPINNER – U.K.

53"   36" OUTSIDE DIAM. YELLOW. 32" O. DIAM. BLUE.

32" COCARDE ON SAME CENTRE AS R.A.F. ROUNDEL WAS ON UPPER PORT WING. COCARDE OF SIMILAR SIZE AND POSITION UNDER STARBOARD WING. 2" YELLOW OUTLINE TO UNDERSIDE COCARDE ON SOME AIRCRAFT.

FIN FLASH OFTEN RETAINED IN M.T.O.

DARK EARTH   MID STONE

N. OTTAWAY.

AZURE BLUE   TROPICAL LAND SCHEME CAMOUFLAGE – M.T.O.

and that, further to guard against trigger-happy anti-aircraft gunners when this radial-engine monoplane approached, an enlarged national insignia should be applied to the undersurfaces of both wings. These were to be 59in in diameter, with the centre line of the star 82in from the wing tip, 17in further in than the original factory-applied position. The fuselage insignia was notified as 36in in diameter with a 2in wide yellow encircling band, and the centre of the star was to be 20in from the rear edge of the intercooler door. As the original insignia was 35in in diameter and close up to the intercooler door, the general practice was simply to paint in a yellow border. These markings were notified by VIII Fighter Command on 20 February 1943; their application

was the task of base air depots. An attempt in April 1944 to have this work carried out in the US on new P-47s before shipment to Europe did not meet with success as Materiel Command objected to any changes that did not meet the current Technical Order on insignia. Depots continued to meet the theatre requirement until January 1945, at which time it was deleted from the list of required modifications on new P-47s.

While the 8th Air Force had been dulling its star insignia, opinion in other theatres of operations held that the national marking was not conspicuous enough and needed enlargement. The high incidence of misidentification of friend and foe resulted in modifications to the insignia approved by both US

Army and Navy on 28 June 1943 and notified during the next two days to all commands, effective immediately. The new device, known as AN-I-9a, was detailed in a revised T/O 07-1-1 as follows:

'The straight line forward by the top edges of the two star points, parallel with the leading edge or top of the fuselage, is continued for a distance of one radius of the blue circle out from each side thereof. Two rectangles, each one radius long and a half radius wide, the inner ends of which remain concave to conform to the circle, are blocked in on each side of the blue circle, solid white, using the extension line as the top edge of the rectangle. The entire design is then outlined with a red border, one eighth radius wide.'

This change endorsed a lesson first realised in the First World War that, at a distance, shape can be discerned before colour. The new insignia, soon commonly known as the 'star and bar', took several days to apply to the majority of fighter aircraft in the 8th Air Force and several weeks in the hard-pressed heavy bomber Groups. In those B-17 Groups using squadron code letters, the 'bars' added to the fuselage insignia overlapped the nearest letter of the code. This remained so on many Fortresses but some units took the opportunity to repaint the codes on the rear fuselage, where they were more discernible. The bars added to the fuselage insignia of many 322nd Bomb Group B-26B Marauders also extended over the individual aircraft letter. On the B-26s of the 386th and 387th Bomb Groups, which arrived around the time the new insignia was introduced, the existing fuselage cocarde was painted out and a completely new insignia positioned some 40in further forward in order to bring the aircraft call-letter clear of the tailplane. The position of fuselage national insignia on Marauders varied between sources of production and models at this time.

No sooner was the 'star and bar' insignia applied to the majority of 8th Air Force aircraft than another revision was notified. Again this stemmed from experience in the war with Japan, whose aircraft were marked with red. To avoid any mistakes likely to occur in combat, where a flash of red might actually come from a friendly aircraft, the red outline of the US insignia was changed to blue. The 8th Air Force notified its units of the change on 14 August 1943, to be effective by 17 September. The comparatively long period allowed for units to carry out this work indicated that the outline colour was of no great importance in the ETO. In fact, many 8th Air Force aircraft were still to be seen with the red-bordered insignia months after the introduction of the blue. This was particularly so on upper wing surface insignia, which was not so noticeable when aircraft were on the ground and thus tended to be overlooked. Officially, the blue-bordered insignia was AN-I-9b.

No further changes were made to the national insignia during the war. Factory positioning of the marking was altered on some models, notably P-47Ds, where the 'star and bar' was painted completely aft of the intercooler doors. This added more work to the depot modification list with the re-siting of the fuselage insignia to make room for the individual aircraft letter.

While not an official USAAF insignia, for the 'Torch' invasion of North-West Africa in November 1942 all participating combat aircraft despatched from the UK carried the British-type nationality fin flash of red, white and blue. Approved as an Allied insignia for this campaign, the fin flash was applied to the B-24Ds of the 93rd Bomb Group that were detached to operate from North Africa during the winter of 1942/43. On return the Liberators so adorned continued to carry this red, white and blue fin flash until it was obscured by other markings in the autumn of 1943.

Individual Aircraft Identities

To distinguish one identical production-line machine from another, manufacturers usually bestow serial numbers. From the earliest days of powered flight aircraft were so identified, the term 'Constructor's Number' becoming the general reference in Britain and the United States. The number was normally carried on the constructor's or maker's plate fixed to the instrument panel or in some suitable position in the cockpit. As different manufacturers often used the same runs of numbers, military organisations, employing several makes of aircraft, required their own systems giving unique identities, independent of any manufacturers. The United States Army Air Service's practice of prefacing a serial number with 'A.S.' was replaced following the Air Corps Act of July 1926 by the system perpetuated by the USAAF and USAF. It consists of the last two digits of the fiscal year in which the government order for the aircraft was placed, followed by a hyphen and a number related to that year. An exam-

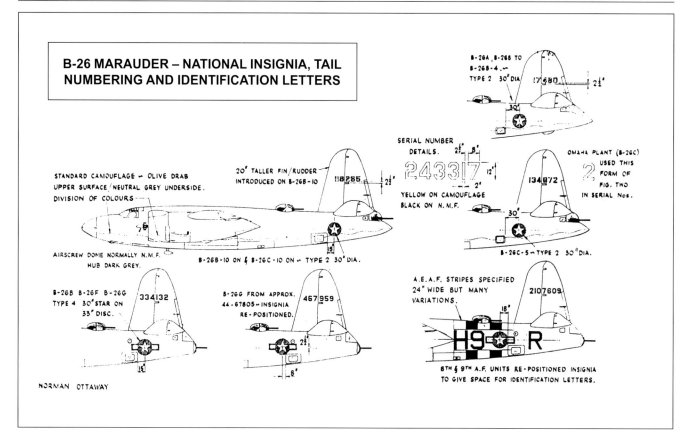

B-26 MARAUDER – NATIONAL INSIGNIA, TAIL NUMBERING AND IDENTIFICATION LETTERS

STANDARD CAMOUFLAGE – OLIVE DRAB
UPPER SURFACE / NEUTRAL GREY UNDERSIDE.
DIVISION OF COLOURS

20' TALLER FIN/RUDDER INTRODUCED ON B-26B-10

AIRSCREW DOME NORMALLY N.M.F. HUB DARK GREY.

B-26B-10 ON & B-26C-10 ON – TYPE 2 30" DIA.

B-26B B-26F B-26G TYPE 4 30" STAR ON 35" DISC.

B-26G FROM APPROX. 44-67805 – INSIGNIA RE-POSITIONED.

B-26A, B-26B TO B-26B-4. – TYPE 2 30" DIA

SERIAL NUMBER DETAILS.
YELLOW ON CAMOUFLAGE BLACK ON N.M.F.

OMAHA PLANT (B-26C) USED THIS FORM OF FIG. TWO IN SERIAL Nos.

B-26C-5 – TYPE 2 30" DIA.

A.E.A.F. STRIPES SPECIFIED 24" WIDE BUT MANY VARIATIONS.

H9 R

8TH & 9TH A.F. UNITS RE-POSITIONED INSIGNIA TO GIVE SPACE FOR IDENTIFICATION LETTERS.

NORMAN OTTAWAY

ple is Boeing B-17B serial number 39-1. The '39' indicates that funds for the purchase of the aircraft were made available in 1939, and the '1' that it was the first aircraft serial number allocated for that year.

By then it was a standard requirement for the manufacturer to include an aircraft's Army serial number in the Technical Data Block painted on the external skin of the left fuselage side, below or forward of the cockpit area. Stencilled in 2in high black characters, the data block had been reduced to give the aircraft's model designation, serial number and crew weight. Below these, in small characters, was information relating to the fuel rating to be used in replenishment. These markings were usually positioned in the same place on aircraft of the same model from the same factory, unless repainted by a service unit following the removal or application of a paint finish.

As the serial number in the technical data block could only be read at close proximity it was necessary to provide an indication of individual identities that were visible at some distance. Operational units were therefore permitted to use large numerals painted on fuselages or tail fins. In 1937 an authorised system, known as Designators, was introduced,

featuring three or four characters on tail fins which identified the unit and the aircraft within the unit. In 1941 this gave way to a new form of designator that remained in use for many years. This consisted of the aircraft's serial number prefixed by the last digit of the fiscal year without the hypen. For example, Martin B-26 serial 40-1498 had the designator 01498. Painted on the fin, but extending across the fin and rudder on some aircraft models, the numbers were in yellow on dark paintwork and in black on light colours or bare metal finishes. Their size was sufficiently large to allow the designator to be read at 150yds. The details in the Technical Order specifying these requirements, T/O 07-1-1A, dated 28 October 1941, are confused by other published specifications mentioning requirements for blue and red designators.

The designator also came to be known as the 'radio call-number' as it was used for identification purposes in radio transmissions. Owing to the designators usually being composed of five or six figures, it soon became normal practice to use only the last three in radio communications. The term 'designator' was eventually dropped from official publications in favour of 'radio call-number' or 'tail number'; in fact, the latter became the common term in the 8th Air Force. Identification Yellow 48 used for tail numbers was a bold shade, inclined towards orange, that varied in appearance through slight differences in manufacture and application on different camouflage backgrounds. With the discontinuation of camouflage finishes at the end of 1943 the tail number was painted in black on bare metal or 'silver' doped fabric.

The majority of the aircraft arriving in the UK from the United States, assigned to service units or replacements, had no major individual identification markings other than the radio call-number on their vertical tail surfaces. Once assigned to a combat unit it was the practice in some Groups to paint the last three digits of the serial number on both sides of the nose to assist identification on the ground. As aircraft were normally parked on hardstands facing towards the perimeter track, nose numbers aided truck drivers delivering to a particular aircraft. The 'last three' was also the common form of aircraft identification on bomber loading lists. These nose numbers were generally some 6 to 10in high on B-17s and ranged from 6in high to as much as 36in on B-24s. P-38s also often carried the 'last three', 9in high, on their noses. To confuse matters, another number of four digits, 3in high, was also to be seen on P-38 noses, but this was a manufacturer's number with no relevance to service use.

Yet another nose marking, often seen on 8th Air Force B-17s and B-24s, was a number prefixed 'P', painted in black on the left side. The size of the characters varied: on some aircraft these were no more than 2in high, on others 4–6in. Known as the Project Number, it was for identification of an aircraft prepared by modification centres for assignment to a particular organisation for overseas movement from the United States. Although the code had no relevance once the aircraft was assigned to an operational station in the UK, this Project Number was rarely painted out. The same went for other pre-overseas dispatch numbers most commonly found on B-24 noses.

Unit Identification Markings Prior To Overseas Movement

Pre-war Army Air Corps unit markings usually consisted of an organisation's approved insignia—commonly known as its 'patch'—positioned on both sides of the fuselage, and a coloured engine cowling band.

In the case of pursuits (fighters), white, yellow and red were normally the colours of a Group's three squadrons. Where aircraft were operated with bare metal finishes, blue often replaced white to obtain a better contrast. In bomber or other four-squadron Groups the squadron cowling bands were white, red, yellow and blue, with green being sometimes preferred to white or blue. With the introduction of camouflage finishes the coloured cowling bands were retained by many units but often reduced in area to just the leading edge. In other units only spinners or propeller bosses carried the squadron colour.

Following the United States' entry into hostilities, Groups receiving aircraft for combat service overseas were not permitted to apply squadron colours and no unit markings were authorised. However, a very few of the bomber Groups, joining the 8th Air Force in 1942–43, did carry unofficial markings peculiar to individual squadrons. Most notable were those arriving in the UK in the spring of 1943, several of whose B-17Fs had coloured bands and symbols adjacent to the tail numbers.

Individual Aircraft Letters

From the outset it had been necessary for the USAAF in the UK to use the British system of flying control to ensure complete integration with British services. Multi-engine aircraft, primarily bombers, used wireless telegraphy (W/T) and radio telephony (R/T) for communication, the former being Morse code, the latter voice. An aircraft had a four-letter W/T identification code, the first three letters usually being common to all aircraft of a squadron but changed frequently for security purposes. The last letter usually remained constant, being the individual letter of the aircraft within its unit. R/T featured a two-syllable code word for the squadron, changed periodically, followed by the phonetic call of the aircraft's individual letter in establishing an audio identity. In October 1942 the four operational B-17 Groups of VIII Bomber Command were advised that the individual aircraft letter used in W/T and R/T could also be used as a means of visual identity and to this end painted on the tail fins in yellow.

In assigning individual aircraft letters to the four squadrons of a bomber Group, the operational instruction required two squadrons to use the first half of the alphabet and two to use the last half; most Groups arriving during the first year of 8th Air Force operations complied with this instruction.

23

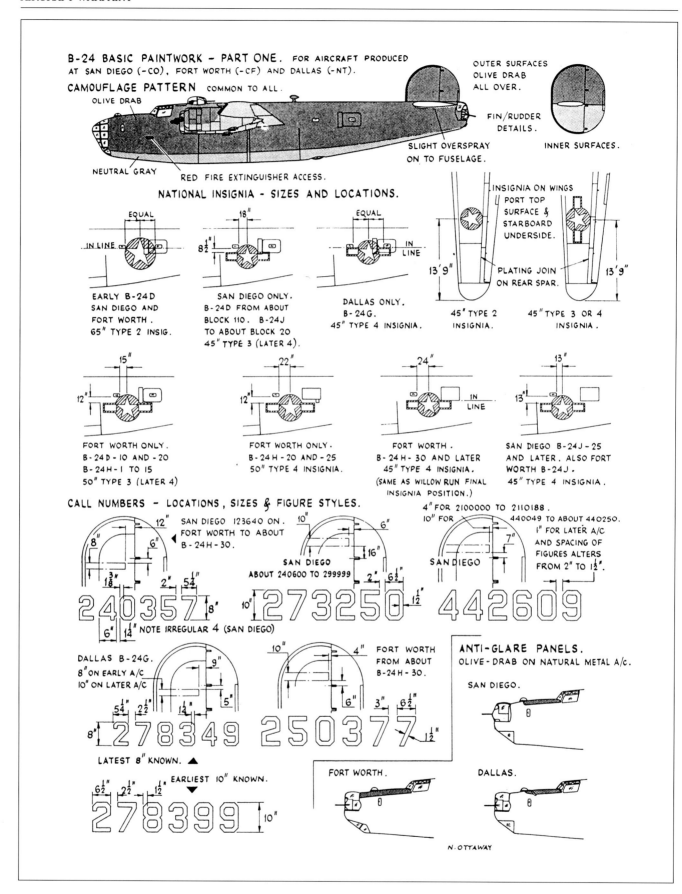

B-24 BASIC PAINTWORK - PART ONE. FOR AIRCRAFT PRODUCED AT SAN DIEGO (-CO), FORT WORTH (-CF) AND DALLAS (-NT).

CAMOUFLAGE PATTERN COMMON TO ALL.

OLIVE DRAB

NEUTRAL GRAY   RED FIRE EXTINGUISHER ACCESS.

SLIGHT OVERSPRAY ON TO FUSELAGE.

OUTER SURFACES OLIVE DRAB ALL OVER.

FIN/RUDDER DETAILS.

INNER SURFACES.

NATIONAL INSIGNIA - SIZES AND LOCATIONS.

EQUAL   IN LINE

EARLY B-24D
SAN DIEGO AND FORT WORTH.
65" TYPE 2 INSIG.

18"   8½"

SAN DIEGO ONLY.
B-24D FROM ABOUT BLOCK 110. B-24J TO ABOUT BLOCK 20
45" TYPE 3 (LATER 4).

EQUAL   IN LINE

DALLAS ONLY.
B-24G.
45" TYPE 4 INSIGNIA.

INSIGNIA ON WINGS PORT TOP SURFACE & STARBOARD UNDERSIDE.

13'9"   PLATING JOIN ON REAR SPAR.   13'9"

45" TYPE 2 INSIGNIA.

45" TYPE 3 OR 4 INSIGNIA.

15"   12"

FORT WORTH ONLY.
B-24D-10 AND -20
B-24H-1 TO 15
50" TYPE 3 (LATER 4)

22"   12"

FORT WORTH ONLY.
B-24H-20 AND -25
50" TYPE 4 INSIGNIA.

24"   IN LINE

FORT WORTH.
B-24H-30 AND LATER
45" TYPE 4 INSIGNIA.
(SAME AS WILLOW RUN FINAL INSIGNIA POSITION.)

13"   13"

SAN DIEGO B-24J-25 AND LATER. ALSO FORT WORTH B-24J.
45" TYPE 4 INSIGNIA.

CALL NUMBERS - LOCATIONS, SIZES & FIGURE STYLES.

12"   8"   6"

SAN DIEGO 123640 ON. FORT WORTH TO ABOUT B-24H-30.

3"   2"   5¼"
1⅛"

240357   8"

6"   1¼"   NOTE IRREGULAR 4 (SAN DIEGO)

10"   6"   16"

SAN DIEGO ABOUT 240600 TO 299999

2"   6½"

10"   273250   1½"

4" FOR 2100000 TO 2110188.
10" FOR 440049 TO ABOUT 440250.
1" FOR LATER A/C AND SPACING OF FIGURES ALTERS FROM 2" TO 1½".

7"

SAN DIEGO

442609

DALLAS B-24G.
8" ON EARLY A/C
10" ON LATER A/C

9"

5¼"   2½"   1½"

8"   278349

LATEST 8" KNOWN. ▲

10"   4"

FORT WORTH FROM ABOUT B-24H-30.

6"   5"

250377   1½"

3"   6½"

EARLIEST 10" KNOWN. ▼

6½"   2½"   1½"

278399   10"

ANTI-GLARE PANELS.
OLIVE-DRAB ON NATURAL METAL A/C.

SAN DIEGO.

FORT WORTH.   DALLAS.

N. OTTAWAY

B-24 BASIC PAINTWORK — PART TWO. FOR AIRCRAFT PRODUCED AT WILLOW RUN (-FO) AND TULSA (-DT).

CAMOUFLAGE PATTERN - WILLOW RUN.

OUTER AND INNER SURFACES OF FINS AND RUDDERS ARE FINISHED AS SHOWN IN PART ONE FOR A/C PRODUCED AT BOTH WILLOW RUN AND TULSA.

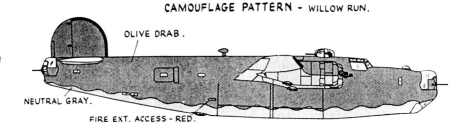

OLIVE DRAB.

NEUTRAL GRAY.

FIRE EXT. ACCESS - RED.

CAMOUFLAGE PATTERN - TULSA.

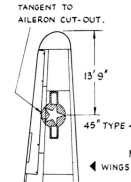

TANGENT TO AILERON CUT-OUT.

13' 9"

45" TYPE 4 INSIGNIA.

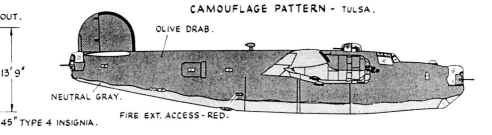

OLIVE DRAB.

NEUTRAL GRAY.

FIRE EXT. ACCESS - RED.

NATIONAL INSIGNIA - SIZES AND LOCATIONS.

◀ WINGS   FUSELAGE ▼

WILLOW RUN A/C (EXCEPT AS NOTED BELOW).

TULSA A/C AND WILLOW RUN A/C BEFORE ABOUT 27600 - AS DIAGRAMS IN PART ONE.

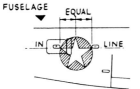

EQUAL

IN —— LINE

WILLOW RUN B-24E AND FIRST FEW B-24H. 65" TYPE 2 INSIGNIA.

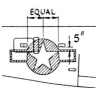

EQUAL

5"

WILLOW RUN B-24H FROM ABOUT 42-7475 PROBABLY TO 42-7718. TULSA UP TO ABOUT 41-28800. 65" TYPE 3 OR 4.

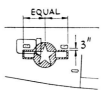

EQUAL

3"

WILLOW RUN B-24H 42-7718 (?) TO 42-7769. 42-50277 TO 42-52776. 42-94729 TO 42-94794. 45" TYPE 4 INSIGNIA.

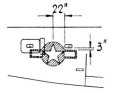

22"

3"

TULSA B-24H FROM ABOUT 41-28800 TO 41-29006 : 42-51077 TO 42-51103.

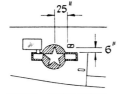

25"

6"

TULSA FROM FIRST B-24H-25 42-51104 TO FINAL B-24J 42-51430. BOTH 45" TYPE 4 INSIGNIA.

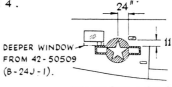

24"

11"

DEEPER WINDOW FROM 42-50509 (B-24J-1).

WILLOW RUN - ALL A/C FROM 42-94795 ONWARD. 45" TYPE 4 INSIGNIA.

CALL NUMBERS - LOCATIONS, SIZES, FIGURE STYLES.

WILLOW RUN ▲   15" FOR SIX FIG. Nos., 12" OTHERS.   TULSA ▲

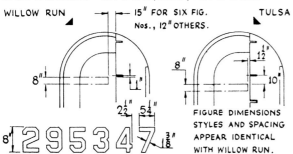

8"

8"

1"

2 1/2"   5 1/4"

3/4"

8"

1 1/2"

10"

FIGURE DIMENSIONS STYLES AND SPACING APPEAR IDENTICAL WITH WILLOW RUN.

ANTI-GLARE PANELS.

OLIVE-DRAB ON NATURAL METAL FINISH AIRCRAFT.

WILLOW RUN

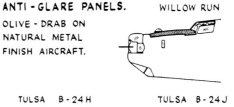

TULSA B-24H   TULSA B-24J

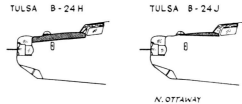

N. OTTAWAY

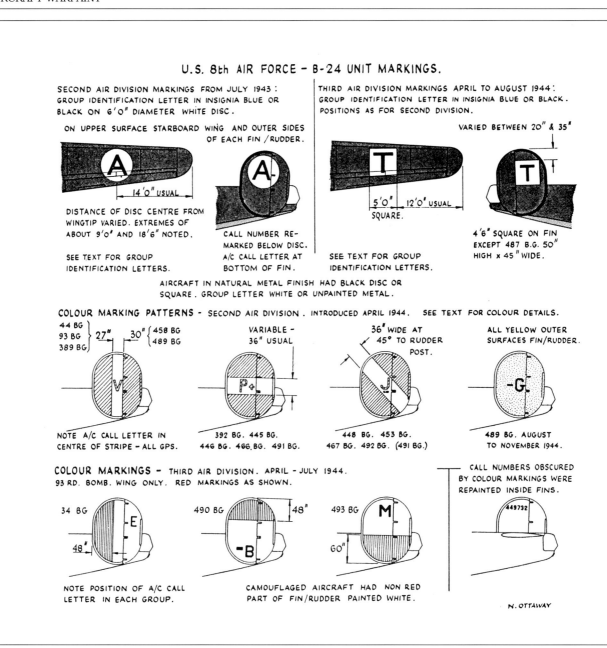

U.S. 8th AIR FORCE – B-24 UNIT MARKINGS.

SECOND AIR DIVISION MARKINGS FROM JULY 1943 :
GROUP IDENTIFICATION LETTER IN INSIGNIA BLUE OR
BLACK ON 6'0" DIAMETER WHITE DISC.

THIRD AIR DIVISION MARKINGS APRIL TO AUGUST 1944 :
GROUP IDENTIFICATION LETTER IN INSIGNIA BLUE OR BLACK.
POSITIONS AS FOR SECOND DIVISION.

ON UPPER SURFACE STARBOARD WING AND OUTER SIDES
OF EACH FIN / RUDDER.

VARIED BETWEEN 20" & 35"

14'0" USUAL

5'0"   12'0" USUAL
SQUARE.

DISTANCE OF DISC CENTRE FROM
WINGTIP VARIED. EXTREMES OF
ABOUT 9'0" AND 18'6" NOTED.

CALL NUMBER RE-
MARKED BELOW DISC.
A/C CALL LETTER AT
BOTTOM OF FIN.

4'6" SQUARE ON FIN
EXCEPT 487 B.G. 50"
HIGH x 45" WIDE.

SEE TEXT FOR GROUP
IDENTIFICATION LETTERS.

SEE TEXT FOR GROUP
IDENTIFICATION LETTERS.

AIRCRAFT IN NATURAL METAL FINISH HAD BLACK DISC OR
SQUARE. GROUP LETTER WHITE OR UNPAINTED METAL.

COLOUR MARKING PATTERNS - SECOND AIR DIVISION . INTRODUCED APRIL 1944. SEE TEXT FOR COLOUR DETAILS.

44 BG
93 BG   27"   30" { 458 BG
389 BG }   489 BG

VARIABLE -
36" USUAL

36" WIDE AT
45° TO RUDDER
POST.

ALL YELLOW OUTER
SURFACES FIN/RUDDER.

NOTE A/C CALL LETTER IN
CENTRE OF STRIPE - ALL GPS.

392 BG. 445 BG.
446 BG. 466 BG. 491 BG.

448 BG. 453 BG.
467 BG. 492 BG. (491 BG.)

489 BG. AUGUST
TO NOVEMBER 1944.

COLOUR MARKINGS - THIRD AIR DIVISION. APRIL - JULY 1944.
93 RD. BOMB. WING ONLY. RED MARKINGS AS SHOWN.

CALL NUMBERS OBSCURED
BY COLOUR MARKINGS WERE
REPAINTED INSIDE FINS.

34 BG

48"

490 BG

48"

493 BG

60"

449732

NOTE POSITION OF A/C CALL
LETTER IN EACH GROUP.

CAMOUFLAGED AIRCRAFT HAD NON RED
PART OF FIN/RUDDER PAINTED WHITE.

N. OTTAWAY

There were exceptions, but generally the first and third squadrons of a Group used letters from A and the second and fourth squadrons letters from O. The letter I was not to be used, but most Bomb Groups evolved their own policy regarding what letters to employ, and this was often influenced by the visual appearance of the letter. C was often eliminated due to the possibility of confusion with G; likewise E was not used by a few Groups, presumably as it was similar to F.

With 36 to 40 aircraft on hand, some Bomb Groups sought to distinguish aircraft displaying the same letter by different positioning relative to the tail number—above or below. During the summer of 1943 a few B-17s appeared with the numeral 1 or 2 adjacent to the radio call-letter to indicate their being the second aircraft to bear that letter in the Group. This practice seems to have been short-lived, although no official condemnation has been found in records.

In the summer of 1943 two Liberator Groups, the 44th and the 93rd, introduced a different marking for duplicated call-letters. A solid horizontal stroke, the same width as the strokes of the letter, was painted below the call-letter and was known as a bar. For example, in the 93rd Group the 328th Bomb

Above: The placement of the individual radio call-letter B above the tail number indicates that this B-24D was assigned to the 93rd Bomb Group's 328th Bomb Squadron. The yellow surround to the dulled cocarde has been painted out with a camouflage green, probably the same shade as used for the blotching round the fin and rudder. The RAF-style fin flash was added when on detached service in North Africa. (USAAF)

Squadron had a B-24D marked A and the 330th Bomb Squadron had one with A̲ . At first barred letters were used as required by all squadrons, but a policy soon developed of having them in just two squadrons. A further variation, necessitated by increases in the aircraft complements, was to have a bar above to distinguish the third aircraft of a Group with the same letter.

In November 1943 heavy bomber squadron complements were raised to 14 aircraft and new Groups arriving in the UK thereafter had squadron strengths of 16–19 aircraft. Some of the newcomers followed the early instruction of lettering two squadrons from A onwards and two from Z back, but some Groups simply started with A in all squadrons. The 2nd Division then introduced a plus symbol, to couple with a call-letter, giving four different visual identities for a specific letter. For example, there could be a plain A, A with a bar below, A with a bar above and A with a plus sign. The instruction did not require these to be assigned so as to give a form of squadron identification, but in practice this was what occurred: one squadron would have no symbols, one would have a bar below the letter, another the bar above the letter and the fourth the letter and the plus sign. In some B-24 Groups, instead of the bar being above or below, it was used in front of or following the letter on the tail. Each Group being left to its own devices in this matter, there was no common pattern of symbol assignment to squadrons within a Group. While in most Groups the lowest numbered squadron was normally that without a symbol to the letter, there were exceptions. The 445th Bomb Group was unique in eventually having a system which employed two symbols for a single identity. Other 2nd Division Groups made no use of these symbols or abandoned their use, and the 448th Bomb Group preferred to use geometric shapes around the call-letters to indicate squadron assignment. Two Bomb Groups of the 3rd Division, the 452nd and the 490th, also utilised the bar and plus markings on their B-17s.

When sufficient radar-equipped B-17s and B-24s were available for all combat Groups to employ them, these pathfinders were often allocated radio call-letters at either the beginning or the end of the alphabet (mostly the latter) to give distinction in radio communication.

The painting of the radio call-letter on the tail fins of heavy bombers became a Standing Operating Procedure requirement and common to all combat Groups. The letter was also required to be painted on the fuselage when squadron codes were introduced, except in the case of 2nd Division B-24s. Additionally, the letter was sometimes placed on some forward part of a bomber, particularly the nose area, but this was not an official requirement. It was applied to the side of the tail turret of a few B-17s to aid observation from below when the tailplane obscured the fin marking.

On fighters the individual aircraft letter was purely for visual identification. When squadron complements were increased to over 25 aircraft barred letters were used. The bar was usually painted below the letter, but, as always, there were exceptions.

The 4th Fighter Group used double letters—AA, BB, etc.—instead of barred letters on its Mustangs during its last months in England. These were rarely seen in other units. With the introduction of an operational training section in all 8th Air Force fighter Groups late in 1944, the War Weary aircraft used for this purpose were often identified by numerals rather than letters in several squadrons.

Unit Code Markings

The first fighter units joining the 8th Air Force during the spring of 1942 received Spitfire Vs from the British and were tutored in combat operations by RAF Fighter Command. The squadrons of both the 31st and 52nd Fighter Groups were given code letter identifications in the system used by the RAF, and later the P-38 Lightnings of the 1st and 14th Fighter Groups were given squadron code letters when these units came under RAF Fighter Command operational control.

Following standardisation on camouflage finishes, in April 1939 the RAF introduced a simple means of visual identification for squadron aircraft. Security dictated that the identity and disposition of squadrons should be concealed from the potential enemy. The code letter system involved two paired letters as the squadron identification followed by a third letter which represented the individual aircraft within that squadron. Painted on the fuselage side, the squadron letters were separated from the individual aircraft letter by the national marking, the roundel. In addition to giving a squadron identification, the three letters together also gave a unique

Above: The placement of identification letters on each side of a Fortress with staggered waist gun positions is well illustrated in these two photographs of B-17G 42-38156 JW:E of the 326th Bomb Squadron, 92nd Bomb Group. *Mary B* overran the runway at Podington early in August 1944, finishing up in a wheatfield. Worthy of note is the darker green of the main fin section and black instead of blue for the letter B. (W. Furniss)

individual identity for an aircraft within the RAF. Painted in as large a size as comfortably permitted by fuselage sides, the code letters provided recognition of an individual aircraft from a far greater range than was possible with the five-character serial number. The original instruction required the squadron letters to be painted forward of the roundel on the left side of the aircraft and the individual aircraft letter on the tail side, the positions being reversed on the right side of the fuselage. This led to the practice of referring to observed codes by the squadron letters preceding the individual letter. Later, the configuration of some aircraft types caused the squadron letters to be placed in the same position on both sides of the fuselage or the individual letter to be located on the nose; even so, it was usual to refer to aircraft codes by squadron letters first.

Initially, the letters C and I were not used in code letter combinations, the reasoning being that C could easily be confused with G, and I with the stroke of L or T. The letter shapes were to be 'block capitals' although the actual configuration to be used for each letter of the alphabet does not appear to have been officially detailed, leading to much in-the-field variation following the changing of all squadron code letter combinations on the outbreak of war. An original intention, to aid security and confuse enemy intelligence, was periodically to change code letter allocations. However, following the changes of September 1939, it was clear that regular changes would demand considerable man-hours and be an unnecessary burden on operational units. Thereafter selective changes were made, but many RAF squadrons retained the same code letter identifications throughout the war. Enemy intelligence was soon fairly conversant with the identities of codes to squadrons, which largely negated the RAF's security objectives. However, the three-letter code remained the popular means of service identity within the RAF and is probably the simplest and most efficient form of combining a unit and individual aircraft identity ever devised and employed.

The British Air Ministry issued the code combinations in S.D.0110 (hereinafter referred to by the common form SD110), a publication classified as secret. The combinations issued to the four USAAF Fighter Groups stemmed from this source. On the Spitfires of the 31st and 52nd Fighter Groups they were painted 24in high in the light blue-grey Sky, commonly referred to as duck-egg blue. This was a British paint, and if unavailable another, slightly darker shade, called Light Sea Grey, was used. Applying code letters to the P-38s proved more difficult owing to the depth limitations of the twin booms and the coolant radiators thereon. The 1st Fighter Group grouped all three letters together, 18in high, on the radiator coolant cover, most with a hyphen separating the squadron code from the individual aircraft letter. The 14th Fighter Group used slightly larger letters in Sky with the squadron code on the radiator cover and the aircraft letter on the rear boom. Other fighter Groups arriving from the US and fostered by the 8th Air Force before being transferred to the 12th Air Force for Operation 'Torch', the Allied invasion of North Africa, were apparently never issued with squadron code letters as they did not operate under RAF Fighter Command control.

Below: A 450th Bomb Squadron B-26B with its radio call-letter F positioned completely under the tailplane. The revised national insignia was achieved by extensions to the existing cocarde. Despite the requirement to provide a more visible marking the white portions were still dulled! (Roland Scott)

The 8th Air Force's heavy bomber Groups, equipped with B-17s and B-24s, commenced combat operations without any form of unit identification on these aircraft. The need for easier plane-to-plane visual identification when assembling formations and for flying control operatives monitoring aircraft movements on airfields persuaded 8th Air Force HQ to adopt the British code letter system for all its squadrons. This, first notified in Operational Instruction 11 on 8 October 1942, was brought into use in December. For B-17s these letters were detailed to be 48in high block capitals painted in light blue-grey, the squadron code forward of the national insignia on both sides of the fuselage and the individual aircraft letter aft. The positioning of the national insignia meant that the squadron code was not clear of the trailing edge of the wing and not easily observed from some angles. The 91st Bomb Group evidently felt grey too bland and that the codes would be better seen in yellow. In some units those aircraft which had already received a painted individual letter on the tail fin had it painted out. While there are no written records to verify the ploy, it appears that, in allocating codes to US bomber Groups, the Air Ministry staff responsible for SD110 deliberately selected combinations giving two squadrons of a Group the same positioned letter, most probably to confuse enemy intelligence during initial contacts as to whether a Group had three or four squadrons. Codes allocated to the squadrons of the four B-17 Groups in December 1942 included

Below: Repositioned national insignia on a 552nd Bomb Squadron B-26B, with code letters in what would become the standard position for Marauders from the summer of 1943. (USAAF)

LG and LL in the 91st Bomb Group and BN and GN in the 303rd Bomb Group. This was even more pronounced in allocations to Groups arriving in the spring of 1943, with the 100th Bomb Group having LD and LN, the 379th Bomb Group FO and FR, the 381st Bomb Group VE and VP and the 384th SO and SU. All four B-26 Marauder Groups assigned to the 8th Air Force had two codes with the same positioned letter. The 322nd Bomb Group had DR and ER, the 323rd VT and WT, the 386th RG and RU and the 387th KS and KX.

Many of the code-letter combinations issued for 8th Air Force units during the winter of 1942/43 were those previously worn by units in RAF Coastal Command and Army Co-operation Command. An example is the 67th Reconnaissance Group at Membury which was given AX, DA, VX and ZM for its four squadrons, combinations previously used by Catalina, Hudson and Sunderland aircraft in Coastal Command squadrons.

It was also Air Ministry practice to use the same code combinations of squadrons sent overseas to the Middle or Far East theatres of war for new or re-coded units in the UK. This again was intended to confuse enemy intelligence as to the movement and location of units. Thus, after the 1st, 31st and 52nd Fighter Groups went to North Africa with the 12th Air Force late in 1942, the code combinations they had used were allocated to the three Fighter Groups equipping with P-47 Thunderbolts in England during the following spring. The 4th Fighter Group at Debden, which had been formed from the three RAF Eagle Squadrons and had retained its code letters during its operations with Spitfires, received the same letters used by the 52nd Fighter Group, QP, WD and VF; the 56th Fighter Group was given HV, LM and UN as used by the 1st Fighter Group; and the 78th Fighter Group were allocated MX, HL and WZ, which 31st Fighter Group Spitfires carried. The 14th Fighter Group, having only two assigned squadrons while in the UK, had its code combinations later allocated to the 7th Photographic Group, but these were never displayed on the unit's F-5 Lightnings during hostilities. Both the 1st and 14th Fighter Groups abandoned code letters early in 1944 in favour of colours and numerals for identification purposes, but the 31st and 52nd Fighter Groups continued to carry code letters throughout their operational service in the MTO. This eventually led to two 8th Air Force and two 15th Air Force P-51

Above: With the staggered waist gun positions several units grouped the squadron code and the individual letter together on the rear fuselage for better visibility. This 602nd Bomb Squadron B-17G has a hyphen separating the code from the call-letter. (R. Welty)

Groups often operating in the same area bearing the same code letter combinations.

Code letters on P-47 Thunderbolts were regularised by an instruction dated 15 June 1943 requiring the letters to be white on camouflage, 24in high and 12in wide, with 3¹/₂in strokes. The squadron codes were forward of the national insignia and the individual aircraft letter aft on both sides of the fuselage. This presentation was fairly rigidly maintained, with very few deviations. When bare metal-finished P-47s arrived the letters were painted in black. In fighter units the individual aircraft letter was for visual identification only, and unlike bombers, where it came to be known as the call-letter, it did not feature in radio communication. Fighter squadrons used two-syllable code words as identification in radio broadcasts but individual aircraft within a squadron were identified by their position within a formation, or the pilot's two-digit call-number. Individual letters were at times those of the regular pilot's surname, particular in the case of senior officers. Examples were Colonel Hubert Zemke's LM:Z and Lieutenant-Colonel John Meyer's HO:M.

Code letter positioning, size and colour for P-51 Mustangs when they entered service late in 1943 was as advised for P-47s. When P-38 Lightning fighters reappeared in the UK that autumn some initial variation in application gave way to 18in high white letters. The squadron code was painted on the boom aft of the radiator housing and the individual letter on the radiator housing on both sides of the aircraft.

Whereas the squadron was a more defined and independent unit in Fighter Groups, it was less prominent in Bomb Groups simply because operations were always conducted on a Group basis with a mixed formation normally drawn from three of the four squadrons. Thus visual identification of squadron aircraft was not so important and the code letters were chiefly used as a means of positioning within a formation. For this purpose they were far from ideal, and with the introduction of Group and Wing markings in mid-June 1943 their use for identification purposes was questionable. The 4th Bomb Wing, apparently seeing little value in burdening combat Groups with the work of application, did not pass on instructions for applying SD110 codes to new Groups. The 385th, 388th and 390th Bomb Group B-17s all commenced operations without squadron markings. Codes for the 385th and 390th were issued, but for some unknown reason the squadrons of the 388th Bomb Group did not appear in SD110. Two of the 4th Wing Groups that had displayed codes began to omit them from replacement B-17s at this time, applying only the individual aircraft letter. In some cases the individual letter was followed by the numeral 1 or 2, indicating that it was the first or second aircraft with that call-letter in the Group.

With the large number of USAAF units arriving in the UK, plus the expanding RAF, the 576 combinations available for SD110 were practically exhausted by the autumn of 1943. It was then decided to use C and I, thus adding another 100 combinations and explaining why four bomber and five fighter Groups arriving in England during the final months of 1943 all had squadron codes featuring the letters C or I. There were still insufficient combinations to meet the forecast increase in units, both British and American, so in December 1943 SD110 included code combinations featuring a letter followed by a numeral and vice versa. All letters or the alphabet were used but the figure 1 was not as it could obviously be confused with I.

With the exception of three night flying squadrons, all combat squadrons of the US 9th Air Force were issued with, and displayed, SD110 codes— some 175 combinations. All units joining the 8th Air Force in 1944 received letter/numeral or numeral/letter codes and it appears that most of the combinations available were eventually issued. There were a few cases of duplication, which might sug-

gest that this system became exhausted but for the fact that the combinations involved were issued to units round about the same time and which were by no means the last to arrive in the UK. In the 8th Air Force 4N, used by the 833rd Bomb Squadron, was also carried on the P-38s of a 9th Air Force unit. Interestingly Z5, the code used by the 754th Bomb Squadron Liberators at Horsham St Faith, was in July 1944 displayed on the re-formed RAAF No 462 Squadron's Halifaxes operating from an airfield only a few miles away.

Although 8th Air Force Liberator Groups had been allotted codes in SD110 from the earliest days, they were not displayed by the two original Groups or any of the 2nd Bomb Division until their Divisional HQ issued Instruction 15, dated 3 March 1944, amended by 15A of 24 April. This suggests that no instructions were issued by the Division (or the earlier Bomb Wing) to effect the requirement until this date, although the intention to display SD110 codes was under review in February 1944. Hitherto some Groups used symbols adjacent to call-letters to dis-

Above: When the high-visibility colour tail markings were introduced on 2nd Bomb Division Liberators in May 1944 the tail number was repainted on the inward-facing sides of the fins as shown on the 752nd Bomb Squadron's *Liberty Lad*. The squadron codes on 458th Bomb Group aircraft were usually extra large, approximately 54in high. The colour of those depicted is Sky S. (USAF)

tinguish squadron assignments. Owing to limited space forward of the national insignia on B-24s, and to ensure uniformity, squadron codes were painted on the rear fuselage, aft of the waist gun window. These were 48in high in most Groups, although the 467th Bomb Group regularly used a 36in size and the 458th and 492nd Bomb Groups generally went to 54in. The colour for display on camouflaged aircraft was first advised as yellow, quickly amended to grey. The shade varied but is known to have been Sky Grey from British sources in some cases. On bare metal finishes the codes were in black. The individual letter was only carried on the fuselage by two Groups, the 389th and the 445th, and then in small size adjacent to the squadron code. By the autumn of 1944 the 448th Bomb Group ceased applying squadron codes to its aircraft and eventually deleted those on aircraft already in service. The 453rd Bomb Group also abandoned the use of squadron codes towards the end of the war, presumably considering them unnecessary.

All but one of the 1st Bomb Division B-17 Groups carried squadron codes, the exception being the 457th Bomb Group, which, like the 388th Bomb Group, was apparently overlooked by SD110. The 3rd Bomb Division continued to neglect squadron codes until the arrival of the B-24-equipped 486th and 487th Bomb Groups for the 92nd Combat Bomb Wing. These carried codes in a similar position to the 2nd Bomb Division Liberators but additionally had an individual aircraft letter forward of the fuselage national insignia. It is evident from this and similar actions that the decision whether or not to implement the displaying of these codes and other unit markings was vested in the Combat Wings controlling the Groups so far as the 3rd Division was concerned.

Although the 94th and 95th Bomb Groups had resumed applying codes to their B-17s in the winter of 1943/44, both abandoned their use completely in the early months of 1945. The 486th Bomb Group also discontinued the painting of squadron codes in favour of colour markings during the same period.

Several 1st Bomb Division Groups sought to improve the clarity of squadron codes on their B-17s by repositioning them on the rear fuselage. This occurred when the enlarged national insignia was introduced. In fact, the 381st Bomb Group used this location from the outset. In July 1943 the 91st Bomb Group placed all three letters on the rear fuselage with a space or hyphen between the code and the call-letter. Around the same date the 306th and 379th Bomb Groups transferred their squadron codes to the rear fuselage position, and in March 1944 the 306th dispensed with squadron codes completely—the only 1st Division Group to do so during hostilities. An anomaly, which persisted with the 384th Bomb Group, was the splitting of the squadron code on the right side of the fuselage, the first letter being on the rear fuselage and the second coupled with the call-letter forward of the national insignia. Splitting the squadron code also occurred in the 351st Bomb Group on some aircraft. That this practice continued throughout the Group's service

gives some indication of how little importance 8th Air Force bomber organisations placed on squadron code markings. The use made of squadron codes in visual identification and reference varied from Group to Group. Some Group records fail to mention them at all, whereas others, particularly the 91st Bomb Group, regularly list them, indicating a valuable reference.

The most uniform application of squadron code letters among the bomber units was that to the B-26 Marauders, no doubt due to the precise nature of the instruction, issued on 18 May 1943, which was as follows:

'Identification Letters. Locate fuselage station 559 3/8, which is the second station aft of the aft edge of the camera hatch. Measuring from the lower longitudinal member along the outside skin adjacent to station 559 3/8 lay out a point 7 inches above the longeron. Locate station $434\frac{1}{4}$ which is the station at which the fuselage centre section is spliced to the fuselage tail section. Measuring from the top edge of the aft bomb bay along the outside of the skin surface adjacent to the splice, lay out a point 13 inches above the bomb bay edge. Draw a line connecting the two points laid out as directed above. This line will be the base line for all identification letters. To locate the edge of the single letter, aft of the National Insignia, measure along the base line to a point 6 inches aft of the rearmost point of the National Insignia. Lay out the appropriate letter in a block 40 inches high and approximately 29 inches wide using 6 inch strokes. The double letters located forward of the National Insignia. Locate station $486\frac{1}{4}$, which is the first station forward of the waist gun window. Using this station as the aft edge, lay out the rearmost double letter in a 40 inch high and approximately 29 inch wide box along the base line using 6 inch strokes. Measure 6 inches from the forward edge of the rear letter to locate the rear edge of the first letter.'

This instruction was soon to be made obsolete by the revision of the national insignia the following month, bringing a need for wider spacings.

All Fighter Groups continued to use squadron codes to the end of their service in the UK. The application of 'D-Day stripes' prior to the cross-Channel invasion of June 1944 saw many codes overpainted. On the P-38s these were not restored, possibly because of the pending conversion to P-51s. In restoring individual letters the 352nd Fighter Group

Above: The standard size and positioning of Lockheed Lightning identification letters on a 38th Fighter Squadron P-38H. The stained and bleached paintwork aft of the boom turbosuperchargers also shows well in this photograph taken at Nuthampstead in November 1943. (Robert Sand)

chose to paint them on the tail fins of its aircraft instead of the rear fuselage. On converting from P-38s to P-51s the 364th Fighter Group carried squadron codes aft of the fuselage 'star and bar', with the individual letter on a geometric symbol on the vertical tail.

Changes in the allocation of codes to USAAF units were few. Apart from the 4th Fighter Group on conversion to P-47s, the only other known changes occurred in the 381st Bomb Group and 359th Fighter Group. For some unknown reason, but probably because the combinations allotted were already in use by RAF units, the 381st Group's squadrons changed their codes a month after the original application. This appears to have been due to some error in transmission rather than a planned change. The change of the 359th Group's 370th Fighter Squadron from CR to CS was also probably through some clerical error. The only other known changes came about through the redesignation of an organisation; for example, VIII Fighter Command's Air Technical Section at Bovingdon, on becoming Operational Engineering Section, exchanged VQ for Q3.

Several complaints concerning the violation of flying regulations by very low flying in the immediate post-VE days prompted the 8th Air Force to issue on 17 May 1945 teletype order D-60.611 requiring the grounding of all aircraft until codes had been painted on the underside of the left wing. The unit code followed by the individual aircraft letter were to read from left to right, when facing the front of the aircraft, with the tops of the letters towards the leading edge of the wing. Generally the size was to be as large as could be accommodated in the space available and the colours black on bare metal and yellow on camouflage. The actual size varied considerably, although the 3rd Air Division specified 72in high characters in 10in strokes on its B-17s, starting outward from wing station 15. At this date some aircraft of the 1st and 2nd Divisions had already been redeployed and did not receive these markings. For several units, particularly Bomb Squadrons, this post-war application was their only display of allotted codes. Interestingly, the squadrons of the 388th and 457th Bomb Groups applied their current four-letter W/T codes to the under surface of their B-17's wings. This suggests, as previously mentioned, that they were never included in the SD110, or in CD302, the confidential document that superseded it at the end of hostilities.

Authorised holders of SD110 were instructed to destroy the document on receiving a new issue. An apparent strict adherence to this direction has resulted—as far as can be ascertained—in no war-time copies of SD110, or its successor, surviving in historic archives. In consequence the identity of some units with displayed codes still remains unknown.

Bomber Group Identification Markings

As 8th Air Force bombers operated on a Group ba-sis, it was important that Groups could recognise each other when manoeuvring their formations to gain the briefed position in the bomber stream. This sometimes proved difficult, particularly in poor vis-ibility. With the doubling of the B-17 force in the spring of 1943, and with the advent of longer-range missions which often entailed assembling formations in the half-light of dawn, it became increasingly nec-essary to have some form of visual Group marking. Squadron codes were of limited value in that they could usually only be clearly seen at distances less than 1,000ft, and with four combinations per Group correct identification could be confusing for other units. To give a more positive identification of Groups, and so facilitate the assembly of Group and Combat Wing formations, VIII Bomber Command issued a requirement on 20 June 1943 for individual Group markings to be carried on the tail fins and wings of its heavy bombers.

A geometric shape identified each Bombardment Wing and a letter within the device the Group—an idea taken from the brand marks of the western cattle ranches. The 1st Bomb Wing was to use an equilateral triangle with 6$\frac{1}{2}$ft sides, the 2nd Bomb

Below: The 40th Combat Bomb Wing Groups were alone in carrying the Group geometric device under the left wing, a practice introduced in the spring of 1944. B-17G *El Lobo*, 42-102424 NV:B of the 325th Bomb Squadron, 92nd Bomb Group, had landing gear failure at Chilham on 24 April 1944. Repaired, the aircraft had to be ditched in the sea in October that year. (W. Furniss)

Wing a 6$\frac{1}{2}$ft diameter circle and the 4th Bomb Wing a 6$\frac{1}{2}$ft square, to be painted above the tail number.

Each Group in a Wing was assigned a letter to be placed within the Wing marking, starting with A and running consecutively with the order of the numeri-cal designations of Groups. Letters that were not used, because they might cause confusion, were E/F, D, O, Q and M/N. The device was painted on each side of the tail fin and on the upper surface of the right wing near the tip. The colour of the geometric devices was white, with the Group letter in Identifi-cation Yellow. The radio call-letter on the tail fin, which hitherto had been arbitrary, was to be car-ried on the fins of all B-17s and B-24s in tactical units, painted below the tail number in 28in high yellow characters.

Implementation of this requirement took several days and the original detail was soon subject to change. Space limitations on B-17 fins reduced the triangle to 6ft per side. Similarly, the 4th Wing sym-bol became a rectangle, with varying dimensions, but mostly 5ft high by 4ft wide. The Command in-struction also called for the device to be dulled to a one-mile visibility. This involved adding a small amount of grey to the white on application or a light grey water paint wash over the dry paintwork. It was soon found that the yellow Group letter was not clearly seen at distances beyond half a mile. At the beginning of July a revision of the instruction called for this Group letter to be painted in Insignia Blue, the same colour as used in the surround to the white star. As in most Groups the task of apply-ing the Group/Wing marking was still far from com-plete, those aircraft which had already received this marking tended to be left with yellow Group letters until all other aircraft had been dealt with. Some B-17s were still to be seen with yellow Group letters a month after the change had been ordered.

Compliance with the detail of instructions on markings issued by commands often did not ap-pear on aircraft in tactical units. Sometimes the in-structions were refined by intermediate commands or by the Groups themselves. Apart from different dimensions from those listed for the Group/Wing devices, the 4th Wing instructed the 100th Bomb Group to use the letter D, which was to have been eliminated according to the VIII Bomber Command instruction. The 2nd Bomb Wing's B-24s, detached to North Africa at this time, would not display these Group/Wing markings until their return.

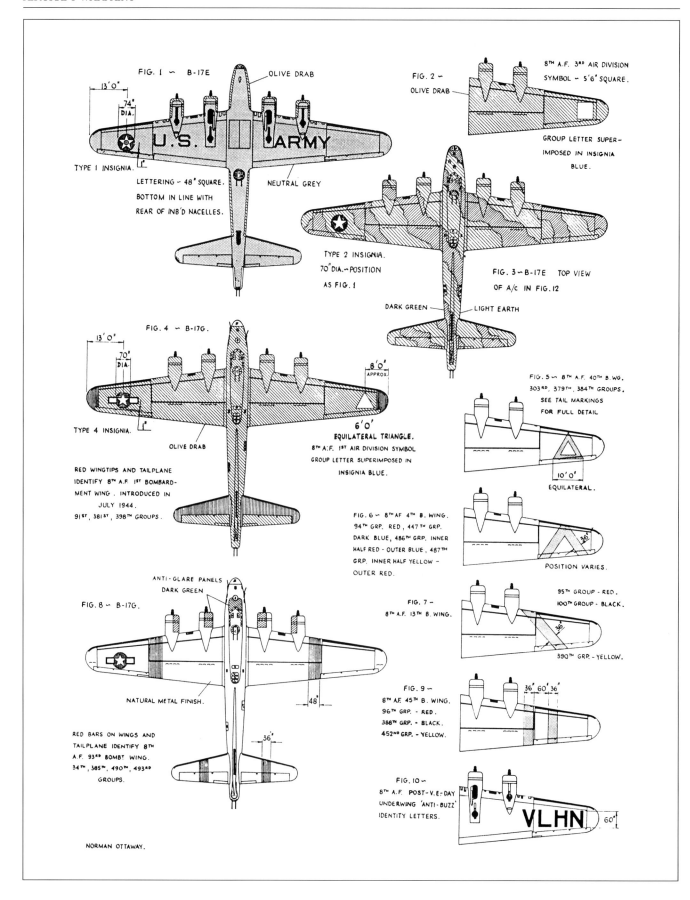

FIG. 1 ~ B-17E

OLIVE DRAB

13'0"

74" DIA.

U.S. ARMY

TYPE 1 INSIGNIA.

LETTERING - 48" SQUARE.
BOTTOM IN LINE WITH
REAR OF INB'D NACELLES.

NEUTRAL GREY

FIG. 2 ~ OLIVE DRAB

8TH A.F. 3RD AIR DIVISION
SYMBOL - 5'6" SQUARE.

GROUP LETTER SUPER-
IMPOSED IN INSIGNIA
BLUE.

TYPE 2 INSIGNIA.
70" DIA.~ POSITION
AS FIG. 1

FIG. 3 ~ B-17E   TOP VIEW
OF A/c IN FIG. 12

DARK GREEN   LIGHT EARTH

FIG. 4 ~ B-17G.

13'0"

70" DIA.

TYPE 4 INSIGNIA.

OLIVE DRAB

RED WINGTIPS AND TAILPLANE
IDENTIFY 8TH A.F. 1ST BOMBARD-
MENT WING. INTRODUCED IN
JULY 1944.
91ST, 381ST, 398TH GROUPS.

8'0" APPROX.

6'0"
EQUILATERAL TRIANGLE.
8TH A.F. 1ST AIR DIVISION SYMBOL
GROUP LETTER SUPERIMPOSED IN
INSIGNIA BLUE.

FIG. 5 ~ 8TH A.F. 40TH B.WG.
303RD, 379TH, 384TH GROUPS.
SEE TAIL MARKINGS
FOR FULL DETAIL

10'0"

EQUILATERAL.

FIG. 6 ~ 8TH AF 4TH B. WING.
94TH GRP. RED, 447TH GRP.
DARK BLUE, 486TH GRP. INNER
HALF RED - OUTER BLUE, 487TH
GRP. INNER HALF YELLOW -
OUTER RED.

36°

POSITION VARIES.

FIG. 7 ~
8TH A.F. 13TH B. WING.

95TH GROUP - RED.
100TH GROUP - BLACK.

36°

390TH GRP. - YELLOW.

FIG. 8 ~ B-17G.

ANTI-GLARE PANELS
DARK GREEN

NATURAL METAL FINISH.

RED BARS ON WINGS AND
TAILPLANE IDENTIFY 8TH
A.F. 93RD BOMBT WING.
34TH, 385TH, 490TH, 493RD
GROUPS.

48"

36"

FIG. 9 ~
8TH A.F. 45TH B. WING.
96TH GRP. - RED.
388TH GRP. - BLACK.
452ND GRP. - YELLOW.

36" 60" 36"

FIG. 10 ~
8TH A.F. POST-V.E-DAY
UNDERWING 'ANTI-BUZZ'
IDENTITY LETTERS.

VLHN

60"

NORMAN OTTAWAY.

Bombardment Wings became Bombardment Divisions in September that year but aircraft markings remained unchanged. Instruction 55-14, issued by VIII Bomber Command on Christmas Day 1943, repeated the original requirements for Group markings but revised the dimensions. On tail fins the 1st Division's equilateral triangle was to have 6ft sides, the 2nd Division's 'circle' to have a diameter of 5ft 9in and the 3rd Division's 'square' to be 4ft in height by 5ft wide. On the upper right wing surface the 1st Division triangle was specified as 8ft with a $4^3/_4$ft letter, the 2nd Division disc $6^1/_2$ft with a 4ft letter and the 3rd Division 'square' $4^3/_4$ft chordwise and 6ft spanwise with a $3^3/_4$ft letter—all to be of 7in strokes. In practice most 2nd Division 'circles' were 6ft and 3rd Division 'squares' 5ft high by 4ft wide or a true 4ft square. The instruction stated that the letter within the device was to be 3ft high with 6in strokes. The same instruction detailed the radio-call letter as 2ft high with 4in strokes for all fin positioning. The divisional device, less letter, and the repositioning of tail numbers, if necessary, became a task undertaken by the air depots prior to delivering an aircraft to a combat unit.

These dimensions for the geometric-form Group markings remained little changed to the end of the war. The introduction of bare metal-finish aircraft brought an instruction for the divisional device to be painted in black and the Group letter white thereon. Eighth Air Force Headquarters Instruction 55-21 of 23 June 1944 gave the colour for the Group letter on camouflaged aircraft as black instead of blue. Black had been used for some time in lieu of blue by some tactical units. This issue also gave dimensions for the Group marking on 3rd Division B-24s. The 'square' was 4ft high and 5ft wide, with other details as for B-17s of that organisation.

In the spring of 1944 the three Groups of the 40th Combat Wing commenced painting the Group triangle/letter device on the underside of the left wing in addition to the upper surface of the right wing. The colours and size were the same. B-17s of the 92nd, 305th and 306th Bomb Groups were the only aircraft to carry underwing markings of this type.

There was only one change to this form of Group marking and that occurred when the 486th Bomb Group of the 3rd Division converted from B-24s to B-17s. It was soon apparent that the Square O marking of the Group placed on its B-17s could easily be confused with the Square D marking already in use by the 100th Bomb Group. To avoid this possibility the 486th used the Square W on its Fortresses. As mentioned previously, the detail of command instructions was not always applied by a unit, and often the markings of a unit were in use before being endorsed by a Command instruction. When the 489th and 491st Bomb Groups were scheduled to arrive in the UK the 2nd Bomb Division originally assigned the letters S and T respectively to these Groups, in compliance with the standing instructions. However, these were changed to W and Z and there is no evidence that S and T were ever used. The reason for this change is apparently unrecorded and speculative reasons are that W and Z were more distinctive shapes, less likely to be confused with other letters, and also that S and T were in use by 3rd Division B-24 Groups at nearby bases. A stylised Z in a square was applied to the B-17 used by 3rd Bomb Division headquarters, and this symbol is listed for that headquarters although no other instance of its use is known.

'A' and 'B' Group Markings

In November 1943 VIII Bomber Command commenced expansion of Group complements, raising the aircraft numbers in squadrons from nine to fourteen. With another 20 aircraft on hand in each Group, it was planned that they would fly two formations on some combat missions, distinguished as 'A' and 'B' Groups. This expansion began in the 3rd Bomb Division, firstly in the 45th and then in the 13th Combat Bomb Wing. The latter Bomb Wing decided that aircraft of its 'B' groups would be identified by a special marking, detailed as follows in an instruction dated 5 December 1943: 'A white stripe 16 inches wide from the white square on the horizontal stabiliser to the trailing edge of the rudder. A second white stripe 17 inches wide and 36 inches long extending from the white square on the right wing panel towards the wing tip.' Other 3rd Division Combat Wings did not take up this marking, protesting that it was not large enough to be an identification at any great distance and that with repair and maintenance the Groups would not have sufficient aircraft available to segregate into 'A' and 'B' groups on a permanent basis. The 95th, 100th and 390th Bomb Groups did identify a number of their aircraft with this 'B' Group marking but the practice was short-lived for the objections raised by the other Groups.

SQUADRON
LETTERS

A
46324
R

LL R

91ST BG
(401ST B S)

B
48735
C

C

92ND B G

SQUADRON No.

C
Y

Y

303RD B G
(427TH B S)

G
46300
K

K

305TH B G

SQUADRON
COLOUR

H
2102578
D

D

306TH B G
(367TH B S)

J
338277
O

O

351ST B G

SQUADRON No.
SQDN. LETTERS

K
48438
I

FO

379TH B G
(527TH B S)

SQUADRON
LETTERS

L
48963
C

MS

381ST B G
(535TH B S)

SQUADRON No.
SQDN. LETTERS

P
46135
H

S   OH

384TH B G
(547TH B S)

SQUADRON
LETTERS

S
338738
N

IW N

401ST B G
(614TH B S)

U
339195
J

457TH B G

SQUADRON
LETTERS

M
2102555

30M

398TH B G
(601ST B S)

A
2107160
K

K

94TH B G

B
46838
E

95TH B G

SQUADRON
LETTERS

C
48382
V

MZV

96TH B G
(413TH B S)

D
337686
G

G

100TH B G

H
46597
M

388TH B G

J
338945
N

N

390TH B G

K
46511
B

447TH B G

SQUADRON SYMBOL

L
337905
O

452ND B G
(729TH B S)

P
337901
B

487TH B G

U.S. 8TH A.A.F.
FIRST & THIRD AIR DIVISIONS
UNIT IDENTIFICATION MARKINGS

BG = Bombardment Group   BS = Bombardment Sqdn.

NORMAN OTTAWAY

W
338148
M

486TH B G

A

34TH B G

E
48368

385TH B G

SQUADRON SYMBOL

L
48492

490TH B G
(848TH B S)

SQUADRON LETTER

T
46808

P   T

493RD B G
(863RD B S)

Markings of the Day

On numerous occasions, particularly during the summer of 1943, heavy bomber crews reported single B-17s and B-24s suspected of being enemy-operated. The facts are that there is only one recorded instance of the *Luftwaffe* trying to infiltrate an 8th Air Force formation with captured aircraft, this occurring near the end of hostilities. It must therefore be assumed that the vast majority of these suspect B-17s and B-24s were friendly aircraft that had become separated from their units. Nevertheless, the threat of the enemy using captured B-17s and B-24s with hostile intent was considered real enough for VIII Bomber Command Instruction No 55, in the 25 December 1943 issue, to detail measures to be taken to distinguish friend from foe. This involved temporary markings valid for only one mission and detailed the action to be taken if an aircraft devoid of these markings attempted to join a formation. The relevant paragraphs covering these markings ran as follows:

'1/ Whenever it is believed necessary, there will be included in para. 3.x of each Field Order issued by this Headquarters, a Bomber Command identification symbol for the mission being planned. This marking, in turn, will be made known by a special notation on the "J" form submitted by the Division A-3 Sections to the NLO Fighter Command just prior to each mission.

'2/ This identification symbol will consist of a marking which will be painted on each side of the fuselage of all aircraft participating in the mission. These markings will be painted on the participating aircraft just prior to each mission and will follow the general form of crosses, squares, X's, circles, half circles, etc.

'3/ These markings will be painted with white Kalsomine paint, and will be placed on each side of the fuselage between the waist windows and the leading edge of the horizontal stabiliser. No size will be set for these markings but they will be as large as is consistent with the space available, with the idea in mind that they must be distinguishable as far distant as possible.'

The Markings of the Day remained in further issues of this instruction during 1944, unchanged but for the addition of use of black Kalsomine paint on bare metal aircraft. However, as far as is known, Markings of the Day were only actually applied for one combat mission, in late December 1943, and then only by the Fortress Groups. This marking, consisting of an X, was still being carried by B-17s participating in several following missions. The water-based paint stipulated being unavailable in some units, a more permanent material had been used. That no further use was apparently made of this instruction probably relates to the complaints that the application of such markings was an unwanted chore for hard-pressed ground crews.

Bomber Squadron Colour Markings

Despite a ban on bright colours that might compromise camouflage, a few bomber Groups did reintroduce the practice of using them to distinguish their squadrons. The first 8th Air Force Group to do so was the 44th Bomb Group, which dubbed itself 'The Flying Eight Balls' and painted a comic winged bomb on the side of its B-24Ds' noses which became an unofficial Group marking. The noses of the bomb markings were painted in a different colour for each squadron. This was no more than a decoration and was not intended as a serious means of identifying unit assignment. In the autumn of 1943 the squadrons of the 385th Bomb Group began to apply a squadron colour to the propeller bosses of their B-17Fs. Again these markings were more a decoration than of any real value as identification markings as the bosses were but 9in in diameter and 10in long, and only seen from close to the frontal area. Moreover, when the boss was turning, a shimmer could ensue, making the colour difficult to identify. The use of squadron colours in the 385th appears to have been a casual business and not directed from Group HQ as many B-17s never received this adornment in 1943.

A more rigorous application of squadron colours to propeller bosses was in force in the 457th Bomb Group, arriving in the UK early in 1944, and thereafter several Groups took up this practice, particularly B-24 Groups which did not carry the SD110-allotted codes. In August 1944 the 306th Bomb Group at Thurleigh, which had ceased using squadron code letters the previous spring, painted the tops of its B-17s' tail fins in squadron colours. The following month the 447th Bomb Group at Rattlesden became the first 8th Air Force B-17 Group to paint the engine cowlings in squadron colours, a practice that thereafter was taken up by several other Bomb Groups. Some B-17 Groups, when adopting squadron colours, painted a band round the nose directly

aft of the Plexiglas nosepiece; a few painted a band round the tail turret as well.

High-Visibility Colour Markings on Bombers

While the geometric shape and letter devices introduced during the summer of 1943 for Group identification greatly aided air leaders in positioning formations, there was still a need for markings that could be distinguished at greater distances. While camouflage was considered essential little could be done, but the situation changed with the arrival of unpainted aircraft early in 1944. Hitherto there had been a number of proposals for using bright markings. In radio communications involving the three Groups composing a Combat Wing, a two-syllable code word identified the Wing and a suffix colour the Group within the Wing. These spoken colours were normally red, yellow and green.

In December 1943 the 385th Bomb Group suggested that Groups in a Wing paint the fin and top side of the horizontal stabiliser in their radio call colours as a means of eliminating some of the confusion that arose in assembly patterns, but this was

Above: The 1st Combat Bomb Wing was the first Fortress-equipped organisation to introduce high-visibility markings, all three Groups using the same colour and layout. This 323rd Bomb Squadron, 91st Bomb Group formation includes both camouflaged and bare metal-finish aircraft, the former having the tail number and call-letter reinstated in yellow and the latter in black. The lead aircraft is the famous *Nine O Nine*, which completed more combat missions (140) than any other 8th Air Force B-17 without an 'abort'. The other camouflaged B-17G is *Betty Lou's Block Buster*, 42-31579 OR:D.

not approved by high command. In the following February, when the first 'silver' finished aircraft arrived in the UK, the 56th Fighter Group was given permission to paint the cowlings of its P-47s' engines with bright colours for squadron identification, and within a month VIII Fighter Command introduced a system of coloured nose markings to identify its Groups. With camouflage no longer a consideration on heavy bombers, in late March 1944 the 2nd Bomb Division devised high-visibility colour markings for all its Groups. Owing to the close proximity of its B-24 bases and the spread of its assembly area, this Division had been particularly troubled by aircraft from one Group joining the formation of another in the half light of dawn. This was not critical when the whole Division was briefed for the same target, but with the veritable flood of new Groups reaching the Division during the early months of 1944 the force was large enough to be given several different targets for one mission. If aircraft from one Group mistakenly joined a formation briefed for another target a difficult situation could arise. The letter within the Division's white disc marking was often difficult to distinguish in the early morning light, where shade and glare predominated because of the low angle of the sun.

Early plans called for both vertical and horizontal tail surfaces to carry bright markings, with an estimated 24 man-hours per aircraft needed to remove existing paint and add new. Eventually it was decided to use only the vertical surfaces, and the new markings were first issued in 2nd Bomb Division instruction 55-25 dated 1 May 1944. Combat Wings were to be identified by a basic colour painted on the outboard surfaces of the fin and rudder. Groups were to be identified by a distinctive stripe superimposed on the basic colour. To facilitate association with Group numbers and identification stripes, Groups within a Combat Wing were to be marked as follows: the lowest number Group—vertical stripe; next lowest number—horizontal stripe; third lowest number—diagonal stripe. The diagonal stripe was to be placed with its top forward on both port and starboard surfaces. The Wing colours allotted were: 2nd Combat Bomb Wing—black with white stripe; 14th Combat Bomb Wing—bare metal and fabric painted silver with black stripe; 20th Combat Bomb Wing—yellow with black stripe; 95th Combat Bomb

Wing—green with white stripe; and 96th Combat Bomb Wing—red with white stripe. The vertical stripe was detailed as $2^{1}/_{2}$ft wide and the horizontal and diagonal stripe width as 3ft. In practice many camouflage-finished B-24s in the 14th Combat Bomb Wing had white-painted fins and rudders for the base colour as this consumed fewer man-hours than removing the existing paintwork. The disc/letter Group marking was to be retained on the upper surface of the right wing and continued to be applied to all aircraft assigned to a Group.

Radio call-letters were to be painted in the Combat Wing colour on the stripe 2ft high and with 4in strokes. The tail number, removed or painted over on the outboard surface, was to be placed on the inboard surfaces of B-24 fins with the base of the numbers 2ft from the top of the fin. These numbers were to be 10–12in high in yellow. While some bare metal B-24s did have the numbers painted in yellow, in the majority of cases the colour was black, although the published instruction does not appear to have been amended to specify black for bare metal finishes. The paint for these bright markings was obtained from RAF sources via the Watton depot.

As the change of markings involved considerable man-hours and could not be allowed to compromise operations, it was realised that it might take several days or weeks to apply to all aircraft in a Group. It

Below: The radio call-sign for the 306th Bomb Group in the 40th Combat Bomb Wing was 'Foxhole Yellow'—hence the yellow tail band for Group-in-Wing identification. The coloured tail tip came into use as an additional squadron marking at the same time as the yellow band in August 1944. Hitherto the only squadron acknowledgement was the coloured propeller bosses. (Ben Marcilonis)

Above: Awaiting disposal. B-17Gs that landed in Sweden display a variety of markings. In the foreground is 42-97467 LL:F of the 91st Bomb Group, which arrived on 18 July 1944 and has the red high-visibility markings and a blue letter in the Triangle A. Next is 42-97212 QJ:G of the 96th Bomb Group, with the first letter of the code back to front, a not uncommon feature on this squadron's aircraft. The letter in the Square C is white. This Fortress arrived on 11 April 1944. Third in line is 42-39994 LD:D, a 100th Bomb Group aircraft which escaped the débâcle that befell that Group on 6 March 1944. The letter in the Square D is Insignia Blue. In the distance is a 305th Bomb Group aircraft with white code letters. (Flodin Collection)

was also apparent that some aircraft might be used on missions following the removal of the old markings but before the new could be applied. In these circumstances a 3ft diameter black (on bare metal) or white (on camouflage) disc was to be painted forward of the waist window and above the national insignia on both sides of the fuselage. There is no record of this being used, probably because the work time entailed could better be utilised for the application of more permanent markings.

The new markings on the 2nd Division's Liberators proved highly successful and Combat Wing colours could often be distinguished at distances of five miles. In late June 1944 the 93rd Combat Bomb Wing of the 3rd Bomb Division also adopted high-visibility colour markings, officially notified by 8th Air Force HQ on 25 June to be effective within a week. The three Groups of the Wing were distinguished by having one-third of the outboard vertical tail surfaces painted red: the 34th Bomb Group the forward third, the 490th Bomb Group the top third, and the 493rd Bomb group the bottom third. The remainder of the surface was to be painted white or remain bare metal with the aircraft's call-letter and call-number applied. The 8th Air Force instruction required the square/letter Group marking to be retained on aircraft wings but the 93rd Combat Bomb Wing removed or painted out the device on its aircraft. In July 1944 the 93rd Combat Bomb Wing painted the entire outer surface of the vertical tails red on those B-24s equipped as radar lead aircraft. The extent to which this continued is not clear as some B-24s in this category carried standard Group markings. The 92nd Combat Bomb Wing was to have used similar markings in yellow on its B-24s, but the imminent conversion to B-17s caused this plan to be abandoned.

The first 8th Air Force B-17s to use high-visibility colour markings were those of the 1st Combat Bomb Wing, which painted wing tips, tailplanes and an area of fin bright red. This was officially notified by the 8th Air Force on 18 July 1944, although the markings had then been in use for some days. The existing Group markings were retained and the red decor was the same for all three Groups. Both top and bottom surfaces of the horizontal stabilisers, excepting the elevators, were painted. An 80in wide red band extended from the top of the fin to the fuselage, the tail number, individual letter and Group device being either painted round or reinstated. No colour being specified for the call-letter and number, individual Groups made their own decisions, the 91st Bomb Group mostly using black, the 381st white and the 398th yellow.

Other 1st Division Combat Wings did not follow suit until late August that year when, on the 28th, 8th Air Force HQ issued notice of colour markings for all. The 40th Combat Bomb Wing was to have a 4ft wide horizontal band painted across the vertical tail surfaces, the bottom of the band level with the base of the triangle marking, which was not obscured. Each Group sported a different colour, as used in their radio call-signs, the 92nd's being red, the 305th's green and the 306th's yellow. The 41st Combat Bomb Wing had a 3ft wide band painted round the triangle markings to form a 12ft equilateral triangle. The colour for the 303rd and 379th Bomb Groups was as their radio call-sign, red and yellow respectively, while the 384th Bomb Group's colour was black. To obtain contrast the Triangle C device on 303rd Group B-17s was white with a black letter, the 379th's Triangle K black with a white letter and the 384th's Triangle P white with a black letter. The tail number was to be repositioned on the lower part of the bordering triangle and at its apex a figure, 1, 2, 3 or 4, indicating the squadron in numerical order, was to be applied. These border markings were in yellow on 303rd and 384th aircraft and black on 379th. The individual call-letter of the aircraft was painted below the base of the 12ft triangle in the standard colour and size. The 3ft wide border marking was applied to the wing

Below: Awaiting disposal. B-24s at Sandia, New Mexico, in 1946. The red 224 on the high-visibility tail marking of the 93rd Bomb Group is a post-war storage number. The other sun-baked 93rd Bomb Group aircraft carries the 409th Bomb Squadron patch on its nose. This was the only squadron in the 8th Air Force to make use of its official insignia on some of its aircraft throughout hostilities. (NASM)

triangle/letter device on 41st Wing B-17s but without the number given. The 94th Combat Bomb Wing was distinguished by a 4ft wide diagonal band running through the triangle marking, but not eliminating it, with the high point to the rear and the low point to the fore. The colours were red for the 351st Bomb Group, yellow for the 401st and medium blue for the 457th. Why the 384th and 457th Groups did not use their radio call colour green is not known, although one veteran believes the reason was the lack of sufficient bright green paint from the depot. Neither the 40th nor the 94th Combat Bomb Wings had high-visibility colour markings on the wings of their aircraft.

With the exception of the 93rd Combat Bomb Wing, which introduced bright colours on its B-24s at an early date, the 3rd Division Bomb Groups were the last to embrace high-visibility markings, although then in a quite substantial fashion. The 93rd CBW converted from B-24s to B-17s in the late summer of 1944 using the same one-third red tail markings to distinguish its Groups. Additionally a 4ft wide chordwise red stripe was painted on both upper and lower surfaces of the B-17 wings outboard of the engines, and a similar marking 3ft wide chordwise across the tailplane surfaces. Although still listed in Divisional publications, the square/letter devices of these Groups were not applied to the upper surface of the right wing.

a small scale. To avoid compromising camouflage, from 4 July the stripes were removed from the upper surfaces of the wings and the fuselage top from above the national insignia. This was applicable to 8th Air Force fighters but initially to air units detailed for operating from Normandy landing strips. It took some days to effect in full on all 8th Air Force fighters. A further instruction from SHAEF dated 19 August required the 'Distinctive Marking – Aircraft' (the official terminology) to be removed from the all wing surfaces between 25 August and 10 September, cautioning that, owing to the difficulty of removing the paint from fabric-covered aircraft, these markings might still be seen after that date. The remaining under-fuselage stripes were of dubious value. There was some favour for their retention as an aid to recognition by anti-aircraft gunners, although in a low-flying approach the striping was not clearly seen until an aircraft was nearly overhead. Eventually, in a memo of 6 December, SHAEF ordered the remaining markings removed, effective 31 December 1944. In practice these stripes remained on many 8th Air Force fighters well into the New Year and were still to be seen on some as late as March 1945.

Type and Duty Identification Markings

Throughout air warfare there are numerous incidents of friend attacking and often destroying friend. Many of these resulted from the poor standard of aircraft recognition that existed, despite endeavours to train combatants to become proficient in the subject. Unfortunately, some individuals do not appear to have had the necessary aptitude for instant and accurate recognition between aircraft types of friend or foe. In consequence it became the practice of both the RAF and *Luftwaffe* to paint conspicuous markings on some types of aircraft to enhance their recognition.

When the P-47 Thunderbolts arrived in the United Kingdom the 8th Air Force was advised by the British that the fighter's radial engine could cause it to be mistaken for the FW 190, despite the fact that in other respects the two types were unalike. The result was special type identity markings, advised by VIII Fighter Command to other commands on 20 February 1943. In addition to enlarged national insignia (as described above, under 'National Insignia'), white identification striping was to be used on the nose and empennage. The instruction required

the leading edge of the engine cowling to be encircled with a 24in wide white band. A 12in wide white stripe, parallel with the aircraft's longitudinal axis, was to be painted across both sides of the fin and rudder, with the centreline 26in from the top of the fin, together with an 18in white stripe, parallel with the longitudinal axis, across both upper and lower surfaces of the horizontal stabilisers and elevators, the centreline being 33in from the stabiliser tips. An amendment in July that year gave the centreline of the fin and rudder stripe as 32in from the fin tip, which was allowed by the lower placing of the tail number on later P-47s. When bare metal P-47s appeared in April 1944 the type identity markings were painted in matt black. Depots continued to apply

Below: The white type identity cowling marking that was applied to all camouflaged P-47s after depot reassembly in the UK. This is P-47D 42-8699 of the 486th Fighter Squadron. Posing by the nose is 2nd Lieutenant Arthur Rowley, a P-38 pilot of the 55th Fighter Squadron. (A. Rowley)

Above: The 353rd Fighter Group's striking black and yellow checkerboard, seen on P-51D 44-72096 LH:F. (Don Kammer)

Division had decided to transfer the 385th Bomb Group from the 4th to the 93rd Combat Bomb Wing, so the new markings then only involved four Groups. All surfaces of both vertical and horizontal stabilisers, including rudder and elevators, were painted yellow on all B-17s of the four Groups, which were individually distinguished by different coloured stripes encircling the rear fuselage: these were a 3ft wide red stripe for the 94th Bomb Group, two 2ft wide green stripes for the 447th and three 2ft wide yellow stripes for the 486th, while the 487th was identified by having no fuselage stripes. Additionally, 3ft of the top and bottom of the wing tips was painted yellow. There was apparently no requirement to remove the chevron wing markings, so these remained. This work, carried out from mid-February 1945, had to be completed by 5 March. The other 3rd Division Groups applied their allotted colour markings from the last week in January, but on 7 March the Groups of the 13th Combat Bomb Wing were given permission to paint the rudder only in the appropriate colour in lieu of the original requirement for a 4ft wide stripe extending from the top of the fin to its base.

On assignment to the 93rd Combat Bomb Wing the 385th Bomb Group was given new markings in line with those sported by its other Groups. These consisted of a red checkerboard on the vertical tail and red stripes across wings and horizontal tail members. The checkerboard consisted of 28in squares over natural metal or camouflage finish, the Square G marking being deleted on both wing and

tail. Marking out and application took a considerable number of man-hours and some of the Group's aircraft had still not received this marking by the end of hostilities.

High-Visibility Colour Markings on Fighters

At the beginning of February 1944 the 56th Fighter Group, at that time the most successful of the USAAF fighter units operating from the United Kingdom, reintroduced the practice of identifying squadrons of a Group by different engine cowling colours.

Permission was obtained from VIII Fighter Command to overpaint the standard white cowling band of its Thunderbolts with red for the 61st Fighter Squadron, yellow for the 62nd and blue for the 63rd, the colours on the Group's P-47Bs flown while training in the US, except that the blue used in England was of a much lighter hue. The purpose of these markings was stated as twofold: first, to provide quicker and more positive recognition of squadron formations when in a combat situation; and secondly, to confuse enemy fighter pilots, whose aircraft often had coloured nose markings, into believing that the P-47s were friendly. The latter reason was probably no more than wishful thinking. The 56th Fighter Group's first use of these colour markings on a combat mission is reported as 6 February 1944.

VIII Fighter Command then received requests from other Groups wishing to adopt bright colour markings and the situation in early March was confused in this respect. On or about 14 March the Com-

Below: The 479th Fighter Group's Mustangs were identified by having no nose markings. Highlighted by spring sunshine, *American Maid*, 44-15317 L2:U, was the personal aircraft of Lieutenant Elmo Sears. (Elmo Sears)

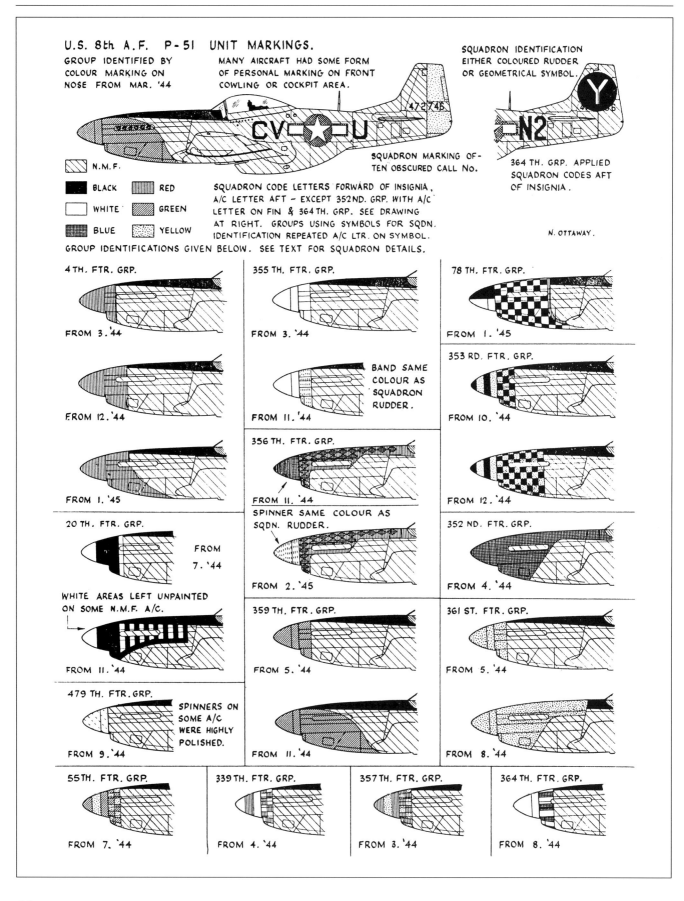

U.S. 8th A.F. P-51 UNIT MARKINGS.

GROUP IDENTIFIED BY COLOUR MARKING ON NOSE FROM MAR. '44

MANY AIRCRAFT HAD SOME FORM OF PERSONAL MARKING ON FRONT COWLING OR COCKPIT AREA.

SQUADRON IDENTIFICATION EITHER COLOURED RUDDER OR GEOMETRICAL SYMBOL.

472746

CV ★ U

N.M.F.

BLACK   RED

WHITE   GREEN

BLUE   YELLOW

SQUADRON MARKING OFTEN OBSCURED CALL No.

SQUADRON CODE LETTERS FORWARD OF INSIGNIA, A/C LETTER AFT – EXCEPT 352ND. GRP. WITH A/C LETTER ON FIN & 364TH. GRP. SEE DRAWING AT RIGHT. GROUPS USING SYMBOLS FOR SQDN. IDENTIFICATION REPEATED A/C LTR. ON SYMBOL. GROUP IDENTIFICATIONS GIVEN BELOW. SEE TEXT FOR SQUADRON DETAILS.

N2

364TH. GRP. APPLIED SQUADRON CODES AFT OF INSIGNIA.

N. OTTAWAY.

4TH. FTR. GRP.
FROM 3.'44

FROM 12.'44

FROM 1.'45

20TH. FTR. GRP.
FROM 7.'44

WHITE AREAS LEFT UNPAINTED ON SOME N.M.F. A/C.

FROM 11.'44

479TH. FTR. GRP.
SPINNERS ON SOME A/C WERE HIGHLY POLISHED.
FROM 9.'44

355TH. FTR. GRP.
FROM 3.'44

BAND SAME COLOUR AS SQUADRON RUDDER.
FROM 11.'44

356TH. FTR. GRP.
FROM 11.'44
SPINNER SAME COLOUR AS SQDN. RUDDER.
FROM 2.'45

359TH. FTR. GRP.
FROM 5.'44

78TH. FTR. GRP.
FROM 1.'45

353RD. FTR. GRP.
FROM 10.'44

FROM 12.'44

352ND. FTR. GRP.
FROM 4.'44

361ST. FTR. GRP.
FROM 5.'44

FROM 11.'44

FROM 8.'44

55TH. FTR. GRP.
FROM 7.'44

339TH. FTR. GRP.
FROM 4.'44

357TH. FTR. GRP.
FROM 3.'44

364TH. FTR. GRP.
FROM 8.'44

mand gave permission for the 4th Fighter Group to paint the noses of its Mustangs bright red as a Group marking. Finally, the Command decided to bring some order to the situation by introducing a system of bright colour noses as a means of distinguishing its various Groups. On 23 March 1944 other commands were notified of these markings, which were being applied to the spinner and a 12in band of the cowling directly aft on P- 51s and a 12in nose band on P-47 cowlings, which amounted to the overpainting of the existing white or black type identity markings. The Groups of the 65th and 67th Fighter Wings were to use 'solid' colours and the 66th Fighter Wing checkerboard. At this date P-47s predominated, with red, green and yellow being allotted to the 56th, 359th and 361st Fighter Groups, while the 78th and 353rd had white and black and yellow and black checkerboard respectively. The 356th Fighter Group was to paint out the white type nose band with camouflage paint and to be recognised by having no special nose colours. For the P-51 Groups the colours were red for the 4th, red and yellow checks for the 357th and white on both camouflage and bare metal finish for the 355th. The 352nd Fighter Group, in the process of changing from P-47s to P-51s, was allocated blue. Red and white checkerboard was al-

lotted for the 339th Fighter Group scheduled to arrive in the theatre in April. On both P-47s and P-51s with checkerboard, the leading checks, having to fit around the curve of the cowling, were not true squares.

Of the P-38 Groups, the 20th's colours were yellow, the 364th's white and the 55th's yellow and white checkerboard. The 364th's colour was advised as red in an initial signal, but this appears to have been in error. As far as is known the 55th Group never applied the allotted checkerboard marking to its Lightnings, probably because it was scheduled to be the first P-38 Group to convert to P-51s.

These markings, applied over a period of two weeks, took longer in the case of the checkerboards

Below: Each Fighter Group established an operational training unit in the autumn of 1944 using War Weary aircraft of the type used on operations. At the end of hostilities, with the prospect of transfer to the Pacific war theatres and re-equipment with a different type of aircraft, the 8th Air Force P-51 units were each assigned two or three Thunderbolts for experience training. These were usually painted in the Group's decor. This P-47D, 42-74676, assigned to the 359th Fighter Group, was shorn of camouflage paint and given a green nose and the codes CS:X. (T. P. Smith)

which required more man-hours and were not a priority task. In changing the nose colours of all its P-47s to scarlet the 56th Fighter Group transferred the squadron colour to the rudders, with the exception of the 63rd Fighter Squadron, identified by having a plain rudder.

Within a month changes to the Group markings were under way, the first being the 352nd Group's extension of the blue cowling band to sweep back and up beyond the engine exhaust manifolds. On bare metal-finish aircraft it was found that the 12in blue band was difficult to distinguish from the standard black type band at distances beyond a quarter of a mile.

Later in the year other P-51 Groups also painted a larger area of the cowling in their colours. This was primarily to increase the distance at which positive identification could be made, but also to avoid confusion with 9th Air Force squadrons which had started to use coloured nose bands and spinners for additional recognition markings. With few exceptions, the 9th Air Force's units did not adopt bright colour markings until the autumn and winter of 1944 when established on the Continent, and there was no overall system detailed from 9th Air Force Headquarters. Combat units were apparently left to their own devices, although Group markings were mostly carried on the tail and squadron decor on the nose, the reverse of the 8th Air Force fighters. Both 12th and 15th Air Force fighter and reconnaissance units also carried Group markings on empennages.

The conversion of the 20th and 364th Fighter Groups from P-38s to P-51s meant that they had to have new Group markings as yellow and white were already in use as 'solid' colours by the 361st and 355th Groups respectively. The 20th adopted a black-and-white striped arrangement, later carried further back to give recognition at greater range. The 364th kept the white spinner and added medium blue horizontal bars to the white nose band. When the 356th Fighter Group replaced its Thunderbolts with Mustangs, late in 1944, a similar situation existed as the 'plain nose' marking was already in use by the 479th Group. An elaborate design of blue and red ringed spinner and blue diamonds on a red background became the 356th's new adornment. Although originally given yellow and white checkerboard as a Group marking, the 55th Fighter Group used yellow and green on its P-51s.

The green was a medium shade, believed to have been the Dark Green camouflage shade used on British aircraft. The result was that the green checks and spinner rings appeared as black from a distance of a few hundred yards. This was not a problem until the 353rd Fighter Group changed to Mustangs in the autumn of 1944. The 353rd, on a neighbouring airfield to the 55th, became aware that if it used the standard two vertical rows of 6in squares confusion would result, so its design featured three rows of checks. This, too, was soon found wanting, and the number of vertical rows was increased to eight.

In August 1944 Colonel Hubert Zemke moved from command of the 56th Fighter Group to that of the 479th, currently equipped with P-38s but scheduled to convert to P-51s. Shortly after assuming command of the 479th Zemke had the geometric symbol markings removed from the P-38s' tails and instead had the rudders painted in a squadron colour, as was the case in the 56th Group. The reason for this change was the greater range at which bright colours could be seen, giving better control of squadron dispositions on combat missions. In the following month the highly successful 357th Fighter Group also adopted bright rudder colours, using red, yellow and no colour to distinguish the three squadrons as was the case in both the 56th and 479th Groups. An appreciation of the visibility range advantage obtained with bright colour led 8th Air Force HQ to detail rudder colours for all fighter squadrons in a document dated 17 October 1944. Some of these colours were changed when the requirement was finalised the following month. The implementation of squadron rudder colours took place over several weeks and it was not until early December that all Groups had their aircraft thus adorned. At this time special colour markings were devised and used on those Fighter Group aircraft employed by the so-called Scouting Forces. All, however, retained the nose markings of the parent Group, all three Scouting Forces being provisional units with no authorised unit establishments.

Special P-38 Lightning Markings

Early operations of the 20th and 55th Fighter Groups highlighted the difficulty of air-to-air recognition by reference to squadron code letters. Beyond 400yds the 18in high letters were not clear and formation leaders requested a better form of identifying the

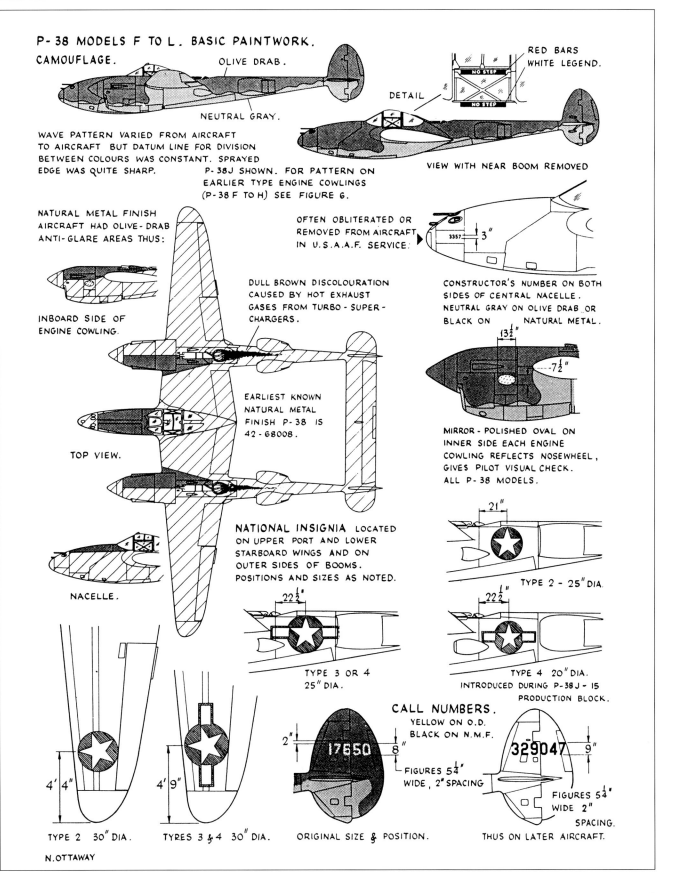

P-38 MODELS F TO L. BASIC PAINTWORK.
CAMOUFLAGE.

OLIVE DRAB.

NEUTRAL GRAY.

RED BARS
WHITE LEGEND.

DETAIL

NO STEP

NO STEP

WAVE PATTERN VARIED FROM AIRCRAFT
TO AIRCRAFT BUT DATUM LINE FOR DIVISION
BETWEEN COLOURS WAS CONSTANT. SPRAYED
EDGE WAS QUITE SHARP.

P-38J SHOWN. FOR PATTERN ON
EARLIER TYPE ENGINE COWLINGS
(P-38 F TO H) SEE FIGURE 6.

VIEW WITH NEAR BOOM REMOVED

NATURAL METAL FINISH
AIRCRAFT HAD OLIVE-DRAB
ANTI-GLARE AREAS THUS:

INBOARD SIDE OF
ENGINE COWLING.

OFTEN OBLITERATED OR
REMOVED FROM AIRCRAFT
IN U.S.A.A.F. SERVICE:

3357   3"

CONSTRUCTOR'S NUMBER ON BOTH
SIDES OF CENTRAL NACELLE.
NEUTRAL GRAY ON OLIVE DRAB OR
BLACK ON NATURAL METAL.

DULL BROWN DISCOLOURATION
CAUSED BY HOT EXHAUST
GASES FROM TURBO-SUPER-
CHARGERS.

$13\frac{1}{2}"$

$-7\frac{1}{2}"$

EARLIEST KNOWN
NATURAL METAL
FINISH P-38 IS
42-68008.

TOP VIEW.

MIRROR-POLISHED OVAL ON
INNER SIDE EACH ENGINE
COWLING REFLECTS NOSEWHEEL,
GIVES PILOT VISUAL CHECK.
ALL P-38 MODELS.

NACELLE.

NATIONAL INSIGNIA LOCATED
ON UPPER PORT AND LOWER
STARBOARD WINGS AND ON
OUTER SIDES OF BOOMS.
POSITIONS AND SIZES AS NOTED.

21"

TYPE 2 - 25" DIA.

$22\frac{1}{2}"$

$22\frac{1}{2}"$

TYPE 3 OR 4
25" DIA.

TYPE 4   20" DIA.
INTRODUCED DURING P-38J-15
PRODUCTION BLOCK.

CALL NUMBERS.
YELLOW ON O.D.
BLACK ON N.M.F.

2"   17650   8"

FIGURES $5\frac{1}{4}"$
WIDE, 2" SPACING

329047   9"

FIGURES $5\frac{1}{4}"$
WIDE 2"
SPACING.

4' 4"

TYPE 2   30" DIA.

4' 9"

TYRES 3 & 4 30" DIA.

ORIGINAL SIZE & POSITION.

THUS ON LATER AIRCRAFT.

N. OTTAWAY

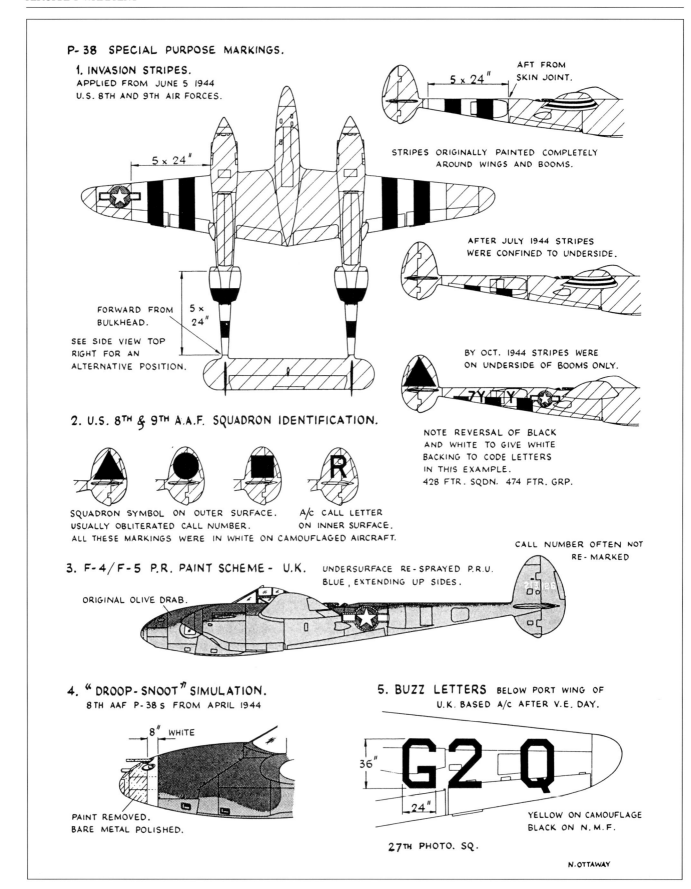

P-38 SPECIAL PURPOSE MARKINGS.

1. INVASION STRIPES.
APPLIED FROM JUNE 5 1944
U.S. 8TH AND 9TH AIR FORCES.

5 x 24"

AFT FROM
SKIN JOINT.

STRIPES ORIGINALLY PAINTED COMPLETELY
AROUND WINGS AND BOOMS.

AFTER JULY 1944 STRIPES
WERE CONFINED TO UNDERSIDE.

FORWARD FROM
BULKHEAD.

5 ×
24"

SEE SIDE VIEW TOP
RIGHT FOR AN
ALTERNATIVE POSITION.

BY OCT. 1944 STRIPES WERE
ON UNDERSIDE OF BOOMS ONLY.

7Y   Y

2. U.S. 8TH & 9TH A.A.F. SQUADRON IDENTIFICATION.

NOTE REVERSAL OF BLACK
AND WHITE TO GIVE WHITE
BACKING TO CODE LETTERS
IN THIS EXAMPLE.
428 FTR. SQDN. 474 FTR. GRP.

R

SQUADRON SYMBOL ON OUTER SURFACE.
USUALLY OBLITERATED CALL NUMBER.
ALL THESE MARKINGS WERE IN WHITE ON CAMOUFLAGED AIRCRAFT.

A/c CALL LETTER
ON INNER SURFACE.

3. F-4/F-5 P.R. PAINT SCHEME - U.K.

UNDERSURFACE RE-SPRAYED P.R.U.
BLUE, EXTENDING UP SIDES.

ORIGINAL OLIVE DRAB.

CALL NUMBER OFTEN NOT
RE-MARKED

4. "DROOP-SNOOT" SIMULATION.
8TH AAF P-38s FROM APRIL 1944

8" WHITE

PAINT REMOVED.
BARE METAL POLISHED.

5. BUZZ LETTERS BELOW PORT WING OF
U.K. BASED A/c AFTER V.E. DAY.

36"

G2 Q

24"

YELLOW ON CAMOUFLAGE
BLACK ON N.M.F.

27TH PHOTO. SQ.

N. OTTAWAY

three squadrons of a Group, particularly in the early stages of a mission when individual aircraft and formations sought to position themselves as briefed. In January 1944 the Groups were instructed to paint 2¹/₂ft wide 'solid' white geometric devices on the outward-facing sides of the P-38s' fins and rudders. One squadron was to use a triangle, another a disc and a third a square, but in no prescribed order relative to the order of squadron designations. With the arrival of the first bare metal-finished P-38s the following month these markings were applied in black. The devices mostly obliterated the designator tail numbers and in many cases these were not repainted. Additionally, the instruction called for an aircraft's individual letter to be painted on the inward facing sides of the vertical tail above the horizontal stabiliser in 2¹/₂ft characters. These markings were generally approved and became a standard requirement for all 8th and 9th Air Force P-38 combat Groups. In January 1944 VIII Fighter Command asked its Group commanders if the same geometric symbols would provide better squadron-in-Group markings for P-47s and P-51s. These and coloured wing tips for flight assignments did not meet with their approval.

In the early spring of 1944 an 'in the field' modification of a small number of P-38s allowed a bombardier and bomb sighting equipment to be carried in the nose section. The purpose was for leading formations of P-38s on fast medium-bombing attacks against heavily flak-defended targets. The modification required the removal of the nose armament and the replacement of the metal nose cap with a Plexiglas moulding. These aircraft were unarmed and thereby vulnerable to enemy fighter interception, and a deceptive camouflage was devised for these so-called Droopsnoot Lightnings. An 8in wide white band was painted round the nose directly behind the Plexiglas nosepiece. Standard armed P-38s in combat Groups were also given an 8in white nose band immediately in front of the gun

Right: All factory-camouflaged P-38 Lightnings had an oval-shaped area of polished bare metal on the lower, inward-facing sides of the engine cowlings. This served to allow the pilot to check on the position of the nose landing gear. A 'mirror' can be clearly seen in this photograph of an Dark Olive Drab and Neutral Gray-painted 20th Fighter Group P-38H. The partly covered four-digit number on the nose is the constructor's number. (Art Rowley)

compartment covers, and any paintwork forward of the band was removed and the bare metal highly polished. This simulation of the Droopsnoot's nose was most effective as only at close range could the difference be clearly seen.

'D-Day Stripes'

Planning for the cross-Channel invasion of Continental Europe in the spring of 1944 included the application of distinctive markings to Allied aircraft. The sheer scale of the operation involving sea and ground forces would inevitably include elements deficient in aircraft recognition, and as strong opposition was expected from the *Luftwaffe* it was imperative that highly conspicuous markings were employed to distinguish Allied aircraft. The form eventually decided upon was a series of black and white stripes encircling both wings and fuselage. Although compromising camouflage, it was felt that Allied aircraft were more at risk in the air than on their airfields in the situations envisaged. Black and white stripes had been a type identification marking carried under the wings of RAF Typhoon and

Above: The five bands of 'D-Day stripes' on a fighter took up a 90in width on wings and fuselage, partly or fully covering any code letters on the latter. This was the case with P-47D 42-8496, *Galloping Catastrophe*, of the Air Sea Rescue Squadron, where the codes 5F:X were still to be reinstated when this photograph was taken. The 96th Bomb Group B-17F in the background, 42-3089 BX:V, had been retired from combat and stripped of armament and was used as a 'hack'.

Tempest fighters, and the deletion of this marking in early February 1944 was a preparatory step. Applying the distinctive marking would entail considerable numbers of man-hours, yet it was imperative that this work be carried out only within a few hours of the launch of the invasion, to avoid enemy observation alerting him to the impending attack. On 3 May HQ Allied Expeditionary Air Force approached RAF and USAAF commands for an estimate of the time it would take to apply these markings, the 48 hours allowed being based on their replies.

The directive to apply the distinctive markings was issued late on the evening of 3 June, effective next day, with a stipulation that no aircraft so painted should fly within twenty miles of hostile territory until instructed. Bad weather delayed the invasion forces for a day, adding a risk that enemy agents, if any, or reconnaissance aircraft crews, might observe the distinctively marked aircraft on their bases and thus the forthcoming assault could be compromised. Fortunately, this did not occur.

The instruction involved only the fighter and reconnaissance units of the 8th Air Force and for single-engine types required five alternating white and black stripes, each 18in wide. On the wings they were to be placed so that the edge of the outer white stripe was 6in from the national insignia. The fuselage stripes were to begin 18in forward of the leading edge of the tailplane but should not obscure the national insignia. On twin-engine aircraft the width of the stripes was to be 24in. Unit identification markings were to remain or, if obliterated in the cause of haste, to be restored at the earliest opportunity. With the exception of the P-38 Groups, most units did retain the squadron codes, either masking them before applying the stripes or, more often, repainting over the stripes. In the four P-38 Groups where the wider stripes completely covered all squadron codes on the fuselage booms, it appears that permission was given not to reinstate them, possibly due to the pending conversion to P-51s, although this would be delayed. On the Mustangs of the 352nd Fighter Group the individual aircraft letter, having been obscured by the stripes, was repainted on the fuselage forward of the leading edge of the wing or on the tail fin. The tail fin soon became the preferred location and individual 'plane-in-squadron' letters were no longer placed on the rear fuselage of the 352nd's aircraft.

The white and black stripes, popularly known as 'D-Day' or 'invasion' stripes, were the most conspicuous tactical markings carried by Allied aircraft of the Second World War and are estimated to have been borne by some six thousand machines.

By mid-July 1944 many RAF 2nd Tactical Air Force and US 9th Air Force fighter units were operating from advanced landing grounds in Normandy. Camouflage against air attack had been reinstated, although *Luftwaffe* daylight activity was usually on

Although General Doolittle was still hoping to move his Fighter Groups to the Continent as late as a few weeks before the Nazi collapse, a shortage of suitable airfields and difficulties with logistics prevented this transfer. The application of camouflage gradually waned, although some Groups had carried out very little anyway.

By late 1944 the practice had ceased in most Groups—with the exception of the 56th which, on receipt of P-47M models, had a distinctive camouflage scheme for each of its squadrons, even though these were more uniforms than camouflage.

Special Duty Finishes

The RAF had found that the best camouflage finish for its unarmed, high-flying photographic reconnaissance aircraft was an all-over azure blue. The shade developed for this purpose was called Deep Sky Blue, but was more commonly referred to as PRU Blue. Influenced by the British work in photographic reconnaissance, the USAAF desired similar colours on the P-38 Lightnings modified for this purpose, designated F-4 and F-5. Lockheed and the Materiel Command fostered a development known as Haze

paint, which had peculiar properties allowing blue and violet shades to be reflected while absorbing other colours. Haze paint was applied to most photographic Lightning models produced between March and October 1942 before several problems in application and wear led to its discontinuation. F-5s were then finished in normal Dark Olive Drab and Neutral Gray, as then carried by fighter Lightnings.

By the spring of 1943 an new form of Synthetic Haze paint had been developed which was applied to F-5s until bare metal finish was introduced at the end of that year. This application consisted of an overall base colour, Sky Base Blue, of a similar shade to PRU Blue. A very light blue, produced to the Synthetic Haze formula and known as Flight Blue, was then sprayed in varying degrees on areas of the airframe where shadows would occur in bright sunlight at a normal flight attitude. The object was to lighten such areas and, as far as possible, maintain an overall blue hue that would be lost in the sky background. Several of the 7th Photographic Group's aircraft at Mount Farm wore Haze paint; others which had arrived in olive drab and grey were painted with Deep Sky Blue in the UK, as were some of the bare metal-finished models received later in 1944. However, by 1945 a 'silver' finish had become acceptable for all occasions.

The Spitfire PR.XI and Mosquito PR.XVI photographic reconnaissance aircraft employed by the 7th

Below: An early Spitfire XI of the 7th Photographic Group in standard PRU Blue with the RAF roundels painted out and replaced by AN-I-9b national insignia. This aircraft carries the nickname *Priscilla* in white on the engine bay.

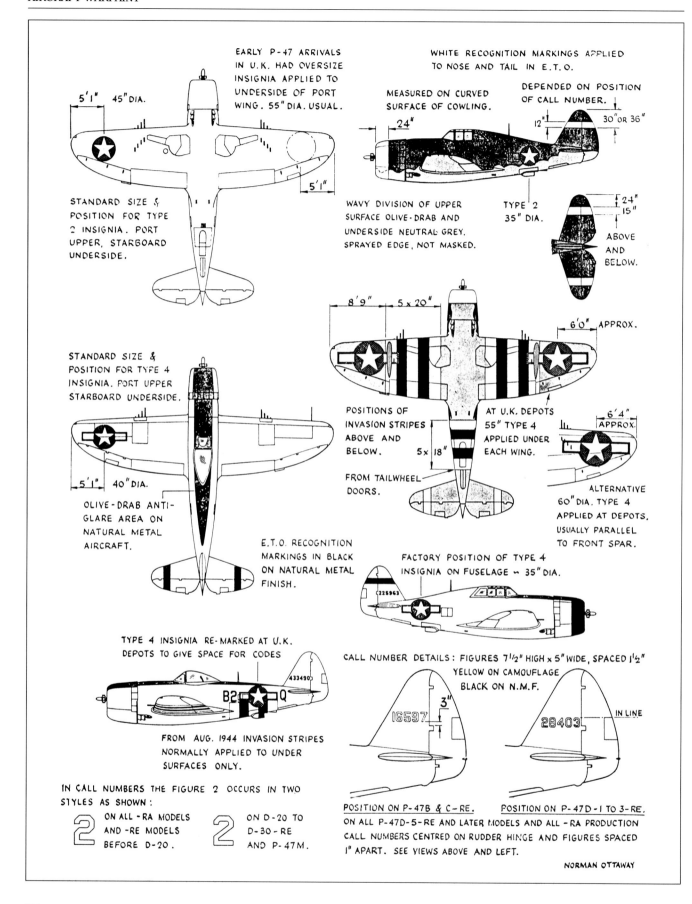

EARLY P-47 ARRIVALS IN U.K. HAD OVERSIZE INSIGNIA APPLIED TO UNDERSIDE OF PORT WING. 55" DIA. USUAL.

WHITE RECOGNITION MARKINGS APPLIED TO NOSE AND TAIL IN E.T.O.

MEASURED ON CURVED SURFACE OF COWLING.

DEPENDED ON POSITION OF CALL NUMBER.

STANDARD SIZE & POSITION FOR TYPE 2 INSIGNIA. PORT UPPER, STARBOARD UNDERSIDE.

WAVY DIVISION OF UPPER SURFACE OLIVE-DRAB AND UNDERSIDE NEUTRAL GREY. SPRAYED EDGE, NOT MASKED.

TYPE 2 35" DIA.

ABOVE AND BELOW.

STANDARD SIZE & POSITION FOR TYPE 4 INSIGNIA. PORT UPPER STARBOARD UNDERSIDE.

POSITIONS OF INVASION STRIPES ABOVE AND BELOW.

AT U.K. DEPOTS 55" TYPE 4 APPLIED UNDER EACH WING.

FROM TAILWHEEL DOORS.

OLIVE-DRAB ANTI-GLARE AREA ON NATURAL METAL AIRCRAFT.

ALTERNATIVE 60" DIA. TYPE 4 APPLIED AT DEPOTS. USUALLY PARALLEL TO FRONT SPAR.

E.T.O. RECOGNITION MARKINGS IN BLACK ON NATURAL METAL FINISH.

FACTORY POSITION OF TYPE 4 INSIGNIA ON FUSELAGE ~ 35" DIA.

TYPE 4 INSIGNIA RE-MARKED AT U.K. DEPOTS TO GIVE SPACE FOR CODES

FROM AUG. 1944 INVASION STRIPES NORMALLY APPLIED TO UNDER SURFACES ONLY.

IN CALL NUMBERS THE FIGURE 2 OCCURS IN TWO STYLES AS SHOWN:

ON ALL -RA MODELS AND -RE MODELS BEFORE D-20.

ON D-20 TO D-30-RE AND P-47M.

CALL NUMBER DETAILS: FIGURES 7½" HIGH x 5" WIDE, SPACED 1½" YELLOW ON CAMOUFLAGE BLACK ON N.M.F.

IN LINE

POSITION ON P-47B & C-RE.   POSITION ON P-47D-1 TO 3-RE. ON ALL P-47D-5-RE AND LATER MODELS AND ALL -RA PRODUCTION CALL NUMBERS CENTRED ON RUDDER HINGE AND FIGURES SPACED 1" APART. SEE VIEWS ABOVE AND LEFT.

NORMAN OTTAWAY

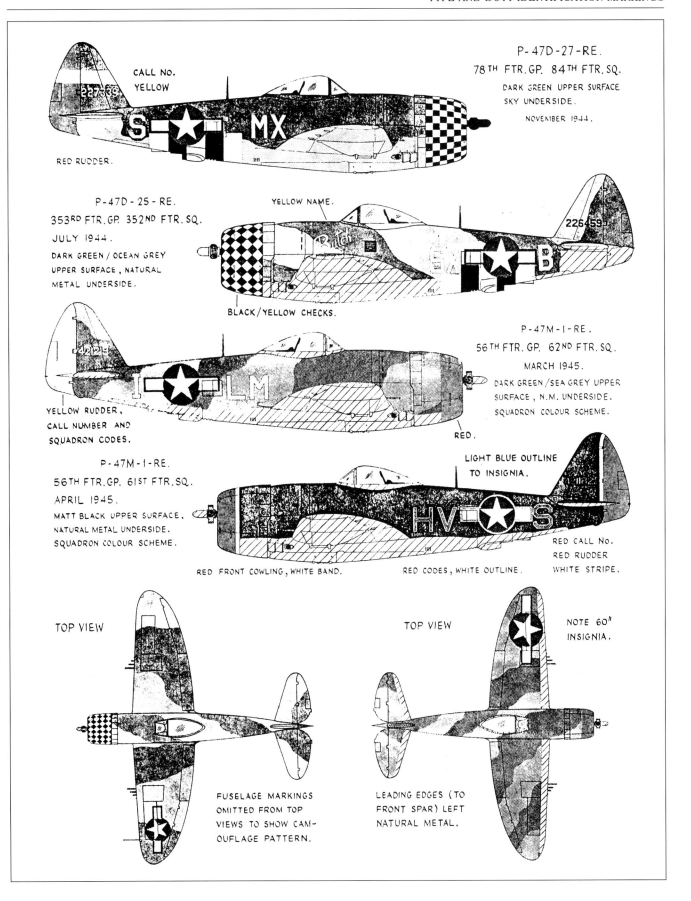

CALL NO.
YELLOW

227339

RED RUDDER.

P-47D-27-RE.
78TH FTR. GP. 84TH FTR. SQ.
DARK GREEN UPPER SURFACE
SKY UNDERSIDE.
NOVEMBER 1944.

P-47D-25-RE.
353RD FTR. GP. 352ND FTR. SQ.
JULY 1944.
DARK GREEN / OCEAN GREY
UPPER SURFACE, NATURAL
METAL UNDERSIDE.

YELLOW NAME.

226459

BLACK/YELLOW CHECKS.

YELLOW RUDDER,
CALL NUMBER AND
SQUADRON CODES.

P-47M-1-RE.
56TH FTR. GP. 62ND FTR. SQ.
MARCH 1945.
DARK GREEN / SEA GREY UPPER
SURFACE, N.M. UNDERSIDE.
SQUADRON COLOUR SCHEME.

RED.

P-47M-1-RE.
56TH FTR. GP. 61ST FTR. SQ.
APRIL 1945.
MATT BLACK UPPER SURFACE,
NATURAL METAL UNDERSIDE.
SQUADRON COLOUR SCHEME.

LIGHT BLUE OUTLINE
TO INSIGNIA.

RED CALL No.
RED RUDDER
WHITE STRIPE.

RED FRONT COWLING, WHITE BAND.   RED CODES, WHITE OUTLINE.

TOP VIEW

TOP VIEW

NOTE 60"
INSIGNIA.

FUSELAGE MARKINGS
OMITTED FROM TOP
VIEWS TO SHOW CAM-
OUFLAGE PATTERN.

LEADING EDGES (TO
FRONT SPAR) LEFT
NATURAL METAL.

55

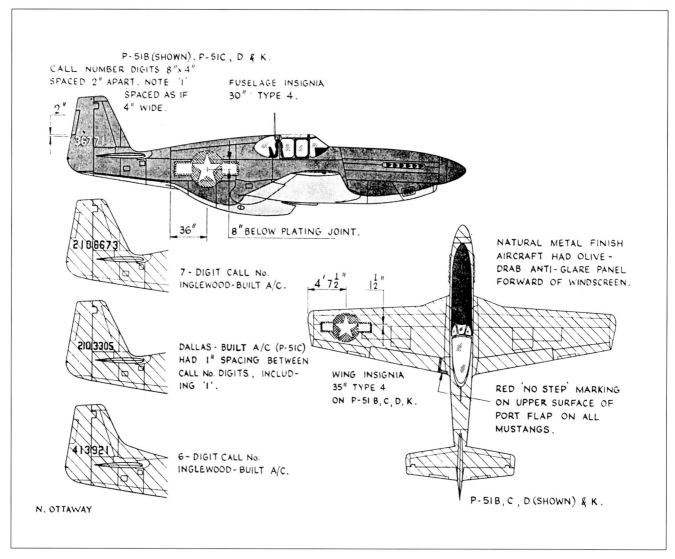

P-51B (SHOWN), P-51C, D & K.
CALL NUMBER DIGITS 8"x 4"
SPACED 2" APART. NOTE 'I'
SPACED AS IF
4" WIDE.

2"

FUSELAGE INSIGNIA
30" TYPE 4.

367 71

36"   8" BELOW PLATING JOINT.

21 06673

7 - DIGIT CALL No.
INGLEWOOD-BUILT A/C.

210 3305

DALLAS - BUILT A/C (P-51C)
HAD 1" SPACING BETWEEN
CALL No. DIGITS, INCLUD-
ING 'I'.

WING INSIGNIA
35" TYPE 4
ON P-51 B, C, D, K.

4 13921

6 - DIGIT CALL No.
INGLEWOOD - BUILT A/C.

N. OTTAWAY

4' 7½"   1½"

NATURAL METAL FINISH
AIRCRAFT HAD OLIVE -
DRAB ANTI - GLARE PANEL
FORWARD OF WINDSCREEN.

RED 'NO STEP' MARKING
ON UPPER SURFACE OF
PORT FLAP ON ALL
MUSTANGS.

P-51B, C, D (SHOWN) & K.

these markings for both the 8th and 9th Air Forces until early in 1945. However, from the spring of 1944 some 8th Air Force Fighter Groups dispensed with all or part of the scheme, indicating that these markings were no longer deemed as important as they were in the previous year when P-47s were new to the scene.

In May 1944 a special P-47 unit was formed at Boxted to carry out air–sea rescue patrols. As these operations would usually only entail two aircraft flying at altitudes below 5,000ft, it was felt that more prominent type identity markings were required which would also indicate the aircraft's duty. In place of the usual white type identity stripe ASR P-47s had the following yellow markings: wing tips, extending 14in from the tips; an 18in wide band round fin and rudder; and an 18in wide band encircling the tailplane, located 25in from the tips. Addition-

ally, the front of the engine cowling was painted with 15in wide encircling red, white and blue stripes. When first specified, an 18in yellow band round the centre of each wing was specified, but this was dropped in favour of the yellow wing tips as underwing racks would obstruct its application.

Allied to the view that a fighter with a radial engine was an FW 190 was the even more ingrained belief that a fighter with square cut wing tips was a Messerschmitt, even though the so-configured Bf 109E model had been withdrawn by the Luftwaffe in the West during 1941. The RAF had given its Mustangs special type identity markings for this reason and with the coming of the P-51B in November 1943 the USAAF was advised to apply a similar scheme. The use of white banding, as with the P-47, was brought into use and advised as follows on 14 December 1943 by VIII Fighter Command, un-

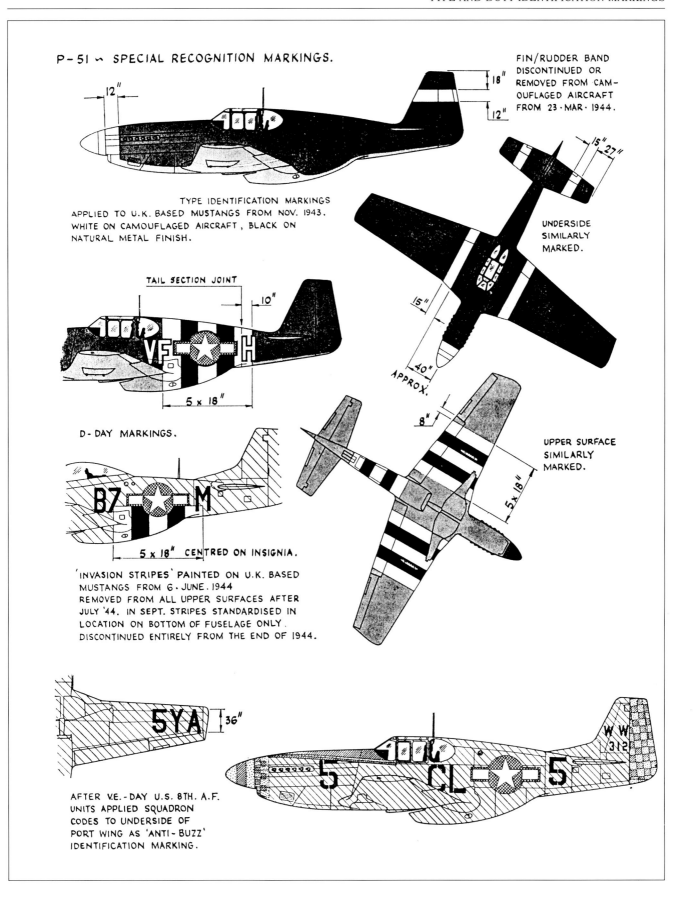

P-51 ~ SPECIAL RECOGNITION MARKINGS.

12"

18"

12"

FIN/RUDDER BAND DISCONTINUED OR REMOVED FROM CAMOUFLAGED AIRCRAFT FROM 23·MAR·1944.

TYPE IDENTIFICATION MARKINGS APPLIED TO U.K. BASED MUSTANGS FROM NOV. 1943. WHITE ON CAMOUFLAGED AIRCRAFT, BLACK ON NATURAL METAL FINISH.

15" 27"

UNDERSIDE SIMILARLY MARKED.

TAIL SECTION JOINT

10"

15"

VF H

5 x 18"

40" APPROX.

8"

D-DAY MARKINGS.

B7 M

5 x 18"

UPPER SURFACE SIMILARLY MARKED.

5 x 18" CENTRED ON INSIGNIA.

'INVASION STRIPES' PAINTED ON U.K. BASED MUSTANGS FROM 6·JUNE·1944 REMOVED FROM ALL UPPER SURFACES AFTER JULY '44. IN SEPT. STRIPES STANDARDISED IN LOCATION ON BOTTOM OF FUSELAGE ONLY, DISCONTINUED ENTIRELY FROM THE END OF 1944.

5YA 36"

WW 312

AFTER V.E.-DAY U.S. 8TH. A.F. UNITS APPLIED SQUADRON CODES TO UNDERSIDE OF PORT WING AS 'ANTI-BUZZ' IDENTIFICATION MARKING.

5 CL 5

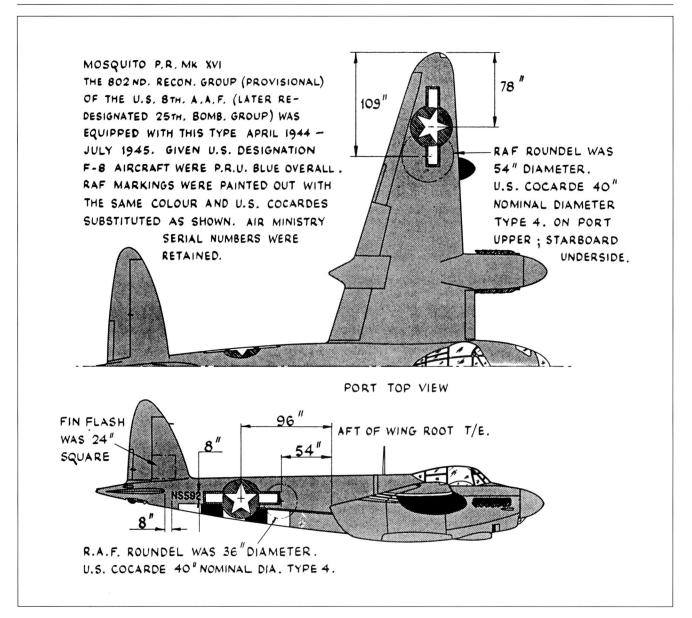

MOSQUITO P.R. MK XVI
THE 802 ND. RECON. GROUP (PROVISIONAL)
OF THE U.S. 8TH. A.A.F. (LATER RE-
DESIGNATED 25TH. BOMB. GROUP) WAS
EQUIPPED WITH THIS TYPE APRIL 1944 -
JULY 1945. GIVEN U.S. DESIGNATION
F-8 AIRCRAFT WERE P.R.U. BLUE OVERALL.
RAF MARKINGS WERE PAINTED OUT WITH
THE SAME COLOUR AND U.S. COCARDES
SUBSTITUTED AS SHOWN. AIR MINISTRY
SERIAL NUMBERS WERE
RETAINED.

109"

78"

RAF ROUNDEL WAS
54" DIAMETER.
U.S. COCARDE 40"
NOMINAL DIAMETER
TYPE 4. ON PORT
UPPER ; STARBOARD
UNDERSIDE.

PORT TOP VIEW

FIN FLASH
WAS 24"
SQUARE

96"

8"

54"

AFT OF WING ROOT T/E.

NS592

8"

R.A.F. ROUNDEL WAS 36" DIAMETER.
U.S. COCARDE 40" NOMINAL DIA. TYPE 4.

der whose operational control the lone 9th Air Force P-51B Group commenced operations on the first day of that month: a white spinner and 12in cowling band immediately aft; a 12in band across the fin and rudder, the centreline 24in below the fin top; a 15in wide stripe round each horizontal stabiliser and elevator centred 33in from the tip; and a 15in wide band round each wing with the inner edge passing through the point where the wing fillet curve begins at approximately 15ft from the wing tips. Following complaints from Fighter Group commanders, on 23 March 1944 the white striping around fin and rudder was discontinued and eventually removed from Mustangs so marked, the reason being that this band was claimed to break up the outline of the

square-cut vertical tail which was considered a valuable recognition feature. As with the P-47, the bare metal-finished Mustangs received these markings in black. Interestingly, the fin and rudder band was then reinstated, but a reason for this does not appear to have been recorded.

A type/duty identification marking was introduced on De Havilland Mosquito XVI scout and photographic reconnaissance aircraft of the 25th Bomb Group (R) in the high summer of 1944. This resulted from a number of attacks by P-51s on Mosquitos while over hostile territory, in most cases where the Mosquito had been mistakenly identified as an Me 210 or Me 410. On 16 August the 8th Air Force signalled that Mosquitos were having their vertical tails painted red as an aid to recognition. Unfortunately, P-51 'bounces' were still reported and on 23 September 1944 another signal advised that the whole tail assembly would be painted red. The red used was RAF roundel red.

The top secret operational experiments with electronic and radio weapons carried out from Fersfield in Norfolk was chiefly concerned with the 'Castor' project. This involved War Weary B-17s, stripped of all armour and armament, being loaded with 20,000lb of explosives. After being flown off by a volunteer skeleton crew, control was taken by a following 'mother' aircraft through radio guidance. When this was achieved the crew parachuted over England and the explosive-filled bomber was headed out towards a target in enemy-controlled territory. As the 'mother' B-17 had to fly some distance behind and above the 'baby', it was essential that the latter was not lost from view. To make the 'baby' highly visible the upper surfaces of wings, fuselage and tail were sprayed white. In most cases, sprayed in haste shortly before an operational launch was made, the white coat was often far from uniform. At some point during these operations, which were carried out from August 1944 to January 1945, yellow was used in place of white as this was found to make the 'baby' more conspicuous.

In the later stages of the strategic bombing campaign a few Groups used special markings to distinguish their radar-equipped pathfinder aircraft. These were Group-originated and not sponsored by higher command. Most notable were the Liberators of the 93rd and 446th Bomb Groups, where the G-H aircraft of the 329th Bomb Squadron had red noses and all H2X-equipped aircraft in the 446th had a black circle superimposed on Group/Wing tail markings.

Formation Assembly Leaders

Daylight bombing operations where deep penetrations of enemy airspace were involved necessitated a launch at first light and, on short winter days, before dawn. With increasing numbers of bombers in the air, during the closing months of 1943 there were a number of occasions when bombers from one Group would mistakenly join the formation of another during the assembly of a task force in darkness or half-light. The chief means of identifying individual Group formations was through the discharge of specified coloured flares by the lead-

Above: Selected B-17s and B-24s, usually War Weary-classified, were used on radio-relay sorties which usually entailed orbiting over the North Sea or liberated areas of the Continent. B-17F 42-30721 VP:I of the 381st Bomb Group, which was utilised for this duty, had red and white stripes painted round the rear fuselage to identify this aircraft to investigative Allied fighters. Most radio-relay 'ships' did not have any special distinguishing markings. (USAF)

ing aircraft, but this had the disadvantage that the leading aircraft, already carrying an extra crewman, was weighed down with a considerable stock of pyrotechnics to allow for their discharge at frequent intervals. Moreover, in conditions of poor visibility, the coloured flare combinations could easily be mistaken. The 2nd Bomb Division, particularly troubled by assembly problems in the congested airspace over East Anglia, devised a means of improved recognition of individual formations. A B-24 retired from operations through high combat hours had all armour and armament removed. An arrangement of

Above: *The Little Garmper* was the 491st Bomb Group's first assembly ship, salvaged in August 1944 not long after this photograph was taken at Metfield. B-24D 42-40722 originally served with the 389th Bomb Group, with whom it flew 52 missions, including the famous low-level attack on the Ploesti oil plants on 1 August 1943. The overall yellow with red polka dots and trim took many man hours, and replacement aircraft for this duty were less exotically decorated. (USAAF)

electric lights was then fitted in the former tail turret position and in the fuselage sides; extra flare chutes were installed and the whole aircraft was painted with bright and distinctive markings. Such aircraft were then used to precede a Group take-off and orbit in the Group assembly area at prearranged altitudes, fully lit and discharging flares. Once the Group formation was completed this special aircraft would return to base.

The origin of this idea and orders covering its introduction cannot be found in 8th Air Force records, nor was there a common name for these special aircraft, which are referred to in various 2nd Division documents as 'beacon ships', 'rendezvous ships', 'forming ships', 'circus leaders', 'monitors' or 'marshalling aircraft' and by other terms, although the commonest was assembly ships. The first docu-

mented use of an assembly ship was by the 93rd Bomb Group on 30 November 1943, but at this date it was apparently still in normal camouflage colours. The first reference to an assembly ship with special markings is early in January 1944 when the 389th Bomb Group refers to its 'Zebra forming aircraft'. It also appears that by this time the Division had accepted the value of these aircraft, for other time-expired B-24s were issued to recently arrived Groups for this purpose. The distinctive colour markings appear to have come into use in most Groups then operational early in March 1944, and by June all fourteen 2nd Division B-24 Groups had an assembly ship. Some of these aircraft were retired or destroyed and replaced by other War Wearies, the colour schemes usually being less ambitious, and towards the end of hostilities a few Groups were using aircraft without distinctive markings for assembly purposes. Only one B-17 Wing adopted the assembly ship idea, but it did not sustain the practice. This was the 40th Combat Bomb Wing, whose three Groups painted up their 'hack' Fortresses in bizarre colour arrangements.

The assembly ship schemes are described later in the book in the section dealing with individual unit markings.

Above: Until retired from combat the 489th Bomb Group's assembly ship served with the 44th Bomb Group and, surprisingly, the original factory-applied national insignia with a red surround was never amended. In addition to the mass of 12in diameter yellow 'polka dots' this B-24H had numerous signal lights, including five forming a cross in the faired-over fuselage end. (W. A. Portouw)

Below: The second 467th Bomb Group assembly ship was painted up with markings that were very similar to those on the first aircraft used for this purpose. B-24H 41-29393 was also known by the same name and had an illuminated letter P on each side of the fuselage. (James Mahoney)

Identification Markings of Transport Units

Although primarily cast as a strategic bombing organisation, the 8th Air Force had a tactical arm until the autumn of 1943. The initial air movement to the United Kingdom in 1942 included three Troop Carrier Groups equipped with the C-47 Skytrain (Dakota) and C-53 Skytrooper, military versions of the successful DC-3 airliner. They were subject to the same flying control as the bomber organisations and radio call-letters were used, these being in most cases painted on the rear fuselage of the aircraft in grey. No official squadron markings were issued and no unit-derived insignia are known to have been applied to these C-47s and C-53s before their movement to North Africa in November 1942. In common with other types destined for the 12th Air Force, a yellow surround was added to the fuselage national insignia.

Shortly after the departure of these three groups the depleted 315th Troop Carrier Group arrived in the UK, having had two of its original squadrons reassigned before overseas movement. The remaining two were issued with squadron codes which were painted on the fuselage in yellow forward of the national insignia. All but half a dozen of these aircraft were then despatched to North Africa on temporary

Above: B-24H serial 41-28697 served the 458th Bomb Group as an assembly ship after the original aircraft employed for this purpose was destroyed by fire. A similar flamboyant paint scheme of red and blue 'polka dots' on the white front half of the fuselage and red and yellow on the rear camouflaged part made this aircraft the most colourful of all these special duty aircraft painted for unmistakable recognition. (USAF)

duty, which endured for several months. The 434th Troop Carrier Group arrived in the UK in September 1943 but received no codes or unit markings before transfer to the regenerated 9th Air Force in October. When code letters were again displayed on C-47s they were painted on the side of the nose. The reason for this placing, which became the standard location on the type, was the need to keep the fuselage sides in the proximity of the troop entry doors clear for a chalked loading number used on combat operations. Furthermore, squadron codes on the rear fuselage were hidden when C-47 loading doors were open.

VIII Air Force Service Command formed its own organisation for transportation to 8th Air Force bases and this was officially established as the 27th Transport Group, although it was erroneously referred to as the 27th Air Transport Group in VIII AFSC documents for most of its existence. No unit identification markings were carried by this Group's aircraft until the 31st Transport Group was organised under IX AFSC in the winter of 1943/44. Then, to distinguish the two Groups, the 27th's aircraft carried

a small white disc on the fin and the 31st a small white triangle similarly located. However, both Groups were at this time taken under the theatre air service command.

Non-Combat Unit Aircraft Markings

There were a great many training and communication aircraft in non-combat units assigned to the 8th Air Force. Generally, until the spring of 1944 these were either devoid of any unit identification apart from the codes allocated in SD110. When the combat organisations turned to using colour markings these began to appear on non-combat types, but in all cases they were unauthorised decorations originated by the unit itself. Wing and Division HQ

Flights all came to decorate their communications aircraft with coloured markings, but they were rarely uniform through not being officially specified. The fighter training Groups were similarly noted for the variation in the decor of their aircraft, in part due to the frequent turn-around in aircraft assignments, most of their complements being War Weary. Tow-target Flights took to painting the extremities of Vultee A-35 Vengeance wings and empennages with yellow, but this again appears to have been a unit-generated marking as it was not used by all the units. Indeed, a good example of the seemingly casual attitude towards aircraft markings that existed in some organisations is exemplified by the 3rd Tow Target and Gunnery Flight, which did not even replace the RAF roundel with the US insignia on the A-35s it used.

The training and communications types assigned to operational Groups were usually decorated with variations of the official markings carried on their combat aircraft. It was again a matter of individual choice, for no instructions were issued by commands on this matter. By 1945 some of the Fighter Groups

Above: It has been estimated that more than 70 per cent of personal motifs on 8th Air Force aircraft featured the female form. The deep-sided nose of the Liberator provided an excellent location for artwork. This voluptuous nude strikes the same pose as a swimsuit-clad girl in the well known Vagas calendar of those days. The aircraft is B-24J *Government Girl*, serial 42-50726, of the 389th Bomb Group. (USAAF)

were giving special training aircraft, specifically fighter types modified as two-seaters, overall coats of bright colour, red, blue and yellow being noted. In a few Bomb Groups overall bright colours were applied to War Weary 'hacks' used for training or communications duties, black and light green B-17s being examples.

War Weary Classification

By the spring of 1944 the 8th Air Force had an increasing number of combat types which were either suffering some performance deficiency that could not be solved or were becoming too worn for further operational use. In the cause of safety a new classification was introduced for these aircraft under the term 'War Weary', operating organisations being instructed to make written application to their command where the condition of an aircraft met these criteria To ensure that the status of War Weary aircraft was evident, its unit was required to paint the letters WW in yellow on the fin, sized the same as the tail number, to which, if space allowed, it was to be placed as a suffix. On bare metal finish the WW was marked in black. These markings were first introduced on P-47s of the air–sea rescue squadron in May 1944 and were extended to other aircraft qualifying under the memorandum, dated 26 June 1944, covering the designation, identification and disposal of aircraft permanently unfit for combat. Although War Weary aircraft were supposedly restricted to non-combat duties, in practice they were occasionally employed on combat missions.

Special Functional Markings

Most aircraft carry markings connected with their function, notably servicing. USAAF aircraft had many instructions in small black characters, only visible from close proximity. There were also red warning panels for 'No Step' areas, first aid kits and

Below: Despite the short average life of a combat aircraft many hours were spent in embellishment with a paintbrush. In addition to the main painting for *Ark Angel*, small green and yellow representations of this were placed close to the position of each of the aircraft's crew members. B-24J 44-40073 T8:–B of the 853rd Bomb Squadron has the outer propeller bosses painted light blue and a yellow bomb-bay door stripe. (USAAF)

the location of fire extinguishers. On natural metal finish aircraft an anti-dazzle panel of matt paint was applied forward of the cockpit windshield, usually extending to the metal extremity of the nose. The specified colour was matt olive drab, although matt black was used by some manufacturers. In addition to these factory-applied markings, there were often others of a functional nature applied by modification centres, depots or combat units.

A special marking for P-38J aircraft which had leading-edge wing tanks installed before delivery to the UK was an 8in cross (as a plus sign) painted on the left side of the fuselage below the aircraft serial number. White was used on camouflaged machines and black on bare metal. The same device was used on P-51B/C models that had the 85 US gallon fuselage tank installed before overseas delivery.

It was found that the roll-up bomb-bay doors of B-24s sometimes failed fully to open or close, which could lead to damage, particularly in the former case when bombs were released. In the spring of 1944, to provide a visual indication so that a crew could be warned by others of malfunctioning bomb-bay doors, Groups were advised to paint an 7in wide yellow stripe along the lower edge of the doors of camouflaged B-24s. For those in metal finish the stripe was advised as green, 13in wide, taking up two sections of the door. In practice the stripe was often white on painted doors and yellow or red on bare metal. The width of the stripe also varied, 13in being the most common.

As an aid in judging a diving turn for dive-bombing, in the spring of 1945 some P-47s and P-51s

had a series of graduated degree lines painted on the leading edges of wings for the pilot to use in sighting a diving turn. The colours were black or red on bare metal and white or yellow on camouflage.

An aid to the top turret gunner of a B-24 was the placing of the figure 9 on the inner side of No 1 engine nacelle and a 3 in a similar position on No 4, to correspond with the clock code, to indicate the location of other aircraft in crew communication. Also, in the heat of battle gunners sometimes became confused and this visual sign helped prevent a wrong direction call. The 445th and 467th Bomb Groups were the only two Groups which employed these markings, the latter organisation proving to be the most efficient Group in the 2nd Air Division.

Bond Presentation Aircraft

The promotion of investment in US government funds included a scheme whereby savings bonds could 'buy' a specific piece of military equipment. Aircraft were a popular choice and commercial or voluntary organisations purchasing bonds to the total value of a chosen type were given an acknowledgement thereon. Most 'bond' aircraft reaching the 8th Air Force were P-47s, and these carried an inscription on the side of the fuselage between the cockpit and national insignia. Usually in black or white 6in high block capitals, the wording was generally in the form of a statement; *Sovereign Senator's Tolerance* and *Spirit of Crawford County, Missouri* are examples, both being P-47Ds assigned to the 63rd Fighter Squadron in 1944. Squadron code

letters were often omitted of the left side of the fuselage when these acknowledgements were displayed.

Personal Markings

Warriors have decorated their equipment for centuries and those of the Second World War were no exception. RAF aircrew bestowed nicknames, motifs and operational achievement signs on the sides of their aircraft and this practice was taken up in more flamboyant form by USAAF personnel. The majority of 8th Air Force combat aircraft were named at some period of their employment. There were changes of name when a new crew did not like the original. In some cases there were two names: removing the first was often considered unlucky. Slogans, rather than names, were not uncommon.

The first bombers arriving from the United States had names neatly rendered in small block capitals, but this command-ordered reserve soon gave way to large, flamboyant styles of presentation. On camouflaged aircraft the predominant colour for names was yellow. Named aircraft mostly had an accompanying motif, of which it is estimated some 70 per cent featured the female form. Here, too, provided such art was not too explicit, command did not object to the amount of space occupied on the nose side by these paintings. The record of an individual warplane's achievement was carried in form of bomb silhouettes for bombing missions completed, mostly in yellow on camouflage and black on bare metal. Crosses or swastikas indicated enemy aircraft claimed destroyed. Many different symbols were employed, particularly on fighter aircraft, where top hats and canes indicated escorts, umbrellas top cover and brooms sweeps. Claims symbols displayed on a fighter were normally for the pilot assigned to this aircraft. Portrayals of locomotives, vessels, and the like were for claims in strafing actions.

While external coloured decorations—other than for names and motifs—were not allowed until the spring of 1944, many aircraft had their main wheel discs decorated. In some cases this was an unofficial squadron or Flight marking but mostly just ground crew fancy. Depending on the strictures of the unit's commanders, fighter pilots were given considerable leeway during the final months of hostilities to add personal markings. These were mostly coloured tail stripes, wing tips and canopy frames, often the choice of a Flight Leader to make his aircraft more conspicuous to the rest of a formation.

INDIVIDUAL UNIT MARKINGS

BOMBARDMENT GROUPS

34th Bomb Group

B-24H/J Liberators, April–August 1944. The majority of original combat aircraft were in Dark Olive Drab and Neutral Gray factory finish. The Group marking, applied soon after arrival at Mendlesham, consisted of a white 'square' which was actually a rectangle as detailed in Instruction 55, being 48in high and 60in wide. Part of the rectangle extended on to the rudder and on replacement aircraft this part was deleted, making the device more a square. The 36in letter S was in black and of narrower strokes than the 6in detailed. The four stencil joins of the S were not usually painted out. The Square S was also carried on the upper surface of the right wing in the same colours on camouflaged aircraft, 57in chordwise by either 60 or 72in. Radio call-letters were 18in high in yellow below the tail number. All letters of the alphabet were used. Bare metal-finished aircraft had call-letters in black and the Group S white on black. The 93rd Combat Bomb Wing chose not to use SD110 codes and the only squadron markings were coloured propeller bosses. These were white for the 4th Bomb Squadron, yellow for the 7th, red for the 18th and bright green for 391st.

In late June 1944 the Group started painting its aircraft with the 93rd Wing high-visibility markings. The front third of the outer surfaces of tail fins were painted red, the remaining two-thirds were left 'silver' on bare metal-finished aircraft and painted white on those camouflaged. The tail number was repositioned on the inward-facing sides of the tail fins in black or yellow as appropriate. The call-letter was repainted in black on the rudder in the area aft of the two central hinges. The Square S device on the wing was not retained although the command instruction did not require its deletion. In July 1944 the 34th Group received some eight G-H B-24Hs relinquished by the 486th Bomb Group to use as 93rd Wing lead aircraft. These B-24s had the outer facing sides of fins and rudders painted all red with white call-letters.

B-17G Fortresses, July 1944–July 1945. These were natural metal finish with 93rd CBW red wing and tail bands to standard dimensions. The front third of the fin was red, with the division from the unpainted section running from where the de-icer boot terminated at the top to a point at the base in line with the rear edge of the tail gunner's door. The tail number was reinstated in black on the red, and individual call-letters, also in black, were 18in high and positioned on the rudder with the base of the letter in line with the top of the trim tab. Propeller bosses were painted in the squadron colours. By October 1944 the squadron colour was also carried as an approximately 24in wide nose band directly aft of the Plexiglas, terminating at the second row of riveting. In December 1944 Pathfinder B-17s had six 12in wide alternating stripes of black leading and the squadron colour around the rear fuselage under the tail gunner's compartment. In the third week of May 1945 SD110 squadron codes, together with call-letters, were painted under the left wing. The codes were 3L for the 4th Bomb Squadron, R2 for the 7th, 8I for the 18th and Q6 for the 391st. The letters, in black, were approximately 72 by 60in.

Communications aircraft included UC-64A Norseman 43-35383 with red cowling, red fin, black B on rudder and R2-B under the left wing in black, post VE-Day.

44th Bomb Group

B-24D/H/J/L/M Liberators, October 1942–June 1945. Original combat B-24Ds were in Dark Olive Drab and Neutral Gray, many with Medium Green blotching along the edges of the flight surfaces. Several aircraft carried the unofficial group 'Eightball' motif on the left side of the nose. This consisted of a

Above: Brilliant colour in the green of the English countryside: a Fortress squadron dispersal area at Mendlesham, spring 1945. Red propeller bosses and engine cowlings identify the 18th Bomb Squadron, red fins the 34th Bomb Group and red wing and tail bands the 93rd Combat Bomb Wing. (Mark Brown/AF Academy)

winged bomb cartoon with an 8 ball superimposed as eyes and the nose of the bomb in the squadron colour. Colours were red for the 66th Bomb Squadron, yellow for the 67th and white for the 68th. Radio call-letters were painted on tail fins in November 1942, positioned below the tail number, 36in high in yellow. The group's 28 aircraft were lettered A to K, except E and I, for the 66th Bomb Squadron; L to U, except O, for the 67th; and V to Z plus A, B, P with bars above and O for the 68th. Replacement B-24Ds and the original B-24Ds of the 506th Bomb Squadron arriving in March 1943 were given available letters with or without bars above or below, regardless of squadron assignment. Although a Group marking was issued in June 1943 this was not applied until the Group's aircraft returned from North Africa in late August 1943. The Circle A device was a 69 or 72in diameter white disc with a 48in high Insignia Blue A painted on the fin. The obscured tail number was repainted directly below the white disc and below that was the call-letter, now reduced in size to 24in high. On the right wing upper surface the device, of 78in diameter, was usually centred 14ft from the wing tip.

In November 1943, when squadron strengths were increased to twelve aircraft, a revision of call-letters was carried out. The 66th Bomb Squadron used A to M, the 67th used A to M with a bar below, the 68th used N to Z, and the 506th used N to Z with a bar below. When squadron strengths were increased still further, bars above were used to distinguish aircraft with the same letter in the same squadron. In March 1944 squadron codes were painted a bluish-grey aft of the waist gun positions in letters 48in high. The combinations for the four squadrons were QK for the 66th, NB for the 67th, WQ for the 68th and GJ for the 506th. On bare metal-finish B-24s arriving early in April the letters were black. The call-letter was also black and the Group marking a white A on a black disc.

In May 1944 high-visibility markings were introduced on tails. The instruction called for all paint to be removed from the outer surfaces of the fins and rudders and a vertical black band 30in wide centred thereon. In practice many camouflaged aircraft had the existing markings overpainted with white and the width of the vertical band was nearer 27in. White 24in high call-letters were centred on the band with the appropriate symbol. With this change of markings the call-letter allocations were again changed. All letters of the alphabet were available to squadrons, but the 68th and 506th never used I. The 66th Bomb Squadron used a plus sign after the letter, the 67th a bar below the letter, the 68th a plain letter and the 506th a bar in front of the letter, although this was soon changed to a bar above due to the narrowness of the black band. At about this time the squadron colours were applied to propeller bosses—red for the 66th, yellow for the 67th, white for the 68th and green for the 506th. In mid-October 1944, following the distribution of G-H pathfinders to all four squadrons, the letters A to E were reserved for them. Non-G-H aircraft, which already had letters in this range, were given another letter from the remainder of the alphabet.

The 44th Bomb Group's assembly ship was B-24D 41-23699 N *Lemon Drop*, painted with alternating black and yellow stripes round fuselage and wings. The black stripes were 2ft and the yellow 4ft wide. A UC-64A Norseman, 44-70289, used by the Group in 1945, had the cowling divided into red, green, white and yellow sections. It carried a black vertical band on the fin with the call letter B thereon.

91st Bomb Group

B-17F/G Fortresses, September 1942–June 1945. Original combat B-17Fs were in Dark Olive Drab and Neutral Gray with some Medium Green blotching along the edges of the flying surfaces. In October 1942 yellow, 24in high radio call-letters were painted on the fins below the tail numbers. The 322nd and 323rd Bomb Squadrons both used letters O to W, while the 324th and 401st used A to J except I. All letters except I were used for call-letters. In early December 1942 squadron codes were painted on the fuselage, forward of the cocarde on both sides of the fuselage. These were: 322nd Bomb Squadron—LG; 323rd—OR; 324th—DF; and 401st—LL. The individual letter was placed aft of the waist gun positions. In contrast to the greys of the other three B-17 Groups then operational, the letters were 36in high in yellow. When the fuselage letters were applied the tail fin letter was deleted.

When the revised national insignia was introduced in late June 1943 the bar of AN-I-9a would have extended across the squadron code. At this time the placing of code letters was changed to the rear part of the fuselage. On both sides the squadron letters were just aft of the waist window and the individual letter just forward of the horizontal stabiliser. There was an approximately 5–6ft separation between the squadron codes and the aircraft letter. During the late June/early July period the Triangle A Group marking was also being applied to the fins and right wing upper surfaces of 91st Group B-17Fs. These were the standard 72in size with an Insignia Blue A. A 24in high call-letter was also painted under the tail number at this time.

When the first natural metal-finish B-17Gs arrived in March 1944 the squadron and call-letters were painted in black and the Group marking white on black. When B-17Gs with staggered waist gun positions were received it was found that the na-

tional insignia on the right side had been relocated to a position between the access door and the waist window. On these the squadron code was placed just forward of the horizontal stabiliser and the individual call letter forward of the waist gun window. This became the standard positioning on the right side of the fuselage, although a few early aircraft of this type had the positions of squadron codes and call-letter reversed. From early July 1944 the 1st Combat Bomb Wing's red scheme was applied to wing tips and tail surfaces. Tail numbers and call-letters were repainted on the red panel, in black on bare metal-finished aircraft and in yellow on camouflaged. The Triangle A device remained unchanged.

92nd Bomb Group

B-17E/F/G Fortresses, August 1942–July 1945. B-17Fs flown to the UK in August 1942 were in Dark Olive Drab and Neutral Gray factory finish and received no unit markings prior to their transfer to the 92nd Bomb Group. The B-17Es received in exchange, to serve as operational trainers under the 11th Combat Crew Replacement Center, were Dark Olive Drab and Neutral Gray factory finish but most had had Dark Earth patterning added and Sky

Left: Detail of 91st Bomb Group tail markings: 72in-sided 1st Bomb Division triangle, standard 15in high number and 28in high call-letter, all on and in the 80in wide vertical red band identifying 1st Combat Bomb Wing aircraft. The battle-damaged tail is that of *The Peacemaker*, which was assaulted by enemy fighters on 20 July 1944. (USAF)

Right, upper: Carrying two Disney rocket bombs, B-17G 43-38069 UX:U taxies out for the mission of 15 March 1945. The propeller bosses are painted light blue, an unofficial marking on most 327th Bomb Squadron aircraft to aid identification in a frontal view. In some units painted propeller bosses were no more than a decorative feature added by the ground crew. (W. Furniss)

Right, lower: Detail of 92nd Bomb Group tail markings on *Belle of Liberty*, 42-31479 UX:L, which crash-landed on 30 December 1944. The water-based paint of the 60in sided triangle shows signs of weathering. There is the usual contrast between the green of the centre fin panel and the faded olive drab of the forward part. The bare metal leading edge of the fin is where the rubber de-icer boot has been removed. Black has been used for the 48in high letter B, and this was common practice in the 92nd Group. Frost patches are evident in several places. (W. Furniss)

undersurfaces. In December 1942 SD110 codes were applied, the two squadron letters being painted in pale grey, 36in high, aft of the waist gun window on both sides of the fuselage. The individual letter was painted forward of the cocarde. The 325th Bomb Squadron used NV, the 326th JW, the 327th UX and the 407th PY. Although the 92nd Bomb Group was re-established as a combat organisation in April 1943 with B-17Fs, the 326th Bomb Squadron B-17Es left with the CCRC continued to carry the JW code for many months.

In late April 1943 the newly received B-17Fs and YB-40s had code letters painted on their fuselages. The squadron letters, 48in high, were painted ahead of the cocarde, with the call-letter aft on both sides in the 325th, 326th and 407th Bomb Squadrons. The 327th, which was initially only equipped with YB-40s, had staggered waist gun windows with the cocarde forward of that on the left and aft on the right. On these aircraft the squadron letters were aft of the waist window on the left side and the call-letter forward of the cocarde. On the right the squadron letters were forward of the cocarde and the call-letter between the tailplane and the entrance door. When this squadron received B-17Fs the codes were

placed in the same positions as with the other squadrons. The letter colour was a bluish-grey. The 325th and 327th Bomb Squadrons used letters in the first part of the alphabet and the 326th and 407th letters in the last part. The letter I was not used and the 327th Bomb Squadron does not appear ever to have used C.

In late June 1943 the Triangle B was introduced as a Group marking and applied to the fin and right wing upper surface. The white equilateral triangle on the fin had 60in sides and that on the wing 72in, both with a 48in letter B thereon. At first some aircraft had the B painted in Identification Yellow but this was soon changed to Insignia Blue. A 28in high yellow call-letter was painted below the tail number. B-17Gs in metal finish had squadron and call-letters in black and the Group device was a white B on a black triangle. By April 1944 the Triangle B was also being carried under the left wing in the appropriate size and colours, but this practice appears to have been discontinued later in the year.

In August 1944 a 48in wide horizontal band was painted across the vertical tail in red, its base in line with the bottom of the triangle, which was not overpainted. By this date the squadrons were also

Top left: Most heavy bomber Groups were given combat time-expired P-47s for use in monitoring formations during mission assemblies. These were usually adorned with a Group's markings, as on 42-8522, where the serial number, less the hyphen, has been used in full. Originally in olive drab and grey finish, the aircraft had all its camouflage removed for its new employment. A direction-finding aerial on the fuselage spine was another feature of these monitor aircraft. (W. Furniss)

Above left: When the first natural metal-finish Liberators were received by the 93rd Bomb Group in April 1944 there was confusion as to the form and colour of the Group markings to be used on these aircraft. For a few days *Shamrock*, B-24H 42-95109

RE:Y, carried a black letter B on the upper fin with no divisional 'circle'. (Amos Golisch)

Top right: A G-H pathfinder of the 329th Bomb Squadron, 93rd Bomb Group, with a distinctive red nose marking. B-24J 42-51968 RE:P also sported a yellow bomb-bay stripe. (Unknown)

Above right: Most G-H-equipped Pathfinder aircraft of the 329th Bomb Squadron were given red noses as an identification feature from the autumn of 1944. The 93rd Bomb Group Circle B can be seen on the right wing of 42-51598 RE:Z, photographed during the mission of 24 December 1944. (Glen Tessmer)

making some use of coloured propeller bosses, the 327th Bomb Squadron using blue.

A monitor P-47D, used by the 92nd Group in the last few months of the war, had all camouflage paint removed and the Group red band and Triangle B painted on the tail above 428522 in black.

93rd Bomb Group

B-24D/ H/ J/ L/ M Liberators, September 1942–June 1945. Original combat B-24Ds were finished in Dark Olive Drab and Neutral Gray, with some Medium Green blotching along the edges of the flying surfaces. Radio call-letters were assigned but these were not painted on those aircraft detached to North Africa until they returned in late February 1943. While in North Africa a 24in by 18in RAF-type red, white and blue flash was painted on the outer side of fins,

under the tail number and close to the rudder. This was, at that time, a standard theatre marking in North Africa. These markings were retained on the aircraft so marked throughout the summer of 1943. With red leading, the width of the vertical colour bands was red 8in, white 2in and blue 8in.

The 328th and 329th Bomb Squadrons both used call-letters from A in alphabetical order, the 329th's having a bar below the letter. The 330th and 409th Bomb Squadrons used letters starting at Z in reverse alphabetical order, the 409th's having a bar below the letter. All letters of the alphabet were used but even when squadron complements rose to nineteen aircraft each in 1945, squadrons continued to use call-letters within their respective parts of the alphabet—that is, the 328th and 330th Bomb Squadrons did not use V to Z nor the 329th and

409th A to E. In the summer of 1943, when aircraft complements were first increased, bars were used both below and above letters to differentiate between aircraft with the same call-letter regardless of squadron assignment. When the Circle B Group insignia was painted on, barred letters appear to have been discontinued.

Although the Group marking was first advised in late June 1943, it was not applied until the 93rd returned from its second African detachment in late August 1943. The white disc was 69 or 72in in diameter and the Insignia Blue B 36in high on both tail and wing. On the fin the obliterated tail number was repositioned under the Circle B and a 28in call-letter was painted below that in yellow. Thereafter, until squadron identification letters were painted on the rear fuselage in March 1944, there was no visual identification for squadrons of the 93rd Bomb Group. Squadron codes for the 93rd had been given in SD110 from late 1942. They were GO for the 328th Bomb Squadron, RE for the 329th, AG for the 330th and YM for the 409th. The letters were 48in high, in white.

With the arrival of bare metal-finish B-24Js in April 1944 the squadron and call-letters were painted in black and the Circle B in black with a white letter. From early May the tail markings were changed to an all-yellow outer face of fins and rudders with a 30–27in wide vertical black stripe thereon. The call-letter was centred on the black stripe in yellow. No bar or plus symbols were used. These markings remained the practice to the end of hostilities.

In the autumn of 1944 the 330th Bomb Squadron commenced a programme of painting a black and white 'whale face' on the noses of the squadron's aircraft, utilising the windows of the bombardier's position as the mouth. This decoration was not applied to all aircraft and neither was the red nose which the 329th Bomb Squadron used to distinguish its G-H pathfinders at around the same time. This red-painted area mostly extended from the rear of the nose turret down to the rear of the bombardire's position. Lead 328th aircraft had a Similar area of the nose in red and black checkerboard. More consistent were the yellow engine cowling bands, introduced by the 409th Bomb Squadron as an additional recognition feature during the winter of 1944/45.

The first 93rd Bomb Group assembly ship was B-24D 41-23667 H *Ball of Fire*, with alternate 2ft red and 4ft white stripes around the fuselage and also on the wings at a 30 degree angle from fuselage to wing tip. It appears that the aircraft was at first painted with 2ft wide red, white and blue stripes, but for unknown reasons the blue stripes were painted out with white, leaving a pale grey effect. This aircraft was replaced with B-24D 42-72869, which had a yellow nose back to the cockpit and a broad yellow band, some 12ft wide, round the fuselage aft of the wing.

Below: The 409th Bomb Squadron painted the engine cowling rings on its Liberators yellow during the last few months of the war. YM:I was a B-24H, serial 42-95204. (Via Mike Bailey)

94th Bomb Group

B-17F/G Fortresses, April 1943–November 1945.
Original combat B-17Fs were in Dark Olive Drab
and Neutral Gray factory finish. Squadron codes
were applied soon after the aircraft arrived in the
UK. They were painted in light grey, 36in high, with
the squadron letters forward of the cocarde on both
sides of the fuselage and the individual aircraft call-
letter aft of the waist gun windows. The 331st Bomb
Squadron used QE, the 332nd XM, the 333rd TS
and the 410th GL. In the 332nd and 333rd Bomb
Squadrons the individual call-letters were from A
onwards and in the 331st and 410th from Z backwards. The letter I was not used and in later months
all the squadrons used all the alphabet except I. In
late June 1943 the Square A device was painted on
the tailfin and upper surface of the right wing, but
the individual aircraft call-letter was not painted below the tail number. The white 'square' was 60in by
48in and the letter 36in high in Insignia Blue. The
wing device was 60in square.

From the late summer of 1943 the fin Square A
was 48in-sided. Soon after this work was started
the national insignia had to have the AN-I-9a modifications which made the white rectangles overlap
the squadron codes. In some cases the codes were
repainted further forward but most replacement aircraft, received in July 1943, only had the individual
call-letter painted on the rear fuselage. Where another aircraft in the Group had the same letter, it
was identified by the figure 2 being painted along-
side, for example A2 and D2.

Above: B-17Gs at Wormingford in July 1945, ready to
transport ground personnel of the 55th Fighter Group
to Germany. In the foreground is 44-8457 with the
yellow engine cowlings of the 410th Bomb Squadron
and a bare metal A in the black square. During
hostilities this Fortress served with the 4th Bomb
Squadron, 34th Bomb Group, and still retains the red
93rd Combat Bomb Wing stripes on its wings. (Robert
Sand)

By mid October 1943 squadron letters were again
being painted forward of the national insignia and
28in call-letters painted under the tail number. The
latter was as the operational instruction, while the
fuselage letters continued to be 36in high and the
same stencils were used throughout 1944. Natural
metal B-17Gs, first received in March 1944, had the
squadron code and call-letter in black and the
Square A white letter on black. In December 1944 a
red chevron was painted on the upper surface of
the right wing and the under surface of the left. The
apex of the chevron was at the wing leading edge,
with the two arms 36 or 48in wide. Positioned opposite the aileron, the Square A marking was removed from the upper right surface prior to painting the chevron.

In January 1945 the 94th Bomb Group experimented with a new 4th Combat Wing marking, and
when this was approved all the Group's aircraft were
so painted during the first weeks of February. Wing
tips and all the tail surfaces were painted yellow.
The Square A was retained on the tail and the tail
number was either reinstated or painted round. The

call-letter was also reinstated on the yellow fin in black. Around the rear fuselage, and encompassing the access door, a 36in wide red stripe was painted to identify the Group within the 4th CBW. When these markings were introduced so were squadron colours. The front of each engine cowling, approximately 24in back, was painted dark blue for the 331st, red for the 332nd, bright green for the 333rd and yellow for the 410th. SD110 squadron codes were gradually removed from fuselages and not painted on replacements, but fuselage call-letters were retained. However, in mid-May 1945, squadron codes were painted under the left wing of the B-17s as part of anti-low flying measures.

95th Bomb Group

B-17F/G Fortresses, April 1943–July 1945. Original combat B-17Fs were in Dark Olive Drab and Neutral Gray factory finish. Several aircraft displayed a 2in wide white line directly under the tail number, with 12in white lines projecting from it downward at 90 degrees. The number of downward projections indicated the four squadrons of the Group by their numerical order. These markings were deleted soon after arrival in the UK and SD110 codes were painted on to the specified size and location—48in high letters with the squadron code forward of the cocarde and the individual aircraft letter aft of the waist windows. The codes given were BG for the 334th Bomb Squadron, OE for the 335th, ET for the 336th and QW for the 412th.

By July 1943 the 412th Bomb Squadron was using 36in high letters on replacement aircraft in a sky blue. As far as is known all camouflaged Fortresses received by the 412th from that date had sky blue codes, making this unit's decor unique in this respect. Individual aircraft call-letters were from A onwards, less C and I, in the 334th and 336th Bomb Squadrons and from Z back in the 335th and 412th, although eventually all squadrons used the full range of the alphabet with the exception of I. When first introduced in late June 1943 the Square B device was first painted with a 40in high yellow letter within an outline square of 48in sides made with 2in strokes directly on the Dark Olive Drab. A 28in high yellow call-letter was positioned under the tail number. The yellow rendering of Square B was only applied to a few B-17s before the standard Insignia Blue B on a white square was introduced. The size on the fin was generally 48in square or 48in high by 56in wide, with a 40in high B. That on the wing was 72in with the span by 60in with the chord and having a 48in letter B thereon. There was considerable variation in both size and letter shape of these markings, which were often hand-painted. From the late summer of 1943 the fin individual

Below: *Snafu*, an early combat B-17F of the 332nd Bomb Squadron, 94th Bomb Group, photographed during May 1943, displays typical Fortress markings prior to the introduction of the Group device. Squadron code letters are in the standard position forward of the cocarde and the call-letter is aft of the waist gun position, all in Sky S shade. The cocarde star has been dulled and the olive drab has yet to fade, the aircraft being not two months off the production line. (AFM)

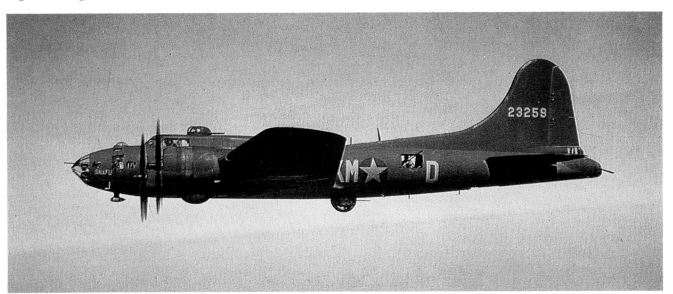

aircraft letter was 24in high and this remained the most common size.

When the AN-I-9a national insignia was introduced at the end of June 1943, the white rectangles extended across squadron codes that were rarely repositioned and were not painted on replacement aircraft. Fuselage letters were reintroduced during the late autumn that year and continued in regular use until the end of 1944. In March 1944, when the first metal-finished aircraft were received, the letters were painted in black and the Square B white on black. When 'A' and 'B' Group formations were first employed a white bar was painted adjacent to the Square B to distinguish these aircraft as 'A' and 'B', but after the initial applications this scheme was discontinued although the markings remained. In July 1944 squadron colours in the form of 12in nose bands were introduced—yellow for the 334th, dark blue for the 335th, bright green for the 336th and red for the 412th. Some aircraft also gained a squadron colour band round the tail gun position, but this marking does not appear to have been a Group-stipulated requirement.

At the end of 1944 the 95th Group discontinued painting code letters on fuselages and eventually removed them from other aircraft. They were, however, painted under the right wing in mid-May 1945. In late January 1945 the Group's aircraft had started to receive a 48in red band following the line of the vertical tail's trailing edge, and a 48in red band on the upper right and lower left wing surfaces, running diagonally from the leading edge by the outboard engines to the trailing edge of the ailerons. This 13th Combat Wing requirement was soon amended to ease application time, with the red tail marking being confined to the rudder, although most aircraft had already received the 48in band. From the summer of 1944 many B-17s had the 'last three' of the serial painted on nose sides 6in high.

96th Bomb Group

B-17F/G Fortresses, April 1943–November 1945. Original B-17Fs were in Dark Olive Drab and Neutral Gray factory finish. SD110 codes were applied soon after the aircraft arrived in the UK, painted in 36in high light grey letters: the 337th Bomb Squadron used AW, the 338th BX, the 339th QJ and the 413th MZ. The actual size of some of the stencils used gave a letter 35in by 20in with a 6in stroke;

later in the war some codes appeared to be hand-painted using a narrower stroke. Following the introduction of the revised national insignia in late June 1943, the painting of codes on 96th Bomb Group aircraft was sporadic, some replacement aircraft going weeks without these markings. The Square C Group insignia, applied in early July 1943, had precedence over the national insignia change. The white 'square' was approximately 48in high by 54in wide but varied considerably. In the summer of 1943 most were 46in high by 56in wide with a 36in high Insignia Blue C. The call-letter was painted under the tail number in yellow, 24in high. The Square C on the right wing was to the instruction size, 72in by 60in.

From the autumn of 1943 the squadrons commenced painting fuselage identification letters in white for clearer recognition, although on some aircraft light grey was still used. When bare metal-finished B-17Gs arrived in March 1944 letters were painted in black and the Group device white on black. When from February 1944 the 413th Bomb Squadron was the Pathfinder lead for 3rd Division Groups, Square C was omitted on these aircraft. With staggered waist gun positions, the uniformity of code letter application gave way to positioning as it took the painter's fancy. On some aircraft all three letters were grouped together and positioned forward or aft of the national insignia on both sides of the fuselage, or only on one side, the other having the squadron letters and call-letter separated by the 'star and bar'. Sometimes there was a space of 18–24in between the squadron letters and the individual letter. The 339th Bomb Squadron had several aircraft with the first or last letter of the QJ code positioned high and close to the bar of the national marking.

In July 1944 squadron colours were introduced in the form of a 5in band aft of the nose Plexiglas; the 337th used red, the 338th yellow and the 339th dark blue, while the 413th did not have a colour. But these markings were not applied to all aircraft of a squadron on hand and their use appears to have been largely discontinued early in 1945. During the winter of 1944/45 some aircraft had the last three digits of the serial number, approximately 6in high, painted on the side of the nose. In late January 1945 two red parallel bands were painted on the upper surface of the right wing and lower surface of the left as well as on both sides of the vertical tail surfaces. The width of the bands was mostly 36in, with a 60in separation. If the red band had not been cut out around the call-letter it was reinstated on the band.

97th Bomb Group

B-17E/F Fortresses, July 1942–October 1942. Some B-17Es had the Dark Olive Drab and Neutral Gray factory finish, but most were finished with Dark Earth disruptive pattering on the olive drab and with Sky equivalent undersurfaces. Although radio callletters were used they were not painted on the aircraft. No squadron markings were carried apart from an adaptation of the squadron insignia on at least two 342nd Bomb Squadron B-17Es. This consisted of two angled bombs on either side of a skull painted in yellow adjacent to the waist gun windows. Most B-17Es had an individual name in small yellow block capitals on the left side of the nose. Several B-17Es had a 6in red stripe under the left wing tip and a blue stripe under the right. Narrower stripes in the same colours, red left and blue right, were also on the undersurfaces of both horizontal stabilisers and elevators.

Below: Veteran of more than sixty combat missions with the 482nd and 379th Bomb Groups, B-17G 42-97667 LD:A has the 13th Combat Bomb Wing coloured rudder—black for the 100th Bomb Group—and the red propeller bosses and nose band of the 418th Bomb Squadron. An H2X radar aircraft, it was assigned to the 100th in May 1945. (NASM)

B-17Fs obtained from the 92nd Bomb Group were in standard factory camouflage finish with yellow tail numbers. No radio call-letters or unit markings were painted on the aircraft prior to the 97th Bomb Group being transferred to North Africa in November 1942.

100th Bomb Group

B-17F/G Fortresses, June 1943–November 1945. B-17Fs were in Dark Olive Drab and Neutral Gray factory finish and SD110 code letters were applied soon after arrival in the UK. The 349th Bomb Squadron used XR, the 350th LN, the 351st EP and the 418th LD. These were painted in 36in high bluish-grey letters, the squadron code forward of the cocarde on both sides of the fuselage and the individual callletter aft. Later in the year a light grey, probably Sky, was used for fuselage letters on several aircraft. Original combat B-17F call-letters were from A onwards, less C and I, for the 349th and 351st Bomb Squadrons and from Z backwards for the 350th and 418th. In late June and early July 1943 the Square D marking was painted on the fin and upper surface of the right wing. On the fin it was 48in square, and on the wing 66in, in white with an Insignia Blue D. A 24in high call-letter was painted in yellow below the tail number. Apart from the use of black instead of blue for the Square D, and black code letters and a white on black Square D, when bare metal-finished B-17Gs arrived in March 1944 100th Bomb Group markings were generally con-

sistent, with few examples of different colours, sizes or positioning. In December 1943 'B Group' formation markings, a white stripe from the Square D, were painted on the vertical tail surfaces and wings but this was discontinued after a few weeks. Late in 1944 propeller bosses were painted in squadron colours: royal blue for the 349th Bomb Squadron, yellow for the 350th, bright green for the 351st and red for the 418th. In February 1945 the squadron colour was also displayed as a 12in wide stripe encircling the nose directly aft of the bombardier's Plexiglas. High-visibility 13th Combat Bomb Wing markings, applied early in February 1945, consisted of a 48in black band down the trailing edge of the fin and the whole of the rudder, which was soon amended to the rudder only, and a 48in back band on the upper right and lower left wing surfaces, extending from the leading edge outboard of Nos 1 and 4 engines to the trailing edges of the ailerons. By 1945 Pathfinder aircraft were being given call-letters from the end of the alphabet in the 349th and 351st Bomb Squadrons and from the beginning of the alphabet in the 350th and 418th.

Monitor P-47D Thunderbolts used by the Group included bare metal 42-8372 WW and 42-25745 WW with red cowlings.

301st Bomb Group

B-17F Fortresses, August 1942–October 1942. The factory finish was Dark Olive Drab and Neutral Gray. Although radio call-letters were assigned to individual aircraft, these were not displayed in painted form on the aircraft and similarly no unit marking was used while in the UK. Most aircraft received a 4–6in wide yellow surround to the fuselage cocarde before transfer to North Africa. Many aircraft had individual names and motifs on their noses.

303rd Bomb Group

B-17F/G Fortresses, September 1942–June 1945. Original combat B-17Fs were in Dark Olive Drab and Neutral Gray factory finish. Radio call-letters, applied in October 1942, were in yellow, 36in high, below the tail number. The 358th and 360th Bomb Squadrons used A to K, less E and I, and the 359th and 427th used O to W. By the winter of 1943 letters from the whole alphabet were in use by all the Group's squadrons. On a few replacement aircraft the tail call-letter was painted in white when yellow was unavailable. In early December 1942 squadron code letters, 48in high, were painted in light bluish-grey on the fuselage; the squadron letters were forward of the cocarde with the individual letter to its rear. The 358th Bomb Squadron used VK, the 359th BN, the 360th PU and the 427th GN. Call-letters were retained on the fin but several replacement B-17Fs did not have this marking. In late June/early July 1943 the Group Triangle C marking was painted on tail fins and the upper surface of the right wing. The white equilateral triangle had 72in sides and the Insignia Blue C was 36in high. On wing and tail the triangle was usually of the same dimensions.

By September 1943 the tail call-letter was reduced in size to 24in high on replacements and from then on this was the standard size for this marking to the end of the war. With the coming of natural metal-finished B-17Gs in March 1944 the Group Triangle C was a white letter on a black triangle with the squadron code and individual letter also black. On B-17Gs with staggered waist gun positions the 427th Bomb Squadron often painted their GN code aft of the waist window and the call-letter forward.

High-visibility markings introduced in August 1944 took some weeks to effect on all aircraft as they required a completely new arrangement on the tails. The Triangle C had to be repositioned lower on the fin with the triangle white and the C black. A 24in wide red border was painted round the Triangle C to give an equilateral triangle with 10ft sides. The tail number was repositioned on the base of the red border in yellow and at the apex of the red triangle a single digit in yellow, 1, 2, 3 or 4, denoted the squadron of the Group. The wing device was of similar dimensions but did not carry the aircraft or squadron number. On some aircraft the letter C was painted directly on a bare metal triangle formed by the red surround. With the introduction of this 41st CBW marking fuselage letters were apparently optional and the majority of replacement aircraft did nor carry them. However, they were usually retained where already painted on aircraft.

B-17E 41-9020, used as an assembly ship in July 1944, had alternating bands, approxiamtely 10ft wide, of red and white on the fuselage and wings.

305th Bomb Group

B-17F/G Fortresses, September 1942–July 1945. The factory finish was Dark Olive Drab and Neutral Gray, but Medium Green blotching was applied to the edges of the flying surfaces in the UK. A few machines were painted with large patches of Medium Green on the fuselage and wings. In early December 1942 squadron codes and individual aircraft call-letters were painted on the fuselage in a light blue-grey, 48in high and with the squadron combination forward of the cocarde and the call letter aft, usually close in. The 364th Bomb Squadron used the codes WF, the 365th XK, the 366th KY and the 422nd JJ. Initially the 364th and 366th used call-letters from A to M, both omitting I and the 364th omitting C as well. The 365th and 422nd Bomb Squadrons used O to W. In August 1943 the 365th and 422nd Bomb Squadrons changed their call-letters to the first part of the alphabet. The whole alphabet range excluding I was later used by all squadrons.

In late June 1943 the Triangle G insignia was painted on the fin and the upper surface of the right wing. The fin device was of standard size, a white equilateral triangle with 72in sides and the letter therein Insignia Blue and 36in high. Yellow call-letters painted below the tail number were initially 28in high and later 24in. The Group marking on the wing was a 96in-sided triangle. The decreed change to the AN-I-9a national insignia in late July was not effected on all the Group's aircraft until November. As this marking was repainted the squadron codes were repositioned further forward, the bases of the letters often extending on to the wing fillet. The first natural metal-finish B-17Gs, received in March 1944, had the code letters painted in black and the Triangle G white on black.

During the winter of 1943/44 code letters were painted in white on replacement aircraft for better visibility. Both fuselage codes and tail markings were generally uniform in size throughout the 305th Group's operational service. In common with the other 40th Combat Bomb Wing Groups, in the spring of 1944 the 305th also painted its Group marking on the under surface of the left wing. When in September 1943 the 422nd Bomb Squadron was assigned to night operations, its B-17s had the grey undersurfaces painted with a non-gloss black. In March 1944 the 422nd became, in effect, a double squadron when in addition to leaflet-dropping it was given the role of Pathfinder unit for the 1st Bomb Division. Its special H2X B-17Gs carried normal 422nd codes but the fin and wing triangles were without the letter G. On 23 May 1944 the Pathfinder aircraft and crews were split between all squadrons and the 422nd Bomb Squadron was re-formed as a normal day bombing unit in late June with the Triangle G on its B-17s. The section that had continued night leaflet operations was transferred and given another designation in June 1944, but, while the Triangle G was deleted, its B-17s continued to display the JJ codes of the 422nd. In August 1944 the 305th Group added a light green stripe across the fin and rudder as an additional recognition marking. The stripe, 48in wide, had its base level with the Triangle G, which was not obscured.

306th Bomb Group

B-17F/G Fortresses, September 1942–December 1945. Original aircraft were in Dark Olive Drab and Neutral Gray factory finish with some Medium Green blotching along the edges of flying surfaces. Several aircraft received a 6in yellow surround to the cocarde in October 1942 which was deleted at the end of the year on most aircraft when the Group was no longer expected to be transferred to North Africa.

Although radio call-letters were issued and used they were not painted on the aircraft until the introduction of SD110 squadron code letters in early December 1942. The letters were painted in a light blue-grey, 48in high, with the squadron combination forward of the cocarde and the individual aircraft letter aft. The 367th Bomb Squadron used GY, the 368th BO, the 369th WW and the 423rd RD. It appears that initially each squadron used the first part of the alphabet, excluding I, for individual aircraft call-letters, but soon the whole alphabet, including I, was available for this purpose.

In late June 1943 the Triangle H was painted on the fin and upper surface of the right wing. On the wing the triangle was equilateral with 96in sides; on the fin, on most aircraft, it was an isosceles triangle of 56in base and 72in sides. The colours were the standard Insignia Blue letter on white but later, in 1943, black was used in lieu of blue. The call-letter was not painted on the fin at this stage. Also in late June 1943 the change to the national insignia was notified. Apparently this was not a priority task as several weeks were to pass before the change was effected on all the Group's aircraft. As the additional white rectangles of the new insignia had to overlap the squadron codes, a new scheme for their presentation was started. The squadron letters were painted on the rear fuselage, in light grey letters, 48in high. On the right side the first letter of the

Above: The Triangle H tail marking of the 306th Bomb Group was noticeable for having a shorter base—56 in—than the sides which were 72in. The yellow band was always outlined in black, even on camouflaged aircraft. (Ben Marcilonis)

combination was painted to the rear of the access door and the second letter between the door and the waist gun window. On the left side the letters were similarly widely spaced. With this change the individual aircraft call-letter was painted on the fin below the tail number, in yellow, 48in high, and was no longer on the fuselage. Eventually all 306th Bomb Group aircraft carried their code letters in this fashion. However, in the week beginning 26 February 1944 squadron letters were discontinued on replacement B-17Gs and over the next twenty days they were removed from all other 306th aircraft. Coloured propeller bosses were now the only means of identifying squadron assignment—yellow for the 367th, white for the 368th, blue for the 369th and green for the 423rd.

The first natural metal-finished B-17Gs arriving in March 1944 were given a tail call-letter painted in black, but no code letters. As with the other 40th Combat Bomb Wing Groups, by April 1944 the Group triangle marking was also painted under the left wing, the same size and colours as the device on the right wing upper surface. The Triangle H was the same shape and size as on camouflaged aircraft but the letter was white on black. In August 1944

the 40th Combat Bomb Wing required a 48in wide yellow band to be painted horizontally across the fin and rudder, approximately 20in below the fin tip. This was actually 44in wide to allow for a 2in wide black border top and bottom. At the same time the area of fin above this marking was painted with the squadron colour. To provide contrast, the 367th Bomb Squadron changed from yellow to red. Propeller bosses continued to be painted with the squadron colour. In mid-May 1945 squadron code letters were reintroduced under the right wing, yellow on camouflaged aircraft and black on bare metal.

UC-64A Norseman 43-35442, used by the Group in 1945, carried the Triangle H and yellow band as tail markings.

322nd Bomb Group
B-26B/C Marauders, March 1943–October 1943. These aircraft carried the Dark Olive Drab and Neu-

tral Gray factory finish. SD110 squadron codes were as follows: 449th Bomb Squadron PN, 450th ER, 451st SS and 452nd DR. These were painted in 40in high, blue-grey letters forward of the cocarde on both sides of the fuselage with the individual aircraft letter aft. The factory positioning of the fuselage cocarde was so far to the rear that the call-letter had to be painted under the tailplane on the B-26B-4 and C-5 models. On the B-26B-10 and C-10 and subsequent production blocks the rear gun hatches were further back and the cocarde centred under the tailplane leading edge, which necessitated the call-letter being painted even further back under the tailplane. When the national insignia was changed in late June 1943 the white rectangles were painted on to the call-letter. The new national insignia did not intrude on the squadron codes: these were not close to the cocarde as the gun hatch intervened. On replacement aircraft the call-letter was positioned around the rearward bar of the national insignia when there was no room to place it further aft. The B-26B-4s of the 450th and 452nd Bomb Squadrons were given call-letters from A in alphabetical order and from Z in reverse alphabetical order respectively. The 449th and 451st Bomb Squadrons used letters from Z in reverse alphabetical order and from A on, respectively, excluding the letters C and I.

323rd Bomb Group

B-26B/C Marauders, May 1943–October 1943. The aircraft had Dark Olive Drab and Neutral Gray factory finish. Squadron code letters used were VT for the 453rd Bomb Squadron, RJ for the 454th, YU for the 455th and WT for the 456th. These were painted in blue-grey forward of the cocarde on both sides of the fuselage with the individual aircraft call-letter aft, 40in high. Owing to the location of the cocarde the call-letter had to be positioned on the fuselage under the horizontal tail surfaces. Not all the Group's aircraft had received these letters when the new national insignia form was introduced. On those that already had fuselage letters the white rectangles of the revised national insignia intruded over the call-letter. In some cases the letter was repainted further back and on others the cocarde was painted out and a new AN-I-9a insignia painted on approximately 40in further forward. Most replacements had the national insignia repositioned further forward so that only about one-third of the call-letter was under the tailplane. On the original B-26C-6s the

453rd and 455th Bomb Squadrons used letters from A in alphabetical order, and the 454th and 456th used letters from Z in reverse order.

351st Bomb Group

B-17F/G Fortresses, April 1943–June 1945. Original B-17Fs were in Dark Olive Drab and Neutral Gray factory finish. Formation leaders' aircraft in three squadrons were marked with special symbols. In the 510th Bomb Squadron these had a red stripe, approximately 72in by 3in, under the tail number. Lead 511th Bomb Squadron B-17s had a small yellow lightning flash painted at the top of the vertical tail, pointing diagonally down from the trailing edge of the rudder. A white triangle, approximately 12in high, on the rudder marked 509th Bomb Squadron leaders. Squadron code letters were painted on soon after the aircraft had arrived at Polebrook. The 508th Bomb Squadron used YB, the 509th RQ, the 510th TU and the 511th DS. The letters were 48in high and light grey (Sky), with the squadron code forward of the cocarde and the individual aircraft call-letter aft. On a few 510th Bomb Squadron aircraft the first letter of the code was painted ahead of cocarde and the second letter aft with the call-letter on the left side, a practice that was continued. The original aircraft complement of the 508th and 510th Bomb Squadrons were lettered A to M excluding I and the 509th and 511th O to Z. Generally, the 508th

Below: The 351st Bomb Group had special markings that identified formation lead aircraft, those with Gee and those with special equipment. The 510th Bomb Squadron used a red bar under the tail number, as on 42-29925 TU:L *The Duchess*, one of the few original aircraft of the Group to survive hostilities. (USAAF)

and 510th continued to use letters from A onward and the 509th and 511th from Z back.

A Group marking was introduced at the end of June 1943, first painted as a yellow J on a white triangle, but very few aircraft received this marking on the fin before it was changed to a white equilateral triangle with 72in sides and an Insignia Blue J thereon. Also carried on the upper surface of the right wing, the Triangle J there was the specified 96in-sided. The radio call-letter was painted in yellow below the tail number, 24in high in the 511th and 28in high in the other squadrons. When the revised national insignia was implemented the white rectangles extended across the squadron code letters, but only a few aircraft had the letters repainted clear of the national insignia, most continuing to operate with code letters thus partly obscured. An unusual practice that continued for some months was the painting of code letters around the rectangular projections of the national insignia.

With the receipt of natural metal-finished B-17Gs from March 1944, the squadron and call letters were painted in black and the Triangle J white on black. Formation lead symbols were painted in black on 509th and 511th Bomb Squadron aircraft but continued to be red on those of the 510th. In August 1944 a 48in wide red band was painted diagonally downward from the trailing edge near the top of the vertical tail without overpainting the Triangle J, tail number or call-letter.

Early in 1945 War Weary B-17G 42-39914, painted overall gloss black with an enlarged white Triangle J on the vertical tail, was mostly used for target-towing and communication work. Other communication aircraft included UC-78 Bobcat 43-22078 with a red nose and carrying a Triangle J on the tail; UC-64A 44-70316 with similar markings; and P-47D 42-7871 WW, used as a monitor.

379th Bomb Group

B-17F/G Fortresses, May 1943–July 1945. Original B-17Fs were in Dark Olive Drab and Neutral Gray factory finish. SD110 squadron codes were painted on soon after arrival at Kimbolton in light grey (Sky), 36in high. The squadron code was painted on the rear fuselage, aft of the waist window, with the individual radio call-letter forward of the cocarde on both sides of the aircraft. The call-letter was repeated on the fin, placed centrally above the tail number in yellow, 36in high. There does not appear to have

been any defined allocation of call-letter use and squadrons selected from the whole alphabet, excluding I. The squadron code combinations were WA for the 524th Bomb Squadron, FR for the 525th, LF for the 526th and FO for the 527th.

When the Triangle K Group marking was introduced in late June 1943 the call-letter was painted over and repositioned under the tail number. The 524th and 525th Bomb Squadrons were fairly consistent in using a 36in letter but the other two squadrons mostly used 28in and, later, 24in high letters. The Triangle K on the fin was of the standard 72in dimensions, with an Insignia Blue K on white. The wing device was also the standard 96in. As with most 8th Air Force Bomb Groups, the display of the new national insignia advised in late June took several weeks to be applied to all the 379th's aircraft. Where a white rectangle obscured part of the fuselage call-letter this was not repositioned, while on replacement aircraft the fuselage call-letter was often omitted.

From November 1943 fuselage code letters were painted in white for better distinction. Bare metal B-17Gs had markings of similar dimensions to those on the camouflaged aircraft but in black. The Triangle K was white on black. In August 1944 work

Below: The 379th Bomb Group placed squadron code letters to the rear of the fuselage, forward of the tailplane, where they were more easily distinguished. As a further aid to this end they were later painted in white rather than light grey. This B-17F, *Paddy Gremlin*, has a 28in high call-letter on the tail whereas 36in letters were more common in this squadron. (Constant Anszperger)

Above: B-17Gs from three of the 381st Bomb Group's squadrons—the 532nd, 533rd and 534th Bomb Squadrons—soon after receiving high-visibility colour markings. Only the 533rd aircraft has a fuselage radio call-letter. (USAF)

started on changing the Group insignia to be within a 24in yellow surround: the specified 36in 41st Combat Bomb Wing requirement could not be met. All existing tail markings had to be removed and the Triangle K sited more centrally, the K white and the triangle black on both camouflaged and 'silver' aircraft. The tail number was repositioned in black on the lower side of the encompassing yellow triangle and a squadron-in-Group number, 1, 2, 3 or 4, was painted in black at the apex. The wing device also had to be completely repainted, there being insufficient room to place even a 24in yellow surround. On both the tail and the wing the remodelled device had 10ft sides. The wing marking did not carry the aircraft number or squadron digit as mentioned above.

At the same time as these markings were introduced identification letters were no longer painted on the fuselage of most replacements. Existing fuselage letters were removed from many aircraft, no-

tably in the 524th, but several aircraft were still to be seen with code letters at the end of hostilities. In mid May squadron code letters were again applied, this time under the left wing in black or yellow as appropriate to contrast.

381st Bomb Group

B-17F/G Fortresses, May 1943–June 1945. Original combat B-17Fs were in Dark Olive Drab and Neutral Gray factory finish. SD110 squadron code letters were applied soon after arrival at Ridgewell in light grey (Sky), 36in high, placed aft of the waist windows on both sides of the fuselage with the individual aircraft call-letter forward of the cocarde. The 532nd Bomb Squadron used VE, the 533rd OQ, the 534th JZ and 535th PL. Within a month the codes of the last three squadrons were changed, the 533rd to VP, the 534th to GD and the 535th to MS. This is the only known change of 8th Air Force bomber code letters. As these combinations were in use at that time by RAF units the assumption is that an error involving SD110 allotments occurred. The call-letters of the 532nd and 534th were from A onwards, including I, and the 533rd and 535th from Z back, and with few exceptions this remained so throughout hostilities. From the winter of 1943/44 fuselage letters were painted more distinctively in white. The original combat aircraft also carried the call-letter, 36in high in yellow, above the tail number. This was deleted when the Triangle L Group marking was introduced in late June. The Group device was to the standard dimensions and colours given in the VIII Bomber Command instruction and was fairly consistently maintained on replacements. With the Group marking, call-letters were placed below the tail number and reduced to a height of 28in.

The change to the new national insignia partly obscured fuselage call-letters and, generally, these were not repainted further forward. The 532nd, 534th and 535th Bomb Squadrons discontinued use of the fuselage call-letter when the Triangle L was introduced, although there were a few exceptions in the 534th and 535th. But the 533rd continued to paint the call-letter forward of the national insignia throughout hostilities. Markings on bare metal B-17Gs which began to arrive as replacements in March 1944 were black squadron and call-letters and a white L on a black triangle. In late June 1944 the 1st Combat Bomb Wing's red high-visibility markings were applied to tail surfaces and wing tips. Tail numbers and call-letters were reinstated in white, the latter being 24in high. In mid May 1945 squadron and call letters were painted under the left wing, 36in high, in black or yellow as appropriate to contrast.

384th Bomb Group

B-17F/G Fortresses, May 1943–June 1945. Original B-17Fs were in Dark Olive Drab and Neutral Gray factory finish. SD110 squadron code letters were applied at Grafton Underwood in early June 1943: the 544th Bomb Squadron used SU, the 545th JD, the 546th BK and the 547th SO. From the initial applications and throughout the operational period the squadrons of the 384th Bomb Group split the squadron code on the majority of aircraft. At first this was only on the right side of the fuselage, where the first letter of the code was placed aft of the waist window and the second letter was forward of the cocarde and coupled with the individual aircraft call-letter. This was most noticeable in the 545th and 547th Bomb Squadrons. There were, however, many examples of the code being split on the left side of the fuselage in other squadrons and, in the following year, of all three letters being grouped together, usually aft of the waist window but sometimes for-

ward of the national insignia. The 384th Bomb Group's display of identification letters was the most inconsistent in the 8th Air Force. At first code letters were painted in bluish-grey, 48in high. On replacements, from the summer of 1943, the height was reduced to 36in. In June 1943 the Triangle P Group marking was applied to the fin and upper right wing surface in the sizes required by the VIII Bomber Command instruction—72in overall on the fin and 96in overall on the wing, in Insignia Blue on white.

Until the national insignia was changed to the AN-I-9a type no call-letter was carried on the fin, and when this was eventually introduced, in the late summer of 1943, it was painted in yellow below the tail number 24in high. Although the 'star and bar' partly obscured fuselage letters, these were not repainted clear of the insignia. When natural metal-finish Fortresses were received the fuselage letters were in black and the Triangle P marking white on black.

The introduction of the 41st Combat Bomb Wing high-visibility markings in August 1944 involved the removal of existing tail markings. The new markings featured a 10ft-sided black triangle, 18 inches wide, circumscribing a 60in-sided white triangle with a 36in high black letter P. The tail number was painted on the lower part of the black triangle in yellow and a squadron-in-Group number, 1, 2, 3 or 4, in yellow at the apex. The call-letter was placed below the base of the black triangle, 24in high and in black. A similar size Group/Wing device was painted on the right wing upper surface but did not have the aircraft or squadron-in-Group digits.

In April 1945 squadron colours came into use on engine cowlings, having previously been used inconsistently on propeller bosses. The 544th Bomb Squadron used dark blue, the 545th yellow, the 546th red and the 547th white. After VE-Day the Group's aircraft were numbered consecutively from 1 to 71, through squadron by squadron, and this number was painted on each side of the nose in black about 24in high. A fuselage cheat line in the squadron colour was also applied to many aircraft when fuselage letters were removed. Code letters, applied in mid May 1945, were retained under the left wing.

B-17F 42-3441, used for assembly ship experiments during July 1944, was painted white overall with sky blue polka dots. A P-47D monitor used late in the war, 42-75154, carried the Group Triangle P insignia on its tail and an SU code in black forward of the national insignia.

385th Bomb Group

B-17F/G Fortresses, June 1943–July 1945. Original B-17Fs were in Dark Olive Drab and Neutral Gray factory finish. Within a week of the aircraft arriving at Great Ashfield a Group marking was notified for painting on the fin and right wing uppersurface. An Identification Yellow letter G, 40in high, was painted on a 'dulled white' (actually light grey) 'square', varying in dimensions but generally 50in by 48in, positioned above the tail number. On some 549th Bomb Squadron aircraft the square was 60in on the horizontal sides and overlapped the rudder. On the wing this marking was 72in with the span and 57in with the chord, again light grey and with a 45in yellow letter. The yellow individual aircraft call-letter, painted below the tail number, was 24in high on some aircraft and 48in on others. The large letters only appeared on the Group's early B-17Fs; in general, replacements had 24in high tail call-letters. On some aircraft the call-letter was also painted on the rear fuselage in bluish-grey, 36in high.

Early in July the instruction for the Group device was amended, the square changed to white and the letter thereon altered to Insignia Blue. The size of the G and the square remained as already established. Exactly how many of the Group's aircraft had received the yellow G before the change is not known, but many 385th Bomb Group B-17s were to be seen with this original device throughout the summer of 1943. The 'white' squares continued to be well dulled while camouflaged B-17F/Gs were received. From early 1944 the dimensions of the Group marking were generally consistent at 48in square. When aircraft without camouflage were received the Group marking was a white letter on a black square, although forming the G by masking bare metal became common. Tail call-letters were black on bare metal but they too remained the same size. Although SD110 squadron code letters were available for the 385th Bomb Group they were not displayed on fuselages during the combat operations period.

By late October 1943 propeller bosses were being painted in squadron colours. The 548th Bomb Squadron used blue, the 549th yellow, the 550th red and the 551st bright green. In December 1944 the Group's aircraft received a yellow chevron mark-

ing on the upper surface of the right wing. Each arm was 48in wide with the apex approximately in the centre of the outer wing section leading edge. At least one aircraft received the all-yellow empennage with which the 4th Bomb Wing experimented in January 1945. On transfer to the 93rd Combat Bomb Wing the Square G marking was deleted from both tail and wing; in its place 93rd CBW red wing and tail markings were applied. A single 48in wide red stripe was painted around each wing outboard of Nos 1 and 4 engines, with the outer edge of the band running just inside the join to the outer wing section. The 36in wide red band round the horizontal tailplane was situated mid way between the two central elevator hinges. The vertical tail markings consisted of 28in squares forming a checkerboard. At the base there were three red squares and at the highest point in the centre of the fin there were also three red squares, giving nine full and five part red squares on each fin surface. The squares separating the red were either olive drab or bare metal. On camouflage the aircraft call-letter was repositioned in white in the top full square and the tail number in white or yellow in its original position over the checkerboard. On natural metal the call-letter was black in the top full bare metal square and the tail number black in its original position. The first 385th Bomb Group B-17s with this marking were to be seen during the third week of February 1945, but it was April before the majority of the aircraft were so painted. In mid May 1945 SD110 squadron codes were used as 'anti-buzz' identification markings under the left wing. Each letter was approximately 72in by 60in, black on bare metal and yellow on Neutral Gray. The 548th Bomb Squadron used GX, the 549th XA, the 550th SG and the 551st HR.

386th Bomb Group

B-26B/C Marauders, June–October 1943. Aircraft were at first in Dark Olive Drab and Neutral Gray factory finish. SD110 squadron codes used were RG for the 552nd Bomb Squadron, AN for the 553rd, RU for the 554th and YA for the 555th. Before these codes were put on the aircraft the old cocarde was painted out and the recently advised AN-I-9a national insignia painted on approximately 40in further forward to allow the aircraft call-letter to be brought nearly clear of the tailplane. The letters were 40in high in light blue-grey. On the original combat aircraft the 552nd and 554th Bomb Squadrons used letters A to S, excluding E and I; the 553rd and 555th Bomb Squadrons used letters from Z to K in reverse alphabetical order.

387th Bomb Group

B-26B/C Marauders, June–October 1943. These aircraft had a Dark Olive Drab and Neutral Gray factory finish. Fuselage cocardes were painted out and the new AN-I-9a national insignia was positioned approximately 40in further forward before squadron code letters were applied. The codes—556th Bomb Squadron FW, 557th KS, 558th KX and 559th TQ—were painted in light blue-grey, 40in high characters with the squadron code forward of the national insignia on both sides of the fuselage and the individual call-letter aft. Selected letters throughout the alphabet, with the exception of I, were used on the original complements of all the Group's squadrons.

388th Bomb Group

B-17F/G Fortresses, June 1943–July 1945. Original B-17Fs were in Dark Olive Drab and Neutral Gray factory finish. The Group marking, a Square H, was applied in early July. A 48in high white 'square', with a 36in high Insignia Blue letter, was the most common form of fin device although there was some variation with the 'square' 60in wide, extending onto the rudder. The letter H had a high bar which, at a distance, made it appear as an M. This same-shaped H was used consistently for all Square H markings throughout the Group's service in England. The individual aircraft letter was in yellow, 24in high, below the tail number. The original squadron complements of twelve B-17Fs were lettered A to N excluding C and I in the 560th and 561st Bomb Squadrons, and O to Z in the 562nd and 563rd. C was not used until numbers were increased in November 1943. When 'silver' B-17Gs arrived in March 1944 the Square H was marked either white on black or a bare metal letter in the black square. The call-letter was also black. Dimensions were as for camouflaged machines.

The 45th Combat Bomb Wing's parallel stripes were first applied early in February 1945, the 388th being given black. Those on the wings were 36in wide with 60in separation, with the outer edge of

Below: Without exception, the letter H featuring in the 388th Bomb Group's marking had a high bar, suggesting that the same stencils were used throughout the Group's stay in the UK. (Robert Astrella)

the inner stripe along the wing section join. On the tail the higher stripe was usually 30in wide and the lower 36in, with the call letter repositioned on the latter in white, 28in high. In mid May 1945 8th Air Force HQ required all aircraft to carry underwing identification markings, but apparently the 388th Bomb Group did not have codes given in SD110. Instead the Group used the current W/T code, consisting of three letters plus the individual aircraft letter. These were painted in black under the left wing with the individual call-letter first followed by the W/T code. The 561st Bomb Squadron is known to have used LHN and two other squadrons used KBZ and PJA, but the fourth combination remains unknown. The 388th Bomb Group is unique in that it was the only long-term heavy Bomb Group in the 8th Air Force whose aircraft had no distinguishing squadron markings during combat operations.

389th Bomb Group

B-24D/H/J/L/M Liberators, August 1943–May 1945. Original B-24Ds were in Dark Olive Drab and Neutral Gray factory finish. Radio call-letters were painted on fins below tail numbers in yellow, 28in high. The 564th and 566th Bomb Squadrons used letters in alphabetical order from A, the 565th and 567th letters from Z in reverse alphabetical order. The 566th and 567th had a yellow bar, approximately 12in by 4in, forward of the call-letter as a means of distinction from the other Group aircraft with the same letter. When the aircraft returned from Africa in late August 1943 the Circle C Group marking was applied to the vertical tail and right wing. On the tail this was of 69 or 72in diameter with a 36in Insignia Blue C, with a similar size on the wing. As the white disc would overlap the tail number this was repositioned lower on the fin, as was the call-letter.

In November 1943, when squadron complements were increased, a new system of distinguishing individual call-letters was introduced. The 564th Bomb Squadron continued to have no symbol with its call-letter, the 565th used a bar before the call-letter, the 566th had a plus sign after the call-letter and the 567th had a bar after the letter. In March 1944 squadron code letters were painted in light grey (Sky), 48in high, on the fuselage aft of the waist gun windows. These were YO for the 564th Bomb Squadron, EE for the 565th, RR for the 566th and HP for the 567th.

Above: Before new instructions were issued for markings on bare metal-finish aircraft the 389th Bomb Group continued to apply the Circle C as on camouflaged machines—an Insignia Blue C on a white disc. An example of this is seen on the tail of a B-24J that crashed at Hethel during an enemy intruder attack on the night of 22 April 1944. The black bar after the individual aircraft letter Z indicates assignment to the 567th Bomb Squadron. (John Driscoll)

The first natural metal-finish B-24Js were received in April 1944 and the code letters were painted in yellow on the first bare metal aircraft received at Hethel but were soon changed to black. The Circle C was white on black and the call-letter black on 'silver' aircraft, but one or two of the early examples were first painted as on camouflage, that is, as an Insignia Blue letter on a white disc. In early May 1944 high-visibility markings were applied to the outward-facing surfaces of the vertical tail. A 27–30in wide white vertical stripe was placed centrally and the remainder of the fin and rudder was painted black. The call-letter, 24in high in black, was positioned centrally on the white stripe. The 565th Bomb Squadron was identified by a bar above the letter and the 567th by a bar below. The 566th placed its plus sign below the letter. In the late summer of 1944 the call-letter was also painted on the rear fuselage of 389th Group Liberators. Positioned just forward of the tailplane, the letter was 36in high and in yellow, with the appropriate symbol below or above, also in yellow.

The 389th Bomb Group had two assembly ships. The first was B-24D 41-23683, known as 'The Green Dragon' and painted with 24in wide alternating concentric stripes of green and yellow, diagonally slanted on both fuselage and wings. Nos 1 and 4 engine

cowlings were yellow and Nos 2 and 3 green. This aircraft was replaced in July 1944 by B-24J 42-99972, which had a series of linked yellow squares over fuselage and wings. A white letter C was placed centrally on the fin.

390th Bomb Group

B-17F/G Fortresses, July 1943–July 1945. Original B-17Fs were in Dark Olive Drab and Neutral Gray factory finish. Their Square J Group marking was applied soon after the aircraft arrived at Framlingham. Most of the original aircraft had a 60in high by 48in wide white rectangle with a 36in high Insignia Blue J thereon. There was considerable variation in the size and shape of the Square J device on tails throughout the Group's stay at Framlingham. Individual aircraft call-letters, 24in high in yellow and placed below the tail number, were fairly consistently marked on camouflaged aircraft. The original complement were also given 36in call-letters on the rear fuselage in blue-grey but many early replacements did not have them. The 568th and 570th Bomb Squadron used letters in alphabetical order from A and the 569th and 571st used letters from Z in reverse alphabetical order. The letter I was not used until late in 1943. Early in October 1943 the Group started painting SD110 squadron code let-

Above: Liberator maintenance line. The 567th Bomb Squadron B-24J 42-50726 carries standard 48in code letters in black on bare metal grouped with a 36in high individual aircraft call-letter and bar in yellow. The 389th and 445th Bomb Groups were the only 2nd Bomb Division Groups that carried their call-letter on the fuselage sides. *Yankee Rebel*, 42-95026 HP:I, in the foreground, was lost a few days after this photograph was taken in July 1944. (USAAF)

ters on the B-17 fuselages forward of the national insignia on both sides. Their colour was bluish-grey and the letters 36in high. The 568th Bomb Squadron used BI, the 569th CC, the 570th DI and the 571st FC. Call-letters were painted on the rear fuselage where required.

With the coming of natural metal B-17Gs in March 1944 the Square J was white on black and all other letters black. Sizes remained as with camouflaged aircraft, although there were a few exceptions, most notably one 571st Bomb Squadron B-17G that had squadron codes on the rear fuselage only 24in high. In July 1944 squadron colours were painted as a 12in nose band just aft of the Plexiglas. The 568th Bomb Squadron used red, the 569th dark blue, the 570th yellow and the 571st bright green. In late January 1945 a 48in yellow stripe was painted down the trailing edge of the vertical tail, soon amended to the rudder only although those aircraft already having the yellow stripe retained it. At the same time a 48in wide yellow stripe was painted diagonally across the upper right and lower left wing surfaces from just beyond the outboard engines to the centre of the aileron. It took several weeks to effect these markings on all aircraft.

392nd Bomb Group

B-24H/J/M/L Liberators, August 1943–June 1945. Original B-24Hs were in Dark Olive Drab and Neutral Gray factory finish. Their Circle D Group marking was applied to tail and wing in late August 1943. On the vertical tail this was a 69 or 72in diameter white disc with an Insignia Blue letter D thereon; on the upper surface of the right wing it was 96in in diameter. Where the tail number was obscured it was repainted below the Circle D in yellow and below this, 24in high, a yellow call-letter appeared. The 576th Bomb Squadron used letters A to M, less I, the 577th used N to Z, the 578th N to Z with a bar below the letter and the 579th A to M, less I, with a bar below the letter. Additional aircraft in all squadrons were distinguished by a bar above the call-letter. In mid-March 1944 squadron code letters were painted 48in high in light grey on the fuselage aft of the waist gun positions. The 576th Bomb Squadron used CI, the 577th DC, the 578th EC and the 579th GC.

When natural metal-finished aircraft arrived as replacements from April 1944 the Circle D was marked white on black with all letters black. At the beginning of May 1944 new tail markings were required by the 2nd Bomb Division. The existing markings were to be removed and a 36in wide black band was to be painted horizontally across the middle of the fin and rudder. The remainder of the outer surfaces of the fin and rudder were to be bare metal or silver finish. However, the black band was painted on aircraft before the existing markings were removed and operations were conducted in this state. On several camouflaged aircraft the existing markings were overpainted with white. Call-letters were placed on the black band in white, 24in high, with the same run of letters for each squadron. To comply with the new instruction, the 577th Bomb Squadron then placed a plus sign after the call-letter, the 578th a bar below it and the 579th a bar above, while the 576th continued to have no symbol with the call-letter.

Above: A 602nd Bomb Squadron Pathfinder with white plastic radome extended. The same 48in high stencils used for the fuselage codes were used for the tail call-letters on most 398th Bomb Group Fortresses, and these letters were with few exceptions painted in yellow. The other two Groups of the 1st Combat Bomb Wing each used a different colour for tail call-letters on the red band of bare metal-finish aircraft: the 91st used black and the 381st white. The W of the Group device is bare metal not white. (Robert Welty)

By June 1944 the Group was painting the last three digits of the aircraft's serial number on both sides of the nose, usually in the area some 3ft above the nosewheel door. The figures were in black on bare metal and yellow on olive drab and varied in size from 15 to 18in high.

The 392nd Bomb Group assembly ship was 41-23689, X, bar above. Painted light grey, it had two black and white outlines of B-24 nose profiles on its nose and two black and white tail turret profiles on the rear fuselage. The stated purpose was to give accompanying aircraft in a formation an indication of how far apart they should position themselves.

398th Bomb Group

B-17G Fortresses, April 1944–June 1945. Original combat aircraft were in natural metal finish and Group and squadron markings were applied soon after arrival at Nuthampstead. Their Triangle W marking was a black equilateral triangle with 60in sides with a white W thereon. The shape and size of the W varied from 24 to 30in and on many replacements it was formed on bare metal, by masking the letter before spraying the triangle. The Triangle W on the upper surface of the right wing also had 60in sides. Squadron codes used were as follows: 600th Bomb Squadron N8, 601st 3O, 602nd K8 and 603rd N7. These were painted in black, 48in high, but there was considerable variation in positioning. On the left side of the fuselage the usual location was aft of the waist gun window with all three letters grouped together. The 602nd Bomb Squadron usually separated the squadron code from the individual letter with a hyphen while the 600th and 603rd left a greater space to distinguish the squadron code from the call-letter. The 601st Bomb Squadron grouped all close together. On the right side the most common placement was the squadron code aft of the waist window and the individual letter forward of the national insignia. The 601st Bomb Squadron frequently placed all three characters forward of the 'star and bar' on the right side and often used an oversize letter O, some 54in high, for their 3O code on replacement aircraft. The call letter on the fin below the tail number was 48in high and in black.

In late June 1944 the red 1st Combat Bomb Wing markings were applied. Both upper and lower surfaces of wing tips and horizontal tail, less the elevators, were painted red. An approximately 80in wide band of red was painted down the fin bordering the leading edge of the rudder. In most cases the Triangle W device was not painted over but there was the odd example of a white triangle with a black letter. The tail number was reinstated in the same location in yellow and the call-letter was also yellow. The latter was 24in high on some replacements and 36in on others, but 48in remained the common size. These variations appear to have been occasioned by

an unusual amount of hand painting rather than spraying using stencils.

401st Bomb Group

B-17G Fortresses, November 1943–June 1945. Original combat aircraft were in Dark Olive Drab and Neutral Gray factory finish. The Triangle S Group marking applied to the fin was an equilateral white triangle with 72in sides and a 36in high Insignia Blue S. The wing marking was of similar dimensions. A 24in high yellow call-letter was painted below the tail number. All four squadrons used letters in alphabetical order from A, initially excluding E and I, although E was used for replacement aircraft from the spring of 1944. Squadron code letters used were SC for the 612th Bomb Squadron, IN for the 613th, IW for the 614th and IY for the 615th. These were painted in yellow, the 612th, 613th and 615th using mostly 48in high letters and the 614th 36in high. On most 612th and 614th Bomb Squadron aircraft the squadron and call-letters were grouped aft of the waist gun position on the left side of the fuselage, with the squadron code forward of the national insignia and the call-letter aft of the waist gun position of the right. Normal practice in the 613th and 614th Bomb Squadrons was to have the squadron letters forward of the national insignia and the call-letter aft of the waist gun positions on both sides of the fuselage.

With the first bare metal-finish B-17Gs, received in March 1944, the Triangle S was then a black triangle with a white or bare metal S. The latter be-

Below: A 401st Bomb Group B-17G with yellow tail 'sash' outlined in black and the S of the Group device formed with bare metal by masking. (Frank Zedon)

came the standard form on replacement aircraft. Code letters were black on bare metal finish. In August a 48in wide diagonal yellow band was painted across both sides of the fin with the lower end to the front. The Triangle S, tail number and call-letter were not obscured, the last two usually being left on a bare metal or olive drab stripe depending on the general finish of the aircraft. The yellow stripe was bordered on both sides by a 4in wide black line. Squadron codes with call-letter were painted under the left wing in black during the third week of May 1945.

445th Bomb Group

B-24H/J/L/M Liberators, November 1943–May 1945. Original combat aircraft were in Dark Olive Drab and Neutral Gray. The Group marking, Circle F, was painted on the vertical tail as a 69in diameter white disc with a 36in high Insignia Blue letter F. This marking on the upper surface of the right wing was of a similar size. Radio call-letters were 24in high and in yellow below the repositioned tail number. The 700th Bomb Squadron used A to M with a plus sign after the letter, the 701st used N to Z with a

Below: A 700th Bomb Squadron B-24H displaying the peculiar use of two symbols to differentiate between other aircraft with a call-letter R in the 445th Bomb Group. This aircraft has a white bomb-bay door stripe. The P-51D in the foreground, 44-14617 D7:C, was the personal mount of Lieutenant-Colonel D. Shafer of the 339th Fighter Group. (James G. Robinson)

plus sign after the letter, the 702nd used N to Z without an adjacent sign and the 703rd used A to M without an adjacent plus sign. Additional aircraft in all squadrons were distinguished by bar signs above or below the call-letter. The bar and the plus arms were approximately 12in long.

In March 1944 SD110 squadron letters were painted on the rear fuselage aft of the waist gun positions on both sides of the aircraft, 48in high in bluish-grey. The 700th Bomb Squadron used IS, the 701st MK, the 702nd WV and the 703rd RN. The call-letter was also painted on the fuselage in yellow at this time, mostly 36in high although smaller sizes, down to 24in, were to be seen. Positioning was beside and aft of the squadron letters on the left side and close to and forward of the squadron letters on the right.

In early April the first natural metal-finish B-24Js arrived as replacements and all lettering except the fuselage call-letter was painted in black. The fuselage call-letter was yellow but later occasionally black. Circle F markings were of the same size as on camouflaged machines but white on black. In May 1944 the high-visibility tail markings were introduced requiring an all-black fin and rudder with a centred white horizontal stripe, 36in wide. On later replacements the stripe was left unpainted. The call letter was painted 24in high on the white stripe and a revised system of accompanying signs was introduced. The 700th Bomb Squadron aircraft used A to Z with a plus sign, those aircraft in the N to Z range also having a bar sign above or below the call-

letter. The 701st also used A to Z with a plus sign but the A to M range also carried a bar above or below the letter. The 702nd used A to Z, with the A to M range having a bar below or above and the N to Z range no adjacent signs. The 703rd used A to M without signs and N to Z with a bar above or below the letter. The 700th and 701st Bomb Squadrons only used the signs on the tails of their aircraft whereas the other two squadrons repeated the sign adjacent to the fuselage call-letter. The 445th Bomb Group's system of distinguishing individual aircraft was undoubtedly the most complicated in the 8th Air Force. Between 17 October and 29 December 1944 the Pathfinder B-24s in each squadron were allocated call-letters at the beginning of the alphabet, A to F, and other aircraft with letters in this range were given other letters.

The 445th Bomb Group's assembly ship, B-24D 41-24215 Z, had alternating bands of black and orange encircling the fuselage and tailplane. The upper surfaces of the wings were also banded black and orange, while the lower surfaces were bare metal-finished. Engine nacelles were black and engine cowlings orange. A 6ft high letter F was formed with white lights forward of the waist windows on both sides of the fuselage.

446th Bomb Group

B-24H/J/L/M Liberators, November 1943–July 1945. Original combat aircraft were in Dark Olive Drab and Neutral Gray factory finish. The Circle H Group marking applied to the vertical tail was a 69in white disc with a 36in high Insignia Blue H. On the upper surface of the right wing the marking was a 78in diameter white disc with a 48in high blue letter. On replacement aircraft the letter was often in black. The tail number, obscured by the Circle H, was repainted below it in yellow. Directly below the number a 24in high individual aircraft call-letter was painted in yellow. All four squadrons used call-letters from A in alphabetical order, excluding I. To distinguish different squadrons, yellow bars were used above or below the letters. It is believed these were added at the end of January 1944, a few weeks after the call-letters were painted on, and resulted in 1½–2in bars, much thinner than commonly used on 2nd Bomb Division aircraft. The 704th Bomb Squadron

Below: *Sugar Baby* 42-50573 FL:S taxies along a puddled perimeter track at Bungay. This B-24H displays the red cowling bands that marked 704th Bomb Squadron aircraft and has a broad yellow stripe along the bomb bay door edges. (Albert Krassman)

was distinguished by not using a bar with the call-letter, the 705th by a bar below the letter, the 706th by a bar above the letter and the 707th by two bars, one above and one below. In March 1944 squadron code letters, 48in high, were painted on the rear fuselage aft of the waist gun positions in pale grey (Sky). The 704th Bomb Squadron used FL, the 705th HN, the 706th RT and the 707th JU. Natural metal-finished B-24Js, first received in April 1944, had code letters painted black with the Group device white on black.

At the beginning of May 1944 high-visibility colour markings were introduced. The outer facing sides of the vertical tail were painted Identification Yellow with a 36in wide black horizontal stripe positioned centrally. A 24in high yellow call-letter was carried on the black stripe but the bar signs were discontinued. From the summer of 1944 call-letters for replacement B-24s were selected from the whole alphabet range excluding I. At the end of May 1944 the engine cowlings, between the cowl ring and the cooling shutters, were painted with squadron colours. The 704th Bomb Squadron used red, the 705th yellow, the 706th white and the 707th dark blue. In the late summer of 1944 the Group's Pathfinder B-24s were given a black ring marking, superimposed centrally on the existing tail markings. Where the ring passed through the black band it was rendered in yellow. The overall diameter was 88in, the ring being 8in 'thick', and the inner diameter was 72in.

The 446th Bomb Group had two assembly ships. The first was B-24D 41-23737, *Fearless Freddie*, described as 'golden orange' in Group records and orange-yellow in official signals. This aircraft was replaced by B-24H 42-7654, in Identification Yellow overall; also named *Fearless Freddie*, it was destroyed in a crash in January 1945.

447th Bomb Group

B-17G Fortresses, November 1943–August 1945. Original combat aircraft were in Dark Olive Drab and Neutral Gray factory finish. Square K Group markings were applied in early December 1943. On the fin the marking was a 48in white square with a 36in Insignia Blue K, and on the upper surface of the right wing a 72in by 57in rectangle with a 48in K in the same colours as on the fin. Individual aircraft call-letters were painted below the tail number 24in high in yellow. Letters used were in alphabetical order from A, excluding I, in all squadrons. No

Above: A well-known photograph of the 447th Bomb Group's worn *A Bit O'Lace*. The white-painted cowlings which identified 709th Bomb Squadron are stained and faded, the olive drab replacement rudder and elevator have not been painted yellow and eleven months' combat service have dulled the once bright metal. The earlier 4th Combat Bomb Wing Insignia Blue chevron remains on the right wing. (Charles Brown)

squadron markings of any kind were carried on the Fortresses for some months although squadron code letters were given in SD110 on the Group's arrival in the United Kingdom. Natural metal-finished aircraft were first received in late March 1944 and the Group markings were painted white on black and the call-letters black.

At some time during the early spring of 1944 propeller bosses were painted in squadron colours. The 708th Bomb Squadron used yellow, the 709th white, the 710th red and the 711th dark blue. In September 1944 the engine cowling ring and some 12in of the primary cowling were painted in the squadron colour. In December 1944, when the 4th Combat Bomb Wing issued directions for coloured wing markings, 447th Bomb Group aircraft carried an Insignia Blue chevron on the upper surface of the right wing outer section and the under surface of the left wing outer section. The arms of the chevron were 48in wide with the apex at the wing leading edge. At the beginning of February 1945 the all-yellow tail markings were introduced, the existing markings not being obscured. Additionally two medium green stripes, 24in wide with a 12in separation, were painted round the rear fuselage and fin fairing well aft of the waist gun positions. Wing tips, both top and bottom, were painted yellow. The blue chevron was discontinued but was not removed from aircraft already painted with this marking. From the winter of 1944/45 the letters X, Y and Z were reserved for Pathfinder aircraft in all four squadrons. In mid May 1945 SD110 squadron code letters were painted with call-letters under the left wing in black. The 708th Bomb Squadron had the letters CQ, the 709th IE, the 710th IJ and the 711th IR.

448th Bomb Group

B-24D/H/J/L/M Liberators, November 1943–July 1945. Original combat aircraft were in Dark Olive Drab and Neutral Gray factory finish with a 12in high white numeral on the lower fin indicating squadron assignment. These were 2, 3, 4 and 5, being the last digits of the squadron numbers. The Circle I Group marking was applied in early December 1943 to the outward-facing sides of the vertical tail and the upper surface of the right wing. The tail marking was a 69in diameter white disc with a 36in high letter I in Insignia Blue; the wing marking, in the same colours, used a 78in diameter disc and 48in letter. Existing squadron markings and the tail number were painted out and the latter was repositioned below the Circle I in yellow. Individual aircraft call-letters were painted below the tail number in a geometric symbol identifying squadron assignment. The 712th Bomb Squadron used a triangle, the 713th a circle, the 714th a square and the 715th a diamond. Each geometric shape was from 24 to 28in overall and formed with a 2in wide yellow outline. The letter within the device, also yellow, was approximately 20in high. All the squadrons used letters from A in alphabetical order.

In March 1944 squadron code letters, 48in high, were painted on the rear fuselage, aft of the waist gun positions, in a bluish-grey. The 712th Bomb Squadron used CT, the 713th IG, the 714th EI and the 715th IO. Natural metal-finished B-24s arriving in April 1944 received black squadron and call letters and a white I on a black disc. At the beginning of May 1944 the existing tail markings were deleted, the entire outer facing surfaces of the fins and rudders being painted Identification Yellow with a 36in wide diagonally inclined black stripe thereon. The forward end of the black stripe was high on the fin leading edge and the rear end low on the rudder. An outline squadron symbol with the call-letter was painted in the centre of the black band in yellow. The size of the letter was then reduced to 12–18in and the geometric device to 24–34in overall, the size

Above: The tail of *Lonesome Lou*, B-24H 42-50677, carries the call-letter J within an outline yellow box of the 714th Bomb Squadron. The 448th was the only Bomb Group that used this form of marking to distinguish its squadrons. (Harold Gage)

and shape varying considerably. As the call-letter was reduced in size due to the width of the diagonal black stripe, it was also painted on the inner facing sides of the fins, below the transferred tail number. On many aircraft this was 36in high but on others 24in and within an outline squadron device. The colour was yellow on olive drab and black on natural metal. The outline geometric symbol surrounding the call-letter on the inward-facing side of the fin was discontinued on replacement aircraft during the summer of 1944. In the late summer of 1944 squadron code letters were also discontinued on most replacement aircraft, and where they were applied the size was reduced to 36in. Squadron letters could still be seen on some 448th Bomb Group Liberators at the end of 1944 but eventually all were removed.

The 448th had at least three assembly ships. The first, B-24D 41-23809 *You Can't Miss It*, was painted with yellow and black checkerboard. In June 1944 it was replaced by B-24D 42-63981 *The Striped Ape*, with yellow markings over camouflage finish. From each tip 15ft of the wings was yellow and the engine cowlings, elevators, fuselage nose and a broad band around the waist were also yellow. A 10ft wide yellow band was painted from the wing root out to the trailing edge on both upper and lower surfaces. When this aircraft was salvaged in February 1945 B-24H 41-29489, known by the same name, was painted up with broad maroon and white bands.

452nd Bomb Group

B-17G Fortresses, January 1944–August 1945. Original combat aircraft were in Dark Olive Drab and Neutral Gray factory finish. The Square L marking was applied to the tail fin and upper surface of the right wing in January 1944. On the fin this was a white rectangle, mostly 60in high by 48in wide with a black letter L, 48in high. There was much variation: on many of the original complement the 'square' was 48in high and 60in wide, overlapping the rudder; on others the device was terminated against the rudder leading edge, reducing the horizontal measurement to 56in. The 728th Bomb Squadron came to use a distinctive 54in high by 42in wide 'square' from the spring of 1944. On the wing the Square L dimensions were mostly 72in with the span and 57in with the chord and the letter L was sized and coloured as on the fin. Here, too, there were variations in size, those given being the most prevalent. When natural metal replacements arrived in March 1944 the Square L was then white on black. On the camouflaged B-17Gs the individual aircraft call-letter was 20in high in yellow below the tail number. Each squadron used letters from the alphabetical range, excluding I. No squadron markings were carried by 452nd Bomb Group aircraft until the summer of 1944, when the bar and plus system, common in the B-24 Groups, was introduced. The 728th Bomb Squadron used a bar before the letter, the 729th used a bar after the letter, the 730th used no sign and the 731st used a plus symbol after the latter. The symbol was painted yellow on camouflage and black on bare metal and was made with approximately 4in strokes with an overall measurement of 12in.

In mid-January 1945 the Group started painting high-visibility colour markings on its aircraft. Two parallel yellow stripes on the outer wing sections, with the inner stripe bordering the section join, were 36in wide with a 60in separation. These markings were on the upper surface of the right wing and under surface of the left wing. On the vertical tail surfaces the lower yellow stripe was 36in wide on some aircraft and 48in on others; the higher stripe was 36in wide and positioned 60in above the lower.

The existing markings were reinstated where obscured, the call-letter being black on the yellow band. In mid-May 1945 Squadron code letters were painted in black under the left wing with the call-letter. The 728th Bomb Squadron used M3, the 729th 9Z, the 730th 7D and the 731st 6K.

453rd Bomb Group

B-24H/J/L/M Liberators, December 1943–May 1945. Original combat aircraft were in Dark Olive Drab and Neutral Gray factory finish. At least nine assigned to the 732nd Bomb Squadron had 'shark mouths' in red and white below the nose turret and encompassing the bombardier's window. The Circle J Group tail marking, applied in early January 1944, consisted of a 36in high Insignia Blue J on a 69in diameter white disc. On the upper surface of the right wing the disc was 78in in diameter with a 48in J, the colours as on the tail. The Circle J on the tail covered the tail number and this was repainted below the Group marking. Call-letters were painted in yellow, 24in high, below the tail number. The 732nd and 734th Bomb Squadrons used the letters A to O, while the 733rd and 735th used letters from Z in reverse alphabetical order to O. As full squadron complements at this date were usually 14–16 aircraft, sometimes four aircraft in the Group carried the letters N or O; but progressively the 732nd and 734th discontinued the use of these letters. Some use was made of bars to distinguish those aircraft serving in the same squadron with duplicated identities.

In the third week of March 1944 the 734th and 735th Bomb Squadrons distinguished their aircraft by the addition of a yellow plus sign after the call-letter. This was at the time squadron codes were being painted in 48in high bluish-grey letters on the rear fuselage. The 732nd Bomb Squadron used E3, the 733rd F8, the 734th E8 and the 735th H6.

Natural metal-finished B-24s were received in April 1944 and the Circle J was then applied as a white letter on a black disc, and the code and call-letters were also in black. In early May 1944 high-visibility markings replaced those on the tail. The new marking was an all-black fin and rudder on the outward-facing sides, with a 36in wide white diagonal stripe thereon. The forward end of the stripe ran from the top corner of the fin to the bottom trailing edge of the rudder. The call-letter, 24in high, was painted in white on the black band. The 732nd and

94

Left, upper: Red propeller bosses indicated an aircraft assigned to the 734th Bomb Squadron, 453rd Bomb Group, and supplemented the SD110 code E8. This photograph was taken in September 1944, before the Group discontinued displaying fuselage codes. The name *Hollywood And Vine* is surrounded by red stars. (S. L. Kitts)

Left, lower: The artwork on *Hazee* was much admired at Old Buckenham. A B-24M, serial 44-50527, the aircraft carried no squadron markings at the time this photograph was taken in March 1945. The call letter T without a symbol indicated the 732nd Bomb Squadron. (S. L. Kitts)

733rd Bomb Squadrons continued to use letters in the A–M and N–Z ranges respectively, with additional aircraft in each squadron distinguished by a bar under the call-letter. The 734th and 735th Bomb Squadrons also continued to use letters within the same respective ranges but discontinued the use of plus signs with the new tail markings, instead using a bar after the call-letter on the black band. Exceptions were aircraft in those squadrons with duplicated call-letters, which were still distinguished by plus signs. However, in the second week of July 1944 the whole system of distinguishing call-letters was rationalised in line with Divisional instruction. The 732nd Bomb Squadron used no symbols with the letter, the 733rd used a plus following the letter, the 734th used a bar following the letter and the 735th used a bar below the letter.

By May 1944 squadrons were painting propeller bosses in a squadron colour, if inconsistently. The 732nd used white, the 733rd blue, the 734th red and the 735th yellow. During the last few operational months several aircraft of the 735th Bomb Squadron carried an unofficial unit insignia on the co-pilot's armour plate panel. It consisted of a red winged, mailed fist clutching a bomb set on a yellow background.

The 453rd Bomb Group assembly ship was B-24D 41-23738 *Wham Bam*, painted with 6ft yellow squares in checkerboard fashion over the existing

Right: Yellow propeller bosses identify aircraft of the 751st Bomb Squadron seen on their way to a target in December 1944. The blue used for the diagonal band was the same Insignia Blue shade as the national insignia. The U in the Group marking is bare metal. (L. R. Peterson)

factory camouflage. A letter J formed with amber lights was positioned on each side of the fuselage aft of the wing.

457th Bomb Group

B-17G Fortresses, January 1944–June 1945. Original combat aircraft were in Dark Olive Drab and Neutral Gray factory finish. Their Triangle U Group marking was a 72in-sided white equilateral triangle with a 36in Insignia Blue letter U thereon. On the upper surface of the right wing the triangle had 96in sides and the letter U was 57in high, with colours as on the tail. An individual aircraft call-letter, either 36in or 48in high, was painted below the tail number in yellow. The 48in letter was the size most commonly used on replacement aircraft but 36in and 24in letters were also to be seen. All four squadrons used letters in alphabetical order from A, excluding C, E and I. These exclusions are not known ever to have been used as call-letters in the 457th Bomb Group.

The first B-17Gs in natural metal finish received by the 8th Air Force as replacements in February 1944 were concentrated in the 457th Bomb Group for a few weeks in the belief that 'silver' aircraft, in a

formation of camouflaged bombers, would be singled out for attack by enemy interceptors. The Triangle U on these aircraft was a white letter on black and the call-letter was also in black. In the summer of 1944 the squadrons were distinguished by coloured propeller bosses. The 748th Bomb Squadron used red, the 749th blue, the 750th white and the 751st yellow. In August 1944 the aircraft call-letter, followed by the last three digits of the serial number, was painted in approximately 12in high characters on both sides of the nose, directly aft of the bombardier's Plexiglas; the colour was yellow on camouflage and black on bare metal. On some aircraft the call-letter was omitted and this later became general practice relative to nose numbers. A number of aircraft had the call-letter, approximately 20in high, painted on the chin turret sides during the final months of hostilities.

In August 1944 a 48in wide Insignia Blue stripe was painted diagonally across the vertical tail, the lower end forward and the higher end at the top of the rudder. On most aircraft the Group insignia, tail number and call-letter were left with a bare metal margin. This was also the process when painting most replacements, although smaller call-letters were more general and 20in high letters were used on several aircraft, most commonly in the 751st Bomb Squadron. In mid May 1945 the current wireless telegraphy codes were used in the anti-low flying programme as an underwing identity marking. This suggests that the 457th Bomb Group squad-

Above: When the 94th Combat Bomb Wing diagonal stripe was applied to aircraft with existing tail markings a bare strip was left round all of these on natural metal finish. B-17G serial 43-38857, D of the 750th Bomb Squadron (white propeller bosses), has the 'last three' painted on the side of the nose, a common practice in the 457th Bomb Group. (L. R. Peterson)

rons had for some reason been omitted from the SD110 publication. The W/T codes used, plus the aircraft letter as a suffix, were as follows: 748th Bomb Squadron RUW, 749th JOB, 750th PPL and 751st MJA.

458th Bomb Group

B-24H/J/L/M Liberators, January 1944–July 1945.
Original combat aircraft were in Dark Olive Drab and Neutral Gray factory finish. Circle K Group markings were applied in early February 1944. On the vertical tail this was a 69in diameter white disc with a 36in high Insignia Blue K thereon. On the wing in the same colours the device was 78in in diameter with a 48in letter. The tail number was repositioned in yellow below the Circle K on the tail and below that a 24in high yellow call-letter was placed. All four squadrons used letters from A in alphabetical order, excluding C, which was not used by the 458th Bomb Group. There was no visual means of distinguishing an aircraft's squadron until SD110 squadron codes were painted on in mid-March 1944. They were in blue-grey, either 48in or 54in high, and placed aft of the waist gun positions

on both sides of the fuselage. The 752nd Bomb Squadron used 7V, the 753rd J4, the 754th Z5 and the 755th J3. When natural metal-finish aircraft came as replacements from April 1944 the squadron codes and call-letter were painted in black and the Group marking as a white letter on a black disc.

At the beginning of May 1944 all existing tail markings were removed or painted over and the new high-visibility colours applied. For this Group they consisted of an overall red fin and rudder on the outward facing surfaces with a 28in or 30in vertical stripe in the centre. A 24in high call-letter was painted in red on the centre of the white stripe. No bars or plus signs were used. In October 1944 all Pathfinder B-24s were concentrated in the 755th Bomb Squadron, which led to some changes of call-letters.

In March 1945 the Group started painting the last three digits of the serial plus a hyphen and call-letter on the sides of B-24 noses. These markings were 24in high, black on bare metal and yellow on olive drab.

The 458th Bomb Group assembly ship was originally B-24D 42-40127 *Z First Sergeant*, which was burnt out in May 1944; it was replaced by B-24H 41-28697, which crashed in March 1945. Both these aircraft were painted in similar fashion. The front half of the fuselage was white with red and blue polka dots, the rear half camouflage-finished with red and yellow polka dots. The wings also had red and yellow polka dots on olive drab. A third assembly ship, B-24J 42-100366, did not have a special paint scheme.

466th Bomb Group

B-24H/J/L/M Liberators, February 1944–July 1945. Original combat aircraft were in Dark Olive Drab and Neutral Gray factory finish. Circle L Group insignia were applied to tails and wings in early March 1944. On the outward-facing surfaces of the vertical tail it consisted of a 69in diameter white disc with a 36in Insignia Blue P thereon. On the upper surface of the right wing the device was 78in diameter with a 48in letter, in colours as on the tail. The tail number, usually obscured by the Circle L, was repainted below it in yellow; below this, also in yellow, the individual aircraft call-letter was positioned. On most of the original complement, where there was sufficient space at the base of the fin, the call-letter was 30in high; otherwise the letter was 24in

Above: The vertical stripe used on 458th Bomb Group aircraft was often wider than the prescribed 30in. Squadron codes were generally larger, with the Z5 on these 755th Bomb Squadron aircraft 54 inches high.

high. Each squadron used letters in alphabetical order from A, excluding C. Before the Group became operational squadron codes were painted on the rear fuselage aft of the waist gun positions. These were in a bluish-grey, 48in high. The 784th Bomb Squadron used T9, the 785th 2U, the 786th U8 and the 787th 6L. When the first replacement aircraft with bare metal finish were received in mid April 1944 the squadron codes and call-letter were painted in black and the Group device white on black.

At the beginning of May 1944 the existing tail markings were replaced by a 36in wide white horizontal stripe across the outward-facing surfaces of the fin and rudder, the remainder of which were painted red. Call-letters, 24in high, were painted in the centre of the white stripe in red. At this time bar and plus signs were employed to distinguish aircraft with the same letter, excepting the 784th Bomb Squadron that did not use a sign: the 785th used a plus sign following the call letter, the 786th a bar above the call letter and the 787th a bar below. During the summer of 1944 a few aircraft displayed coloured engine cowling rings as purely personal decorations. By January 1945 squadron colours had been introduced on the cowling rings: red for the

784th Bomb Squadron, blue for the 785th, yellow for the 786th and white for the 787th.

The 466th Bomb Group assembly ship was B-24D 41-24109, coded T9:Q and later 6L:Q. All camouflage paint was removed and 8in wide red zig-zags were painted on wings and fuselage. The spaces between the zig-zags were also 8in wide.

467th Bomb Group

B-24H/J/L/M Liberators, March 1944–July 1945. Original combat aircraft were in Dark Olive Drab and Neutral Gray factory finish. Circle P group insignia were applied soon after the aircraft arrived at Rackheath. On the vertical tail the insignia was a 69in white disc with a 36in high Insignia Blue P positioned thereon. The device on the upper surface of the right wing was 78in in diameter with a 48in letter P, in colours as on the tail. The tail number was obscured by the Group markings and was repainted the same size directly below the Circle P. The individual aircraft call-letter was painted 24in high in yellow below the tail number. Each squadron used letters from A in alphabetical order, with no exclusions. Bar and plus signs were used to distinguish aircraft with the same call-letter. The 788th Bomb Squadron did not use any symbols, the 789th used a bar after the letter, the 790th used a bar before the letter and the 791st used a plus sign after the letter.

Before the Group became operational squadron codes were painted on the rear fuselage aft of the waist gun positions in 36in high light grey characters. The 788th Bomb Squadron used X7, the 789th 6A, the 790th Q2 and the 791st 4Z. In early May 1944 all existing tail markings were replaced by an all-red outward-facing fin and rudder with a 36in wide white diagonal stripe, its forward end high. A 24in high call-letter and symbol, where appropriate, were painted on the white band in red. The 789th Bomb Squadron then had the bar above the letter and the 790th had the bar below. By October 1944 the last three digits of the serial number were painted on both sides of the nose in black on 'silver' and in white on olive drab. On 791st Bomb Squadron aircraft the numerals were 24in high, while on the B-24s of the other squadrons they were mostly 30in high. Where an aircraft had large decorative motifs or insignia on the nose these numbers were either omitted or reduced in size.

Below: In contrast to the 458th Bomb Group, which used oversize codes on its aircraft, the 467th Bomb Group in the same Combat Wing was the only 8th Air Force B-24 Group to use 36in high characters. The Sky shade 789th Bomb Squadron codes are on *Six Bits*, B-24H serial 42-52525 6A:G, which landed at Bulltofta, Sweden, on 21 June 1944, where it was photographed after the national marking had been deleted. Note the white bomb-bay door edge stripe. (Flodin/NASM)

The first of the 467th Bomb Group's two assembly ships, 42-40370 *Pete, the POM Inspector*, was salvaged in October 1944. The second, B-24H 41-29393, had the same name. Both aircraft were painted black overall with yellow discs outlined in red. Bomb doors were also red, and an illuminated white letter P was superimposed on a yellow disc forward of the waist window on both sides of the fuselage.

482nd Bomb Group

B-17F/G Fortresses and B-24D/H/J/L/M Liberators with H2S, H2X, G-H, AN/APQ-7 and other radar installations, August 1943–June 1945. The original complement was in Dark Olive Drab and Neutral Gray factory finish. No unit markings were carried until October 1943, when squadron code letters were introduced. The 812th Bomb Squadron was allotted MI, the 813th PC and the 814th SI. On B-17s grey squadron letters, 48in high, were painted forward of the national insignia on both sides of the fuselage, with the individual aircraft letter on the rear fuselage. The call-letter was also painted under the tail number on the fin, 24in high in yellow. The B-24s of the 814th Bomb Squadron are not known to have carried squadron letters at this time, although call-letters were painted in yellow on tail fins. A few aircraft that had previously served with Combat Groups before modification still retained the markings of that Group even on operations. The turnover in aircraft was such, particularly when the 482nd Bomb Group became a training and experimental Pathfinder organisation in March 1944, that no unit markings other than call-letters on the lower part of tail fins were used until the autumn of 1944.

In September 1944, when most Combat Wings or Bomb Groups were operating their own Pathfinder aircraft, the 482nd Bomb Group squadrons recommenced using code letters on the fuselage of their aircraft. These were black on natural metal finish and white on camouflage. On B-17s the positioning remained forward of the national insignia for the squadron code, with the call-letter aft. The 24in high call-letter was retained on the fin. At the same time a black 60in-sided triangle without a letter was painted on the fin of most B-17s. The B-24s had the squadron letters in the same position as combat B-24s, on the rear fuselage aft of the waist windows, with the call-letter lower on the fin, 24in high. Colours were as on the Group's B-17s.

Above: A May 1945 photograph of 486th Bomb Group B-17G serial 44-6616 shows the SD110 codes that were required to be displayed under the left wing as part of anti-low flying measures introduced that month. The nose band and fuselage call-letter A are painted with Insignia Blue, the 833rd Bomb Squadron colour. (Cal Sloan)

486th Bomb Group

B-24H/J Liberators, April–July 1944. Original combat aircraft were in Dark Olive Drab and Neutral Gray factory finish. Their Square O Group marking was a white 48in square on the outward-facing sides of the fin with a 36in high black O. On the wing the device was 60in square with a 48in O, in colours as on the tail. The individual aircraft call-letter was painted in yellow, 24in high below the tail number. Each squadron used letters from A in alphabetical order, excluding I. The call-letter was also carried 40in high in light grey on both sides of the fuselage, and squadron codes, the same size and colour, were painted on the rear fuselage aft of the waist gun windows. The 832nd Bomb Squadron used 3R, the 833rd 4N, the 834th 2S and the 835th H8. Natural metal-finish aircraft replaced some of the camouflaged aircraft; these had codes and call-letter in black, with the Group marking as a white letter on a black square.

B-17Gs, July 1944–August 1945. These aircraft were in natural metal finish. To avoid confusion with the 100th Bomb Group's Square D the 486th Bomb Group's marking was changed from Square O to Square W. A few B-17s were painted with the Square O but this was apparently deleted before combat missions were flown. The Square W on the fin was black, 48in square, with a 36in letter W thereon in white. The wing device, in the same colours, was 72in with the span and 57in with the chord. Tail call-letters were black, 24in high, and fuselage code letters, also black, were 48in high. The positioning of the fuselage markings varied, but the most common layout was for the squadron code to be aft of the waist gun position on the left side and the call-letter forward of the national insignia. On the right side the positions were reversed with the squadron code forward of the national marking.

In December 1944 the 4th Combat Bomb Wing chevron marking was painted on the upper surface of the right wing and the lower surface of the left. The arms of the chevron were 48in wide, the inner arm being red and the outer blue. The blue arm obscured most of the Square W device on the right wing and this was not repainted or removed. At the end of January 1945 the 4th CBW's yellow markings were introduced and took approximately three weeks to effect. In addition to the yellow wing tips and all tail surfaces, three 24in wide yellow stripes with a 12in separation were painted round the fuselage aft of the waist gun positions. At this time squadron codes were discontinued and removed. The call-letters on all aircraft, as well as being on the fin in black, were painted in a squadron colour, 36in high forward of the national insignia on both sides of the fuselage. The squadron colour was also carried as a 24in nose band directly aft of the bombardier's Plexiglas. The colours were yellow, with some letters outlined in black, for the 832nd Bomb Squadron, blue for the 833rd, red for the 834th and bright green for the 835th. With the new markings the red and blue chevron remained. In mid-May 1945 squad-

ron codes and call-letter were painted under the left wing, 48in high, in black.

The 486th Bomb Group had a War Weary B-17F, 42-30145 *Green Hornet,* for communication purposes and this was painted a light green overall.

487th Bomb Group

B-24H/J Liberators, April–July 1944. Original aircraft were in Dark Olive Drab and Neutral Gray factory finish. White Square P Group markings, applied to fins, were 48in square with a 36in high blue letter. The wing device, in the same colours, was mostly 72in with the span and 57in with the chord. A 24in high yellow individual aircraft call-letter was painted under the tail number. Each squadron used letters from A in alphabetical order, excluding I. The call letter was also carried on the fuselage 48in high in light grey forward of the national insignia on both sides of the fuselage. Squadron codes were painted on the rear fuselage, also 48in high and in light grey; these were 2G for the 836th Bomb Squadron, 4F for the 837th, 2C for the 838th and R5 for the 839th. A number of natural metal-finish B-24s were assigned to the Group from early May 1944 and on these the squadron codes and call-letters were in black, with the Square P white on black.

B-17G Fortresses, July 1944–August 1945. All these aircraft were in natural metal finish. The Group

Below: Sunlight on the rudder of this 850th Bomb Squadron B-17G gives the false impression that it is painted white and not left in bare metal. The repositioned and smaller-size tail numbers were a notable feature on 490th Bomb Group Fortresses. (A. Delmonico)

marking on the fin was the same size and colour as on metal-finished B-24s. On the wing it was mostly 57in square with a 48in letter. The tail call-letter was 24in and also black. The fuselage codes and call-letter, also black, were mostly 36in high, with the squadron code most commonly aft of the waist gun position on the left side of the fuselage with the call-letter forward of the national insignia. On the right side the squadron codes were mostly positioned forward of the national insignia, with the call letter on the rear fuselage. There was, however, no standard position for these markings and several 837th Bomb Squadron aircraft had the 4F forward of the national marking on the left side. This squadron used both 36in and 48in high characters for its codes. The R5 of the 839th Bomb Squadron appeared to be RS on many aircraft, the top bar of the 5 having a lip.

In December 1944 the 4th Combat Bomb Wing chevron was painted on the upper surface of the right wing and the under surface of the left. Each arm was 48in wide, the inner yellow and the outer red. At the end of January 1945 the 4th CBW yellow tail surfaces and wing tips scheme was introduced. The Group markings and tail number were not obscured but the call-letter was and was not reinstated. Fuselage markings remained the same as there was no requirement for coloured stripes. From March 1945 some aircraft of the 839th Bomb Squadron sported red engine cowlings while others in the same squadron had red chin turrets. At around the same time the 837th Bomb Squadron started to paint its engine cowlings yellow, and most aircraft had received this decoration by VE-Day.

489th Bomb Group

B-24H/J Liberators, April–November 1944. Original combat aircraft were in Dark Olive Drab and Neutral Gray factory finish. Work in applying the Circle W Group marking to the vertical tail began in late April but this was discontinued on instructions that new tail markings were to be issued. The Circle W was applied to the upper surface of the right wing and consisted of a 78–84in white disc with a 48in black W thereon. The new tail markings, issued at the beginning of May 1944, called for an overall green on the outward-facing sides of the fin and rudder with a 30in wide vertical white stripe placed centrally. The shade was a light grass green. An individual aircraft call-letter, 24in high, was painted in

black on the white stripe together with an identifying squadron symbol as detailed. The 844th Bomb Squadron did not use a symbol, the 845th Bomb Squadron used a bar below the letter, the 846th used a plus sign before the letter and the 847th used a bar sign after the letter. The letter I was not used as a call-letter and only one example of E is known (in the 846th Bomb Squadron).

Squadron codes as detailed in SD110 were painted on the rear fuselage aft of the waist gun positions in a light grey. The 844th Bomb Squadron used 4R, the 845th T4, the 846th 8R and the 847th S4. B-24s in natural metal finish were soon received as replacements and on these the squadron codes and call-letters were in black and the Circle W wing device white on black. In August 1944 the 95th Combat Bomb Wing ceased to function and the 489th Bomb Group was transferred to the 20th Combat Bomb Wing. Over the next few weeks the green tail markings were replaced by all-yellow fins and rudders. The call-letter was reinstated in black in approximately the same position on the fin as it had previously occupied.

The 489th Bomb Group's assembly ship, B-24H 42-7552 Z̲ *Lil Cookie*, had 12in yellow polka dots over wings and fuselage camouflage. The code letters NB, from a former assignment, were retained on the rear fuselage.

490th Bomb Group

B-24H/J Liberators, April–August 1944. Original combat aircraft were in Dark Olive Drab and Neutral Gray factory finish, although a few natural metal-finish B-24Js were assigned before operations commenced. The Square T Group marking was painted on the outer surfaces of the tail fins, 48in square with a 40in high letter T. On the upper surface of the right wing the marking was 78in with the span and 57in with the chord, and the letter was 48in high. The colours on camouflaged aircraft were Insignia Blue or black on white, and white on black on those with a bare metal finish. It was also common for the T on a bare metal finish to be formed by masking it when paint-sprayed. Call-letters, 12in high, were painted below the tail number in yellow on olive drab and in black on bare metal. The squadrons used letters in alphabetical order from A without exclusions.

There were no distinguishing squadron markings until the high-visibility markings were introduced

in late June 1944. These featured the top third of the fin and rudder painted red—in practice the top 48in. Natural metal aircraft had the remainder of the fin and rudder left unpainted but camouflaged aircraft had this painted white. The 24in high call-letter was painted in black lower on the fin and where appropriate accompanied by a symbol. The 848th Bomb Squadron used a bar before the letter, the 849th did not use a symbol and the 851st used a plus sign before the letter. The 850th Bomb Squadron was transferred for special duties with the 801st Bomb Group (P) and did not fly combat in the 490th Bomb Group with B-24s. The Square T marking was eventually removed from the right wing on most of the Group's B-24s.

B-17G Fortresses, August 1944–August 1945. All combat aircraft were in natural metal finish. The Group marking of the top third of the vertical tail painted red was applied to its B-17s and extended down 52in, approximately 6in above the top central rudder hinge. For some unknown reason the tail number was removed and the 24in high individual aircraft call-letter positioned to the rudder end of the tail number's original location. The tail number was repainted in 10in high figures above the call-

Above: The 848th Bomb Squadron's bar F, serial 43-38934, leads the 849th Bomb Squadron's H over the clouds. The red wing and tailplane stripes were common to all 93rd Combat Bomb Wing aircraft. (A. Delmonico)

letter. Squadron symbols were painted adjacent to call-letters in bold strokes. The 851st Bomb Squadron's plus sign occupied an area approximately 12in square and the 848th's bar was approximately 18in long by 12in—more a block than a bar. The 850th Bomb Squadron, re-formed in the 490th Bomb Group at this time, had a black block marking as used by the 848th but sited after the call-letter.

All 490th Group B-17s carried the 93rd Combat Bomb Wing red stripes round wings and tailplane to the standard dimensions and positions, that is, 48in wide and placed at the outer wing section join and 36in on the horizontal tail surfaces, halfway along the elevator. In mid May 1945 the Group painted 48in squadron codes with call-letters under the left wing as follows: 848th Bomb Squadron 7W, 849th W8, 850th 7Q and 851st S3.

UC-64A Norseman 44-70226 –Z, used for communications, had a red tail top as a Group marking.

491st Bomb Group

B-24H/J/L/M Liberators, May 1944–July 1945.
Original combat aircraft were mostly B-24Js in natural metal finish but some B-24Hs in Dark Olive Drab and Neutral Gray had been assigned before operations commenced. The Circle Z Group marking painted on the upper surface of the right wing was of 78in diameter in black on bare metal or in white on olive drab. The 48in letter Z was black or Insignia Blue on white or white on black. The vertical tail was green with a 36in wide white horizontal stripe centred thereon. The green was at first a light grass green but later in the year many replacement B-24s had a darker shade which appears to have been British Light Green camouflage paint, similar to USAAF Medium Green. Individual aircraft call-letters were painted, 24in high, with the appropriate symbol on the centre of the white stripe in black. All squadrons used letters from A in alphabetical order, with no exclusions. The 852nd Bomb Squadron did not use a symbol with the call letter, the 853rd used a bar below or forward of the letter, the 854th used a bar above or after the letter and the 855th used a plus sign after the letter.

Squadron codes were painted in 48in high letters on the rear fuselage aft of the waist gun positions. The colour was light grey on camouflage and black on bare metal, although there are reports of the odd 'silver' aircraft with grey codes. The 852nd Bomb Squadron used 3Q, the 853rd used T8, the 854th used 6X and the 855th used V2. In August 1944, when the 95th Combat Bomb Wing became non-operational, the 491st Bomb Group was transferred to the 14th CBW to replace the disbanded 492nd Bomb Group. The 491st continued to use the same

tail markings and not those of the 14th CBW previously carried by the 492nd. Allegedly this was due to a belief that *Luftwaffe* fighters singled out the 492nd Bomb Group for attack. It was not until late March 1945 that the 491st Bomb Group removed the green tail markings and used a 36in wide black diagonal band, forward end high, on its tails. Call-letters and symbols were in white on the black band. By October 1944 852nd Bomb Squadron aircraft had engine cowling rings painted red and those of the 854th yellow, although this marking does not appear to have been applied to all aircraft in these squadrons.

The 491st Bomb Group had three assembly ships. The first, B-24D 42-40722 *Lil Gramper*, was overall yellow with 24in red polka dots at 24in intervals with 6in polka dots midway between. The second, B-24J 44-40165 *Rage in Heaven*, had a series of 18in yellow and green bands around the fuselage and wings. When this aircraft crashed in January 1945 it was replaced with a similarly marked B-24J, 44-40101 *Tubarao*.

492nd Bomb Group

B-24H/J Liberators, April–August 1944. Original B-24Js were in bare metal finish, with a few B-24Hs and Js in Dark Olive Drab and Neutral Gray factory

Below: B-24J serial 42-50770, 5Z:I of the 856th Bomb Squadron, sought sanctuary in Sweden on 4 August 1944, shortly before the original 492nd Bomb Group was disbanded. The black diagonal stripe was painted directly on to bare aluminium in this Group and the code letters were often larger than the standard 48in for B-24s.

finish assigned prior to starting operations. The Circle U markings, being painted on some vertical tails, were discontinued on notification of revised tail markings. The new marking consisted of a 36in wide black diagonal band over the bare metal, the high part to the front of the fin. On some aircraft, where the 69in black disc had already been painted, this was not immediately removed and the aircraft concerned flew with both markings. The Circle U painted on the upper surface of the right wing was a 78in diameter black disc with a white letter on bare metal, or a white disc with a black letter on camouflage. A white individual aircraft call-letter was painted on the black stripe together with the appropriate squadron symbol. The 856th Bomb Squadron used a letter without any symbol, the 857th used a bar above the call letter, the 858th used a bar below the letter and the 859th used a plus sign after the letter. SD110 squadron codes were painted on the rear fuselage in black on bare metal and light grey on olive drab, 48in high. The 856th Bomb Squadron used 5Z, the 857th 9H, the 858th 9A and the 859th X4. The same codes were used by the second organisation of the 492nd Bomb Group later in the war.

493rd Bomb Group

B-24H/J Liberators, May–August 1944. Original combat aircraft were a mixture of Dark Olive Drab and Neutral Gray factory finish and natural metal finish. The Square X Group marking applied to the upper surface of the right wing was mostly 72in with the span and 57in chordwise, with the letter X thereon 48in high. The colours were black on white for camouflaged aircraft and white on black for bare metal. On the vertical tail the white 'square' was 48in high by 60in on camouflaged aircraft, partly extending on to the rudder in some cases. The X was 36in high and black. Later applications used a 48in square marking, as on most of the bare metal-finish aircraft where it was black with a white letter.

Individual aircraft call-letters were mostly 18in high in yellow on camouflage and black on bare metal below the tail number. All squadrons used letters from A in alphabetical order, excluding I. Squadrons were distinguished by bright coloured propeller bosses. The 860th Bomb Squadron used yellow, the 861st white, the 862nd red and the 863rd blue. At the end of June and in early July the existing tail markings were removed or painted over and replaced with the 93rd Combat Bomb Wing high-visibility markings. The bottom 60in of the outward-facing sides of the fin and rudder were painted red and the remainder left bare metal finish or painted white. The call-letter, 18in high in black, was positioned high on the white or bare metal section. The Square X marking was eventually removed from the wing.

B-17Gs, August 1944–August 1945. All combat B-17s were in natural metal finish. The bottom third of the vertical tail, including the fairing, was painted red; in practice this was on a line about 2in below the tail number. The call-letter, still 18in high, was painted in black high on the bare metal part of the fin. At this time, in addition to coloured propeller bosses, a unique squadron marking was added. The initial letter of the squadron radio call-signs was painted on the fuselage in black, 48in high. The 860th Bomb Squadron used S, the 861st B, the 862nd C and the 863rd B. The positioning on the fuselage was most commonly aft of the waist gun position on the left and forward of the national insignia on the right. All 493rd Bomb Group B-17s had a 48in red stripe round each wing, outboard of the section join, and a 36in red stripe round the centre of each tailplane and elevator. In mid May 1945 SD110-originated squadron codes were painted, with the call-letter under the left wing. The 860th Bomb Squadron used N6, the 861st used Q4, the 862nd used 8M and the 863rd used G6.

Above: The lower third of the fin and rudder painted red identifies the 493rd Bomb Group within the 93rd Wing, the red terminating just below the tail number. The black S on the rear fuselage identifies the 860th Bomb Squadron, being the initial letter of the unit's radio call-sign, 'Shunter'. Lieutenant H. Johnson, the regular pilot of '198', called this B-17G *Dollar Ninety-Eight*, his parents owning a general store. (Byron Trent)
Below: Liberators of the 493rd Bomb Group

approaching a runway end for take-off, June 1944. The camouflaged aircraft have Insignia Blue Xs in white squares and the bare metal-finish example a white X in a black square. The bare metal strip round the leading edge of the fins on the leading camouflaged machine is where the rubber de-icer boot has been removed. Red propeller bosses on the aircraft about to make its take-off run identify the 862nd Bomb Squadron. (Mark Brown/AF Academy)

FIGHTER GROUPS

1st Fighter Group

P-38F-1-LO Lightnings in the 41-7552–7680 series with the 8th Air Force, July to October 1942. The standard finish was Dark Olive Drab and Neutral Gray. The only unit markings on these aircraft when they arrived in the United Kingdom were command stripes on the fuselage booms. Situated after of the radiator housing, these consisted of two encircling 5in wide bands, 5in apart, for Squadron COs' aircraft and a single 5in band for the Flight commanders. For A Flight the single band was vertical relative to the boom axis, the top was diagonally inclined forwards for B Flight and the top was diagonally inclined backwards for C Flight. The colours were as used by the 1st Group in the US prior to overseas movement: red for the 27th Fighter Squadron, white for the 71st and yellow for the 94th. In August 1942 a 2in wide yellow surround was added to the fuselage national insignia and squadron code letters were painted on the radiator housings in Sky S. The advised size was 18in high, but the width varied owing to the dimensions of the radiator housing where one letter was placed on the control door. A hyphen separated the squadron letters from the individual aircraft letter. The squadron letters, HV for the 27th Fighter Squadron, LM for the 71st and UN for the 94th, preceded the individual letter when read from either side of the aircraft, and with their painting the command stripes were removed.

4th Fighter Group

Spitfire VBs, September 1942–April 1943. The aircraft were finished in the standard RAF temperate land scheme colours of Dark Green and Ocean Grey in a disruptive pattern, with Medium Sea Grey undersurfaces. Standard British 'friendly aircraft' markings were added: a Sky spinner and 18in wide rear fuselage band and 4in wide yellow stripes on the leading edges of outer wing sections. US national insignia were superimposed on the fuselage roundels, their outer edge corresponding with that of the roundel blue. The yellow surround was retained. Wing roundels were painted out and US national insignia were centred on the position of the roundel on the upper left and lower right wings surfaces. The diameter of the wing insignia varied, most being 32in but others 45in. The 24 or 30in high squadron code letters used by the RAF in Nos 71, 121 and

133 Squadrons, XR, AV and MD respectively, continued in use when these units were redesignated as the 334th, 335th and 336th Fighter Squadrons, that is, the 334th used XR, the 335th AV and the 336th MD. The letters were Sky with the squadron code forward of the national insignia on the left side of the fuselage and aft on the right. The individual letter was painted under the nose in Sky on many aircraft, 6–9in high.

P-47C/D Thunderbolts, February 1943–February 1944. The standard Dark Olive Drab uppersurfaces and Neutral Gray undersurfaces applied. The wing cocarde was of 45in diameter and fuselage cocarde 35in diameter. Identification Yellow radio call-numbers were in $7^{1}/_{2}$in by 5in figures. When the VIII Fighter Command instruction of 20 February 1943 instituted the white type identity markings for Thunderbolts, the last two digits of the serial number were painted on the fuselage forward of the cocarde approximately 20in high in white, and often additionally on the lower cowling lip in black, as temporary recognition markings. Enlarged national insignia of 59in were painted under both wings and the fuselage cocarde was encircled with a 2in wide band of yellow.

In the first week of April 1943, when the Group completed conversion to the Thunderbolt, new squadron code letters were received. These were QP for the 334th Fighter Squadron, WD for the 335th and VF for the 336th—the same combinations previously issued to the 52nd Fighter Group for its squadrons, then removed to North Africa. The squadron codes were painted in 24in white block characters, forward of the cocarde on both sides of the fuselage, with the individual letter aft. The individual letter was also painted in black under the cowling lip on many aircraft, a practice that does not appear to have been sustained. In early July 1943 the revised national insignia caused individual aircraft letters to be repainted nearer the tail as they would otherwise have been partly obscured by an added 'bar'. At least three P-47Ds, received from air depots, that did not have the national insignia relocated had all three identification letters grouped together forward of the 'star and bar' with a hyphen separating the squadron code from the individual letter.

P-51B/C/D/K Mustangs, February 1944–September 1945. The initial complement of P-51Bs were in standard Dark Olive Drab and Neutral Gray camouflage with white type identity bands and spinner. Squadron code letters, as on P-47s, were 24in high in white block capitals. From 14 March 1944 the 4th Group was given permission to overpaint the white spinner and noseband with bright red as a Group marking. The paint used is said to have been obtained from a local civilian source until a suitable shade could be obtained from an air depot. The white type identity bands across fin and rudder were deleted in late March 1944. Arriving at this time were the first bare metal-finish P-51B replacements with black type identity markings. There was no requirement to delete the black horizontal tail stripe on 'silver' Mustangs, although one or two did not have this marking in the spring of 1944. Few 4th Group bare metal Mustangs received the camouflage advised for possible deployment to the Continent after D-Day. Where this did occur a dark green was applied to the top of wings and tailplane and along the fuselage spine. 'D-Day stripes', applied on 5 June 1944, did not obscure fuselage code letters. The first P-51Ds, arriving in the first week of June 1944, had markings applied as used on the earlier models. When more than 25 aircraft were assigned to a squadron the barred letters usually had the bar placed aft of the individual letter. However, at the end of hostilities, the 4th Group also made use of double letters for individual identification.

Only one of the Group's P-51Ds is known to have received camouflage, 44-15347 QP:J, the 334th Fighter Squadron CO's aircraft, in late 1944. Its olive green, applied to upper surfaces, covered approximately the same area as the olive drab on factory-painted P-51Bs. To comply with the 8th Air Force instruction of 17 October introducing rudder colours as an additional squadron recognition marking, the 334th used red, the 335th white and the 336th blue. It became common practice for the white rudder to be given a thin red outline, approximately 1in wide. The 336th's blue rudder appeared in at least two shades, a medium sky blue and a much darker shade which appeared to be a diluted Insignia Blue. In many cases the three digits of the tail number were not reinstated on the rudder; instead, the whole number was repainted on the fin at an angle.

With the introduction of rudder colours the black type identity stripe was removed from the fin and by March was being removed from the horizontal tail surfaces. To distinguish 4th Group P-51s from those of the 9th and 15th Air Force units with red noses, an additional 12in was added to the red nose band in early December 1944. This took the marking back to just beyond the second exhaust pipe. In early January the red nose was made even more distinctive by being swept back to a point just ahead of the wing root, although there was considerable variation in the exact point of termination and the degree of sweep.

Below: A 334th Fighter Squadron P-51D with swept back 4th Fighter Group nose marking, red-outlined code letters and the tail number painted entirely on the fin. (Ed Richie)

During the final months of the war there were a number of embellishments. Most noticeable was the outlining of identification letters in red on the 334th's aircraft, although many had such decoration from the summer of 1944. The 336th depth-edged one side of its letters in red during the final months of the war. Several P-51D/Ks had the cockpit canopy frames painted in the Group or squadron colour, these being personal decorations.

With the establishment of an OTU within the 4th Group in October 1944, numerals were used for individual aircraft identities on the War Weary P-51s. Each squadron had at some time training P-51s marked 2, 3 and 4, 24in high in the same location as individual letters. Other markings were as combat aircraft except for the rudder, which was partitioned horizontally with red, white and blue, red uppermost. In February 1945 two 2-seat conversions of P-51Bs used for training were painted Deep Sky Blue overall (VF:4) and red overall (43-12193 WD:2).

From 17 May 1945 code letters were painted under the left wing of all 4th Group aircraft, in 36in characters on P-51s. A few P-47Ds were received for training and these were given red noses, the red extending back to the cowling shutters. Communications aircraft with red cowlings in use late in the war included AT-6 Texan 42-84602, UC-64A Norseman 44-70392 and UC-61 Forwarder 43-14442. The UC-64 and UC-61 carried the codes VF:AA and WD:AA respectively, in black under their left wings, from mid-May 1945. The UC-61 was finished overall red at that time.

14th Fighter Group

P-38F-1-LO Lightnings in the 41-7552–7680 series with the 8th Air Force, August–October 1942. These aircraft had the standard Dark Olive Drab and Neutral Gray finish. Only two squadrons were on strength while the Group was with the 8th Air Force, the third being retained in Iceland while en route to the United Kingdom. The only unit markings displayed on the 14th's P-38s on arrival were command stripes. The squadron's CO's aircraft had two 5in wide stripes, 5in apart, encircling the fuselage booms aft of the radiator housings. Their colours were red and yellow for the 48th and 49th Fighter Squadrons respectively. Flight commanders had single stripes in the appropriate colours.

In September a 2in yellow surround was added to the fuselage national insignia and shortly thereafter the squadron code letters ES and QU were painted on the fuselage tail booms in Sky S for the 48th and 49th Fighter Squadrons respectively. In most cases the squadron code was painted on the radiator housing and the individual aircraft letter on the rear boom, with a hyphen as added separation. The letters, approximately 20in high, were sometimes outlined in yellow.

20th Fighter Group

P-38H/J Lightnings, September 1943–July 1944. The P-38H was non-operational. The scheme was the standard Olive Drab and Neutral Gray camouflage with yellow tail numbers. Squadron code letters, issued in the first week of October 1943, were painted in white 18in high by 9in wide block letters on the fuselage booms, KI for the 55th Fighter Squadron, LC for the 77th and MC for the 79th. Initially some of these were painted on with one letter of the squadron code on the left side radiator housing and the other aft of this housing, a hyphen separating it from the individual letter. On the right side the squadron code was aft of the radiator housing and the individual letter on it. The standard position for P-38 codes was at this time regularised with the squadron code aft of the radiator housing on both sides of the aircraft with individual letters on the housings. The 77th and 79th Fighter Squadrons placed a hyphen after the squadron code but the 55th did not as far as can be ascertained.

The Group entered combat in December 1943 with P-38Js in standard camouflage colours and squadron codes as used on P-38Hs. Geometric devices for improved squadron-in-Group recognition were carried from early January 1944, the 55th using a triangle, the 77th a circle and the 79th a square. These devices measured approximately 30in at their widest point and were painted in white on the outsides of the vertical tails. Tail numbers were usually obliterated, though repainted in yellow or black on some machines; however, there were more P-38s without than with reinstatement. The individual aircraft letter was painted in white on the inner sides of the fins and rudders when the geometric devices were introduced.

When the first bare metal-finish P-38Js arrived, in February 1944, squadron letters and other markings in white were then rendered in black. With these bare metal aircraft fewer tail numbers were painted over, the space being left in the triangle, disc or square. At the end of March 1944 spinners and a backing 12in band of the engine cowlings were painted Identification Yellow as a Group marking on both engines. Hyphens between codes and individual letters were not used on replacement aircraft after March 1944. April brought Droopsnoot markings, an 8in white band painted round the nose at the station just aft of the gun ports and with the nose cap polished. Camouflaged aircraft had the paint removed from the cap and the metal polished. Some metal-finish P-38s received dark green camouflage on upper wing surfaces and along the top of fuselage booms. The 24in wide bands of the 'D-Day stripes' completely obliterated squadron codes on the booms and these letters were not repainted.

P-51C/D/K Mustangs, July 1944–September 1945. All aircraft received were metal finish and several were given dark green camouflage on wing and tail uppersurfaces and along the fuselage spine. Such applications appear to have been discontinued in the autumn of 1944. Code letters were in standard positioning, their size and colour as usual for P-51s. Additionally the individual letter was also painted on the black squadron geometric device on the vertical tail. Both the 55th's triangle and the 79th's square had 30in sides, while the 77th's circle was of 30in diameter. The letters thereon were white and the same size and shape as those on the fuselage; presumably the same stencils were used. Yellow could not be used as a Group marking as this colour was already in use on 361st Group Mustangs. The new Group marking, somewhat unimaginative, consisted of painting part of the standard P-51 black type identification nose marking on the aircraft with white bands. Precisely, from the tip of the spinner rearward 12in was painted white and the remaining 15in left black. The first 11in of the cowling remained black and aft of this was painted a 5in wide white stripe encircling the nose. It later became common for the white stripe to be painted directly aft of the standard black nose band.

In early November 1944 a more prominent development of the Group marking was introduced. Extending back from the black type identity cowling band along the side of the cowling to a point above the leading edge of the wing, seven white and eight black bars were painted. Each bar, 6in wide, was bordered by a 6in black stripe that curved up from the lower rear edge of the black nose band. There was no black border along the top of the vertical

black and white bars terminating at the edge of the anti-glare panel. Examples of the Group marking were visible where bare metal, between the black bars, remained unpainted.

OTU P-51B/Cs carried standard Group markings except that the spinners of these aircraft were all black. Most had barred letters, the bar below the letter, and the War Weary WW marking was carried on the geometric tail device in white, often split either side of the letter. Communications aircraft in the spring of 1945 included Boston III AL381 with dark green upper and grey lower surfaces. This was marked KI-E on the side of the nose in 36in high white letters; its RAF serial was also in white on the fin. B-17E 41-2578, in repainted olive drab and grey, had yellow engine cowlings. This had been the Fortress that led the 8th Air Force's first heavy bomber mission on 17 August 1942. UC-64A Norseman 44-70290 was in silver finish with a black and white painted cowling. Other types were AT-6D Texan 41-34608 LC:Q and C-78 Bobcat 43-7843 KI:J.

31st Fighter Group

Spitfire VBs, July–October 1942. These aircraft were painted in the standard RAF temperate land scheme of Dark Green and Ocean Grey in a disruptive pattern with Medium Sea Grey undersurfaces. Standard British 'friendly aircraft' markings were as given for 4th Fighter Group Spitfires. The aircraft were received with British insignia and so the wing roundels were painted over and 32in diameter US national insignia were centred on the position of the roundels on the upper surface of the left and lower surface of the right wing. The US national insignia was superimposed on the fuselage roundels, to correspond with the blue portion of the roundel, giving a diameter of 32in. The yellow outline ring was painted out on most aircraft. On many aircraft the serial number was deleted on the normal rear fuselage position and repainted on the fin in approximately 4in high characters. Squadron code letters, generally 24in high in Sky, were forward of the national insignia on the left side of the fuselage and aft on the right. The 307th Fighter Squadron's letters were MX, the 308th's HL and the 309th's WZ.

52nd Fighter Group

Spitfire VBs, July–October 1942. These were in the standard RAF temperate land camouflage colours of Dark Green and Ocean Grey in a disruptive pattern with Medium Sea Grey undersurfaces. Standard British 'friendly aircraft' markings were as for the 4th Fighter Group Spitfires. British roundels were eliminated and replaced in the same way as on the Spitfire Vbs of the 31st Fighter Group. Identification letters, 24in high in most cases, were painted in Sky. The squadron code was forward of the national insignia on the left side of the fuselage and aft on the right. The 2nd Fighter Squadron's code was QP, the 4th's WD and the 5th's VF.

55th Fighter Group

P-38H/J Lightnings, August 1943–July 1944. These aircraft carried the standard Dark Olive Drab and Neutral Gray camouflage. Squadron code letters applied in early October 1943 were CG for the 38th Fighter Squadron, CL for the 338th and CY for the 343rd, painted white in block capitals approximately 18in high and 9in wide. These codes were located aft of the radiator housing on each fuselage boom with the individual aircraft letter on the housing. Similar markings applied to P-38Js, which replaced the H models in December 1943.

Geometric devices were introduced during January 1944 for improved squadron-in-Group recognition, the 38th Fighter Squadron using a triangle, the 338th a circle and the 343rd a square. These were painted on the outward-facing sides of the vertical tail surfaces in white and the size was 30in at the widest point. The yellow tail numbers were painted over in most cases, with some repainted in either black or yellow. The individual aircraft letter was painted on the inward-facing sides of the vertical tail surfaces above the horizontal stabiliser, in white and approximately 30in high. In early March

Below: Forty-five Mustangs of the 55th Fighter Group lined up for review in May 1945. The first row is the 343rd Fighter Squadron, the second the 338th and the rear row the 38th. All the aircraft have the red stripe bordering the anti-glare panel and canopy framing. Some 343rd aircraft have the unit's rearing mustang emblem in red on rudders; in the case of CY:Z, it is in black on the fin. The 338th aircraft have the green and yellow checkerboard backed by a green stripe. Nearly all have had their black type identity stripes removed. (Robert Sand)

1944 some aircraft of the 338th Fighter Squadron were reported to have had some 40in of the fuselage pod nose section painted red. This was evidently a short-lived unofficial marking, removed when VIII Fighter Command issued an instruction on Group colours in the middle of the month. The 55th Fighter Group was detailed to have yellow and white checkerboard, in line with the similar markings detailed for all Groups assigned to the 66th Fighter Wing. However, there is no evidence that these markings were ever used, probably because of the work their application would entail and the impending conversion to Mustangs.

The Group had no Group markings of any kind on its P-38s. When bare metal-finish P-38Js were received in February 1944 black in place of white was used for unit markings. In April the 8in wide white Droopsnoot decoy band was added to the noses of all the Group's Lightnings and the nosepiece forward of this band was cleaned of all paint and polished. The Droopsnoot aircraft used by the Group also had the white band aft of the transparent nosepiece. In May a few bare metal aircraft received 'in the field' dark green camouflage on the upper surfaces of wings, tailplane and fuselage booms. 'D-Day stripes' obscured boom code letters and the latter were not repainted.

P-51D/K Mustangs, July 1944–July 1945. On the Group's first P-51Ds the fins and rudders were sprayed camouflage dark green and 30in diameter squadron symbols were painted thereon in white. Squadron and individual letters were positioned as standard for P-51s, 24in high. The standard black type identity nose markings were retained. On 15 July 1944 VIII Fighter Command devised a new Group marking for the 55th Group. The spinner was striped green/yellow/green of equal widths, backed by a 12in wide cowling band of 6in green and yellow squares. While the yellow used was either Identification Yellow or the British shade, the green was a camouflage shade, Medium Green 42 or a closely matching British colour, possibly Light Green. The result was that at just a few hundred yards the green appeared as a dark shade and was easily mistaken for black. Nevertheless, the 55th continued with this medium green throughout its use of Mustangs. With the introduction of the new Group nose colours the use of geometric symbols on tails was abandoned and those aircraft already so marked had these painted out with dark green.

Above: A 55th Fighter Group P-51B bearing the code CL-6 under the left wing and the yellow and green checkerboard with which OTU aircraft were marked. (Robert Sand)

Later in 1944 a few P-51Ds appeared in a camouflage scheme that was more a form of decoration. The fuselage aft of the wing and empennage was painted dark green, the fuselage paintwork being swept up to the anti-glare panel and the border between the green and bare metal marked with a 5–6in red line. White type identity bands were painted on the upper surfaces of the tailplane, and code letters were also white. This uniform is known to have been applied to at least six of the Group's aircraft in the latter part of 1944. A 343rd Fighter Squadron embellishment, featured on about a dozen P-51s, was a rearing mustang silhouette on the rudder in red and on one aircraft in black on the fin. In mid November 1944 squadron rudder colours were applied—green for the 338th Fighter Squadron (the same green as used on the nose) and yellow for the 343rd. The 38th Fighter Squadron had no rudder colour at this time but in mid March 1945 painted this area red. During December 1944 the 338th Fighter Squadron started to back the nose checkerboard of all its Mustangs with a 6in green border. A red line, 4–6in wide and similar to that bordering the camouflage on the 343rd's aircraft, was applied along the anti-glare panel on some of the squadron's aircraft and in March 1945 this feature was added to all the Group's aircraft. In its final form it ran from the nose checkerboard, skirting the anti-glare olive drab and below and round the cockpit canopy.

OTU P-51Bs were distinguished by yellow and green checkerboard rudders of 6in squares. Other markings were as combat aircraft except that numerals were used for individual aircraft identities; these were 24in high and were often also applied to the side of the nose above the wing root leading edge. The 3rd Scouting Force aircraft were distinguished by red and bare metal checkerboard markings and a red leading edge to the fin.

56th Fighter Group

P-47C/D/M Thunderbolts, January 1943–September 1945. P-47Cs were in Dark Olive Drab and Neutral Gray factory finish. Some aircraft had the yellow surround to the fuselage cocarde on delivery and it was added to others. White type identity markings were painted on from late February 1943. A system of 'plane-in-Group' identification numbers was used from mid February until late March 1943, consisting of approximately 15in high white numerals painted forward of the intercooler doors on both sides of the fuselage. It is believed that 01 to 09 were for Group headquarters, 10 to 39 for the 61st Fighter Squadron, 40 to 69 for the 62nd and 70 to 99 for the 63rd. The 62nd and 63rd Fighter Squadrons prefaced these numbers with 2 and 3 respectively. There are indications that not all the Group's aircraft were painted with these markings before an instruction was received to use codes as detailed in SD110—HV for the 61st Fighter Squadron, LM for the 62nd and UN for the 63rd, the same combinations as those issued for the 1st Fighter Group when in the UK. The codes were carried in the standard size, position and colour for P-47s. With the change in the national insignia of late June 1943, individual aircraft letters had to be moved closer to the tailplane.

At the beginning of February 1944 the 56th Fighter Group was the first unit officially given permission to introduce bright colours as a means of improving in-flight inter-squadron recognition. The 61st Fighter Squadron overpainted the 24in wide white nose band with bright red, the 62nd used yellow and the 63rd a light blue. In late March 1944, following VIII Fighter Command's introduction of coloured nose markings for Group identification, all nose bands were painted red. Not to be deprived of its squadron colours, the Group obtained permission to paint the rudders of the 61st's P-47s red

and those of the 62nd yellow. The 63rd Fighter Squadron's rudders remained in their normal factory camouflage or bare metal. Advised to apply camouflage to the natural metal aircraft, coming as replacements from early April 1944, the 56th Group again promoted its individuality by utilising a variety of paint schemes. Using British Air Ministry paints, several field-camouflaged Thunderbolts were given disruptive patterns; the first is believed to have been in Dark Green and Ocean Grey on the CO's P-47D-25-RE, the first 'bubble-canopy' model to be assigned to the 56th. The aircraft, 42-26413 UN:Z, was in 63rd Fighter Squadron markings, and one other P-47 of the 63rd had similar patterning applied. Generally 'silver' P-47Ds of the 63rd, receiving camouflage, simply had their uppersurfaces coated in Dark Green. The 62nd Fighter Squadron, following its CO's lead, used Dark Green and Ocean Grey patterning on at least eight P-47Ds and the same colours for blotching on four others.

The 61st Fighter Squadron had the most diverse schemes. In addition to plain Dark Green, Dark Green/Ocean Grey patterning and blotched applications of these colours, two aircraft had paints in two shades of grey. P-47D-26-RA 42-28382 HV:S, one aircraft in this scheme, using possibly Light and Dark Sea Grey, had its tail number repainted in black and also its code letters—the latter outlined in white. More flamboyant was P-47D-28-RE 44-19718 HV:M, which, in addition to two shades of grey, had the undersurfaces in a sky blue, possibly Azure Blue, with red codes outlined in white. With this exception and that of a few P-47Ds inherited from the 78th Fighter Group in late 1944/early 1945, undersurfaces were left unpainted. Like other Groups, the 56th always had several aircraft oper-

Right, upper: A May 1944 photograph of Lieutenant Frank Klibbe's *Little Chief*, resplendent in the colours of the 61st Fighter Squadron. Both the red nose and rudder have a white border line on P-47D 42-76179 HV:V. The 56th Fighter Group was the first to introduce coloured rudders for squadron identification. The P-47D in the background is a green-nosed 359th Fighter Group aircraft. (F. Klibbe)

Right, lower: An example of the 'in the field' green and grey blotched camouflage applied to several 56th Fighter Group Thunderbolts. This aircraft, 42-26298 LM:A of the 62nd Fighter Squadron, also has two names, *Stalag Luft III* and *Button Nose*, being individual pilot preferences. (Mark Brown/AF Academy)

Above: With the P-47M the 56th Fighter Group introduced a different colour scheme for each squadron's aircraft. The examples are 44-21182 HV:S, in the matt black with a purplish hue; 44-21219 LM:I, in a dark green and grey disruptive pattern; and 44-21135 UN:A, in a dark and light blue disruptive pattern with tail number and rudder in a medium sky blue. (USAAF)

ating in bare metal finish and most of those that received camouflage from the base paintshop commenced operations in the original guise. In September 1944 the 63rd Fighter Squadron painted its P-47Ds' rudders a medium sky blue as an additional recognition feature.

In January 1945 the 56th Fighter Group began to receive the first P-47M model Thunderbolts and eventually all 130 produced would be assigned at some time or another. In addition to the Group red nose and squadron rudder colours, the P-47Ms were given a different distinctive camouflage for each squadron. The 61st aircraft had matt black upper surfaces, red code letters outlined in white, and red

tail numbers. The black paint, which had a decidedly purplish tinge, does not appear to comply with any Air Ministry approved paints that might have been supplied. To obtain a better contrast the blue outline of the national insignia was repainted in a lighter blue on the 61st's P-47Ms. The 62nd had green and grey patterning, presumably Dark Green and Sea Grey. Code letters were in Identification Yellow, as was the tail number. The 63rd Fighter Squadron also used a patterning employing two shades of blue that appear to have been Dark Mediterranean Blue and Azure Blue, the former being nearly as dark as Insignia Blue and the latter lighter than the rudder blue. Code letters were formed in bare metal, achieved by masking the letter shapes before spraying the camouflage. Tail numbers were in the same shade of blue as the rudder. The undersurfaces of all aircraft were left unpainted, as was the cockpit canopy and the leading edges of the wings and horizontal tailplane. A few P-47Ms arriving at Boxted near the end of hostilities remained unpainted.

OTU P-47Ds had no distinguishing markings other than the WW tag on tail fins. Individual letters were annotated with bars. Communications aircraft used by the Group carried the red cowling band. A P-38J Droopsnoot briefly used by the Group in August 1944 was coded HV:W, with red spinners and cowling bands and the red rudder marking of the 61st Fighter Squadron.

78th Fighter Group

P-38G Lightnings, December 1942–February 1943. These aircraft wore the standard Dark Olive Drab and Neutral Gray camouflage, with 8in high Identification Yellow tail numbers. Similar unit markings to those used while training in the US were applied. 'Plane-in-Group' numerals were painted in the squadron colour, approximately 18in high, on the outer side of each engine cowling below the air intake and on the outer side of each boom radiator housing. The spinners were also painted in the squadron colour, which was white for the 82nd Fighter Squadron, red for the 83rd and yellow for the 84th. Squadron commanders' aircraft were distinguished with two bands, approximately 6in wide and in the squadron colour, encircling the rear fuselage booms. A 2in yellow surround was added to the fuselage cocardes. However, the squadron colours and numerals were soon removed as all P-38s were gradually withdrawn from the Group and sent to North Africa as replacements.

P-47C/D Thunderbolts, January 1943–January 1945. The initial complement of P-47Cs were in standard Dark Olive Drab and Neutral Gray camouflage with Identification Yellow tail numbers. A yellow surround to the fuselage cocarde was added soon after the aircraft arrived at Goxhill. Standard white type identity stripes were applied and wing national insignia changes were also made; later assignments already had these markings. The 'plane-in-Group' numbers were painted on the fuselage ahead of the cocardes in 18in high white numerals. In late March 1943 these numbers were removed and squadron code letters applied, MX for the 82nd Fighter Squadron, HL for the 83rd and WZ for the 84th, in standard white 24in block capitals positioned forward of the cocarde, with the individual letter aft. With the introduction of the revised national insignia in late June 1943 the individual aircraft letter had to be painted out and repainted nearer the tail.

Below: Resplendent with black and white checkerboards, a Flight of 83rd Fighter Squadron P-47Ds awaits refuelling at a bomber station, May 1944. The large national insignia under the left wing, a feature of Thunderbolts serving in Europe, shows well on the nearest aircraft. (Mark Brown/AF Academy)

The increase in squadron strengths to more than 26 aircraft in late October 1943 resulted in the use of barred letters for the additional aircraft, the bar being placed below the letter. In late March the 78th received instructions to apply black and white checkerboard markings to the engine cowlings of its P-47s. Each line of checks, parallel with the fuselage axis, had three black and three white rectangles, each 8in horizontal by 7in vertical. The rectangles around the cowling lip were usually nearer 7in than 8in in width. Indeed, the official description stated that the checkerboard extended 46 inches back from the cowling lip. It took several days for all 80-plus aircraft at Duxford to acquire this striking display.

The first natural metal-finished P-47s were received in early April 1944. In May 1944 the 78th was advised to add camouflage to the upper surfaces of its 'silver' aircraft in case a move was made to Continental airfields at a later date. Dark Green from RAF sources was used, but on most field-camouflaged aircraft the undersurfaces were also painted with Sky S. The 78th was most consistent in this practice, which continued as time allowed until November. There were, however, always a few 'silver' P-47s on hand during this period as replacements arrived. Tail numbers were repainted in yellow on field-camouflaged aircraft. When 'D-Day stripes' were

Above: *Sweet and Lovely*, P-51D 44-72203 WZ:S of the 84th Fighter Squadron, photographed post-VE Day, has the red trim that was used on most Mustangs of the squadron from March 1945. The longitudinal division of the spinner into black and white created a distinct flicker effect when the propeller revolved. (Thomas V. Thain)

Below: Red and white checkerboard and spinner stripes marked 339th Fighter Group Mustangs. *Little One*, fitted with 100 US gallon metal drop tanks, was P-51D 44-14622 D7:E of the 503rd Fighter Squadron. (James G. Robinson)

applied code letters were not obscured. At the end of October 1944 the Group started applying squadron colours to the P-47 rudders. These were red for the 82nd, white for the 83rd and black for the 84th. When camouflage was applied, that part of the white type identity marks painted on the vertical stabiliser remained.

P-51B/D/K Mustangs, December 1944–August 1945. The initial combat equipment was P-51D/K models but P-51Bs, assigned for training purposes, were the first to receive unit markings. The Group black and white checkerboard design applied to the first P-51Bs consisted of 8in squares, three black and three white as on the P-47s, but swept down and forward from the anti-glare panel to eliminate some of the lower squares. This arrangement was soon amended and on combat P-51D/Ks the full rows were increased to eight white and eight black, the size being reduced to 6in, the whole swept back under the wing root where there were six of each colour square per line. A 2in wide red border was later added at the rear of the checkerboard. The spinner had a novel arrangement being half white and half black, longitudinally, to give a distinct flickering effect when turning. Rudder colours were as for the P-47s, although the 83rd Fighter Squadron soon outlined its white rudder in red. On the first P-51s the tail number was left on an unpainted stripe when the rudder was given a squadron colour, but replacements had the whole rudder painted and the number repainted on the fin. The Group's CO's P-51D, 44-72218 WZ:I, was distinguished by black and white checkered wing tips from April 1945. His successor had a black and white checkered rudder on P-51D 44-14251 WZ:I.

OTU aircraft in the 78th Group had individual letters in the normal alphabetical run, some with bars, some without, there being no special distinction from combat aircraft apart from the WW tail marking. P-51B 42-106826WW MX:Z was modified on the base to become a two-seat aircraft and was, when completed in March 1945, given an overall coat of red with no squadron insignia. At least two P-47Ds were on hand in the weeks immediately after VE-Day for training duties. One two-seat conversion, 42-27606, was painted red overall.

339th Fighter Group

P-51B/C/D/K Mustangs, April 1944–September 1945. The first P-51B and C models were in natural metal finish with black type identity stripes. Group nose markings, introduced immediately, consisted of a division of the spinner into three equal portions, with bands being painted white/red/white. The 12in nose band was repainted with two encir-

Below: The 505th Fighter Squadron dispersal area at Fowlmere, late summer 1944. All the Mustangs have 'D-Day stripes' reduced to the lower fuselage only, and black type identity bands are retained. (James G. Robinson)

cling rows of red and white checks, each being 6in square. Squadron codes were also applied at this time—D7 for the 503rd Fighter Squadron, 5Q for the 504th and 6N for the 505th. These were painted in the standard 24in high block capitals except that the tail of the letter Q extended below this measurement. When more than 26 aircraft were assigned to a squadron the bar used for duplicated individual letters was positioned above or below the letter, more often above. In late November 1944 coloured rudders for additional squadron recognition were introduced, the 503rd Fighter Squadron using red and the 504th green (a medium camouflage green), while in the 505th the rudders remained unpainted. The 504th was originally planned to have red and white checkerboard on the rudder but this idea was dropped owing to the time it would take to effect. Black type identity stripes were removed from the fin when rudders were painted or soon afterwards. With the exception of the CO's aircraft in the spring of 1945, which had a 2in wide dark green band backing the nose checkerboard, the 339th's Mustangs had no further embellishments to recognition markings.

The individual identities of OTU aircraft were mostly barred letters. By March 1945 these training aircraft had their rudders painted yellow, apparently regardless of squadron assignment.

352nd Fighter Group

P-47D Thunderbolts, July 1943–April 1944. These aircraft carried the standard factory finish of Dark Olive Drab and Neutral Gray, with white type identity stripes. Code letters were applied to aircraft in late July—PE for the 328th Fighter Squadron, PZ for the 486th and HO for the 487th—painted in 24in high block capitals in the standard location. No natu-

ral metal-finish aircraft are known to have been delivered to the Group prior to its receiving Mustangs. The blue Group marking was not applied to combat P-47s in view of imminent conversion to P-51s.

P-51B/C/D/K Mustangs, March 1944–August 1945. The first P-51B/C models received went initially to the 486th Fighter Squadron and were nearly all in the factory finish of Dark Olive Drab and Neutral Gray. Aircraft of the other two squadrons, which became operational in April, were mostly in bare metal finish. Code letters were as for the P-47s, in standard size and colours. Early in April the white and black type identity nose markings were overpainted with a medium blue on some of the first Mustangs received, but this was found insufficiently conspicuous, particularly on natural metal aircraft where at a distance the blue was difficult to distinguish from black. By 11 May 1944 a lighter blue, possibly Azure Blue, was then used, taken back 18in underneath the nose and then diagonally to a point just aft of the exhaust manifold outlet before being curved to follow the line of the anti-glare panel back to the front of the windshield. The anti-glare panel was completely painted over with blue. There was apparently no on-base application of camouflage to the upper surfaces of natural metal-finish aircraft, yet this was one of two Groups that actually moved to the Continent at the end of 1944.

With the painting of 'D-Day stripes' prior to the 6 June 1944 cross-Channel invasion, the fuselage letters were completely overpainted. While only part of one letter of the squadron code was obscured and eventually restored, the individual letter was completely covered. In the 328th and 487th Fighter Squadrons the letter was later repainted on the fin using the same 24in stencils, first removing the black type identity stripe on bare metal aircraft. In the 486th Fighter Squadron the letter was repainted on the fuselage below and forward of the windshield just behind the blue nose marking, again in 24in high characters. Eventually, following its return from the USSR 'shuttle' mission in late June, the 486th transferred its individual letters to the tail fin. When the 'D-Day stripes' were reduced the 352nd Group continued to display individual letters on Mustang fins and very few examples had the letter on the rear fuselage thereafter. With the coming of P-51Ds in bare metal a darker shade of blue was used for the Group nose marking, believed to be Deep Sky

Top: Blue-nosed Mustangs of the 486th Fighter Squadron, 352nd Fighter Group, ready for the first USSR 'shuttle' mission, 21 June 1944. The individual aircraft letters have been relocated on the forward fuselage as full 'D-Day stripes' are still *in situ*. (Ed Richie)

Above: The 352nd Fighter Group blue nose marking extended back to the windshield and replaced the anti-glare panel dark green. (R. H. Bruner)

Blue, another camouflage shade from British sources. In October 1944 the 352nd Group was issued with the following rudder colours for additional squadron recognition: 328th red, 486th yellow and 487th blue, in the same shade as the nose colour. The three digits overpainted on the rudders were restored in black on 486th Mustangs, usually white in the 487th and normally black in the 328th, although the two last-named squadrons did have examples with the reverse colours. Apart from the underwing location of code letters for low-flying reference in May 1945, no other officially authorised markings were carried by 352nd Fighter Group aircraft.

OTU P-51Bs carried normal Group colours with a numeral as an individual aircraft identity painted on the fin, 24in high. Early in 1945 these aircraft also had their rudders painted with red, yellow and blue in horizontal bands. Three P-47Ds assigned post-war for training had the engine cowling painted blue back to the cooling flaps. Communications air-

craft used by the Group featured blue cowlings, for example AT-6D Texan 43-13584 and C-78 Bobcat 43-32078.

353rd Fighter Group

P-47D Thunderbolts, July 1943–November 1944. The standard factory finish of Dark Olive Drab and Neutral Gray with white type identity stripes was applied to the original combat equipment. Squadron code letters were applied in white in the standard size and position: LH for the 350th Fighter Squadron, YJ for the 351st and SX for the 352nd. Some aircraft had the individual letter on the underside of the cowl front. The first natural metal-finish P-

Below: Probably the most eye-catching Group marking of all 8th Air Force Fighter Groups was that of the 353rd when equipped with Thunderbolts. The arrangement was in 'diamond' pattern, whereas the other P-47 Group with checkerboard, the 78th, had square-set checks. (James Bartley)

Above: *Missy*, a 352nd Fighter Squadron P-51D with yellow outlining to the codes SX:B and the tail number reinstated on the black rudder in white. (James Bartley)

47Ds arrived at the end of March 1944 with black markings in place of white. Group yellow and black checkerboard nose markings were applied from late March to mid April 1944. The checks were arranged in diamond pattern relative to the fuselage axis and were made up of 7in squares. The most common form had four black diamonds per longitudinal row commencing at the cowling lip edge and extending back to the cowling shutters. An alternative form was to have four yellow diamonds per row. Depending on which form was used, the diamonds of one colour were halved at the beginning and end of each row. The Group CO's aircraft, 42-25971 LH:X, had a different form, believed unique in the 353rd, with the checkerboard made up of four yellow and four black squares per row relative to the aircraft's axis. The checks were 6in squares apart from that at the cowling edge, which was reduced to approximately 4in longitudinally. At the same time as the Group nose marking was introduced all type identity stripes were removed from the tail surfaces. When 'D-Day stripes' were applied parts of code letters were painted over, but these were reinstated on the black and white bands in either black or white as appropriate. Few of the natural metal-finish aircraft were given 'in the field' camouflage, and 42-26429 SX:B

is the only example known with grey and green shading.

P-51D/K Mustangs, September 1944–September 1945. These aircraft had a natural metal finish, very few receiving dark green camouflage to their upper surfaces at the Group's paintshop. Code letters were in the standard size, colour and position for Mustangs. Group markings comprised three equal divisions of the propeller spinner painted black/yellow/black and three encircling rows of 6in black and yellow squares on the backing cowling. Although the extra row of checks helped to distinguish 353rd aircraft from those of the 55th Fighter Group, whose green and yellow checkerboard could easily be mistaken for black and yellow, the difference was soon considered insufficient and the number of squares in the checkerboard was extended to eight in December 1944. This addition took approximately two weeks to effect on all the Group's Mustangs. The black type identity stripes were retained on Mustang tails until the introduction of rudder colours in November 1944, which were yellow for the 350th Fighter Squadron and black for the 352nd, the 351st's rudders remaining unpainted. The usual practice was not to overpaint the tail number when painting rudders. Early in 1945 most aircraft of the

Above: A formation of 354th Fighter Squadron Mustangs displaying white flight letters and reinstated tail numbers on their rudders. Part of the black rudder of a training aircraft is just visible on the fourth aircraft in the echelon. (Cal Sloan)

350th Fighter Squadron had their identification letters outlined in yellow, a practice also taken up by the 352nd Fighter Squadron late in the war.

OTU aircraft used numerals for individual aircraft identification, 24in high and placed on the rear fuselage. WW markings were carried on the tail fin. The yellow and black checkerboard was applied to the Group's communications aircraft in 1945, including AT-6D Texan 43-13048, UC-64A Norseman 43-5207 and, post-war, a B-17.

355th Fighter Group

P-47D Thunderbolts, July 1943–March 1944. The standard factory finish of Dark Olive Drab and Neutral Gray with white type identity stripes was originally applied. Squadron code letters, added in August 1943, were WR for the 354th Fighter Squadron, OS for the 357th and YF for the 358th, in white 24in high block capitals in the standard P-47 locations.

P-51B/C/D/K Mustangs, March 1944–July 1945. The first P-51Bs were mostly Dark Olive Drab and Neutral Gray, with a few in bare metal finish. Type identity markings were in the appropriate colours, the white fin and rudder stripes being painted out in late March 1944. Squadron code letters were as for the P-47s, painted in white or black as appropriate and in the standard location and size for P-51s. When in late March 1944 white was given as the Group identification colour, the natural metal-finish aircraft had the black type identity nose markings removed, and the spinner and 12in of the adjacent cowling were painted white. In May 1944 the service squadron commenced giving bare metal P-51B/Cs dark green uppersurfaces and the majority of the Group's aircraft were so painted. At first the dark green coat covered those areas which would have received olive drab on factory-camouflaged aircraft, but by the time the first P-51Ds arrived in June 1944 the dark green was less extensively applied, only the uppersurfaces of wings and tailplane and the fuselage spine receiving this paint. 'In the field' camouflaging, tailing off after June 1944, had ceased by August.

In late October 1944 the Group started painting rudders in squadron colours: red for the 354th Fighter Squadron, blue for the 357th and yellow for the 358th. Tail numbers were repainted in white on most 354th and 357th aircraft. At the same time the 12in wide white cowling band was overpainted with the squadron colour to give a more prominent nose marking. Exceptions were the Group CO, Colo-

Below: P-51D 44-13728 OS:G of the 357th Fighter Squadron, photographed in August 1944 when the 355th Group marking was still an all-white nose. This was an aircraft assigned to the Scouting Force unit attached to the Group and is recognised by the the black bar painted under the squadron code. The Insignia Blue trim tab is a Flight colour. (W. Furniss)

nel E. Stewart's 44-15255 WR:S, assigned to the 354th Fighter Squadron, which had an all-white nose marking swept down and back to the wing root and bordered with a 6in wide red stripe. When Stewart left the Group this aircraft was taken over by the 354th CO, Major G. Graham, the individual letter then being changed to F. The new Group CO, Colonel C. Kinnard's P-51D, 44-73144 WR:A, also had an all-white nose marking which extended back to the exhaust manifold and was then swept up to the anti-glare panel and down to under the fuselage, terminating at· a point directly below the end of the exhaust manifold stack. A number of 354th Fighter Squadron aircraft had the flight letter painted near the top of the rudder in white, approximately 9in high, this being most prevalent in C Flight where the letter was inclined in line with the rudder trailing edge. When squadron numbers were increased to more than 26 aircraft the additional machines used a bar below the individual letter.

OTU aircraft carried standard Group and squadron markings and were at first distinguished by the individual letter being within an outline rectangle, approximately 30in by 24in with 3in strokes, coloured white on camouflage and black on bare metal. In the early spring of 1945 OTU aircraft had their rudders painted black as an additional recognition marking and the outlining of the call-letter was subsequently discontinued. AT-6D Texan 41-34604, used for communications flights, was given a white engine cowling.

P-51s used by the 2nd Scouting Force carried normal markings with a black bar above or below the squadron letters.

356th Fighter Group
P-47D Thunderbolts, September 1943–November 1944. The original aircraft were factory-finished in Dark Olive Drab and Neutral Gray, with white type identity stripes. Squadron code letters were in white, 24in high letters in standard P-47 locations—OC for the 359th Fighter Squadron, PI for the 360th and QI for the 361st. In late March 1944 the Group was given 'no colour' as its distinguishing nose marking and the 24in white type identity nose band was painted out. This was achieved by extending the existing olive drab and grey camouflage, although it appears that dark green was used for the former. The first bare metal-finish aircraft were received at the beginning of April 1944 and a programme of

painting the uppersurfaces in dark green began in May. The extent of this camouflage corresponded approximately with that of factory-finish olive drab. Type identity tail stripes and code letters were reinstated in white and tail numbers in yellow on these field-camouflaged aircraft. Undersurfaces were left unpainted. On P-47D-25-RE and following production models, with 'teardrop' canopies, the framing was frequently left unpainted. Very few 356th Fighter Group P-47s remained in 'silver' finish during their combat assignment. In applying 'D-Day stripes' the fuselage letters were not overpainted, or if they were the letters were reinstated in white and outlined if on a white stripe.

P-51D/K Mustangs, October 1944–September 1945. In contrast to the Group's policy with its P-47s, all P-51s received remained in bare metal finish. Squadron codes were as on P-47s and operations were begun with no other unit markings. As 'no colour' noses were already the distinguishing feature of 479th Fighter Group P-51s, a new marking was devised for the 356th which was also in notable contrast to the former. The rear 9in of the spinner was painted blue and that part forward of the propeller shanks had alternating bands of blue and red, 2in wide, the red at the spinner tip and four other red bands. A 12in wide red nose band was extended back just under the exhaust stacks and then to the windshield. Elongated blue diamonds were superimposed on this red base, strung out in rows from spinner to windshield. Each diamond was approximately 8in long by 4in and there were usually ten in the three longest rows between spinner and windshield with two flanking rows of six above each exhaust manifold stack. Another four diamonds were situated from level with the exhaust stack down on the 12in nose band, although in some cases there were more, extending the arrangement under the nose to meet the diamonds on the other side. There was considerable variation from plane to plane in the number and position of the diamonds. The shade used, a bright medium blue, was probably Deep Sky Blue. These markings were first applied during the latter half of November 1944.

Later that month and in early December the Group added squadron colours to rudders: the 359th Fighter Squadron used yellow, the 360th red and the 361st blue. At first the 359th did not obscure their black type identity band across the rudder and the other two squadrons left the band on the fin. In

Top: The 356th Fighter Group's P-47s were identified by having no cowling nose band, the type marking being painted out in dark green or grey as appropriate. On this 361st Fighter Squadron aircraft the overpainting of the white band has left that part of the cowling a slightly lighter shade. (USAAF)

Above: A 359th Fighter Squadron P-51D, 44-13993 OC:G, with the black type identity band retained on the yellow rudder. The canopy frame is also in the squadron colour in this photograph taken prior to the change in spinner markings.

the 359th and 361st Fighter Squadrons tail numbers were painted over and then reinstated in black. In the 360th most tail numbers were not painted over on the first Mustangs to have red rudders but later this squadron followed suit. In the following weeks several aircraft had the cockpit canopy frame painted in the squadron colour and by March 1945 this had become an accepted part of the decor on all 356th Group Mustangs. In mid February 1945 the squadron colour was carried on the propeller spinner, a less time-consuming scheme to apply than the nine narrow stripes. The group CO's aircraft, however, 44-72435 PI:T, had a spiral of red, yellow and blue on the spinner. Repeated individual aircraft letters had bars either above or below.

OTU aircraft made use of both letters and numerals and carried standard Group markings.

357th Fighter Group

P-51B/C/D/K Mustangs, January 1944–July 1945. Original P-51Bs were in Dark Olive Drab and Neutral Gray factory finish, with white type identity bands and white squadron codes. Codes, applied while the Group was assigned to the 9th Air Force at Raydon in December 1943, were the 362nd Fighter Squadron's G4, the 363rd's B6 and the 364th's C5, in standard colour, size and locations for Mustangs. In late March 1944 the Group applied the Group nose marking consisting of the spinner divided into equal bands of red/yellow/red and the adjacent cowling having a 12in encircling band made up of two rows of alternating 6in red and yellow squares. Bare metal-finish P-51Bs were received from early April 1944 and the following month a programme of giving these aircraft camouflage paint was instigated. The scheme was very similar in layout to that of factory camouflaged aircraft but the colours were dark green upper surfaces and light grey lower surfaces. The shade of both green and grey varied, suggesting access to a range of RAF paints. From June an alternative was applied to several aircraft, mostly P-51Ds, and consisted of dark green on upper wing surfaces, tailplane and

fin and rudder and only the top of the fuselage. The remainder of the aircraft was left as bare metal, the limit of the camouflage on the fuselage being the top of the codes—a continuation of the anti-dazzle panel to the fin. Practically all bare metal P-51B/C/D models received up to September 1944 were field-camouflaged. Different uppersurface schemes were few, although the CO's P-51D, 44-13388 B6:W, with dark green with grey patches, was one. Type identity bands were repainted in white. Field-camouflaging was discontinued in September 1944 and by January 1945 a few of the aircraft that had been so painted had this removed. Fuselage codes were overpainted by 'D-Day stripes', the letters and numerals being reinstated either in outline or on the stripe in the opposite colour. When squadron strengths went to more than 26 aircraft, repeated individual letters carried a bar above them. In October 1944 the rudders of 363rd aircraft were painted red and those of the 364th yellow. The 362nd's rudders, devoid of a special colour, remained either 'silver' or in camouflage.

OTU P-51s had 24in high numerals for individual aircraft identity, and these aircraft appear to have

Below: The bright 357th Fighter Group checkerboard on a P-51D displaying 'D-day stripes' under the wings and light grey 108 US gallon drop tanks. (Harvey Mace)

been concentrated in the 362nd Fighter Squadron. Communications aircraft included UC-64A 43-35444, with four bands of red and yellow checks carrying the underwing code G4-4 in May 1945.

358th Fighter Group

P-47D Thunderbolts, November 1943–February 1944. Originally aircraft carried the standard factory finish of Dark Olive Drab and Neutral Gray with white type identity markings. Squadron code letters, applied in December 1943, were CH for the 365th Fighter Squadron, IA for the 366th and CP for the 367th, in standard locations, size and colour for P-47s. The individual letter was also carried, approximately 9in high in black, on the under lip of the nose cowling of several aircraft. No other unit markings were carried before transfer to the 9th Air Force at the end of January 1944.

359th Fighter Group

P-47D Thunderbolts, November 1943–May 1944. At first the aircraft had the standard Dark Olive Drab and Neutral Gray factory finish with white type identity markings. Squadron codes from November 1943 were in white, 24in high and in standard locations for P-47s. The 368th Fighter Squadron used CV, the 369th IV and the 370th CR. A few P-47Ds in bare metal finish were received in April 1944 with black type identity markings. For unknown reasons, but possibly because of an error relating to the original instruction, the 370th Fighter Squadron code CR was changed to CS. Apart from the 4th Group's change, when relinquishing Spitfires, this is the only known change of an SD110 code issued to a USAAF fighter unit, and it was apparently effected in March 1944. Later the same month the Group was instructed to overpaint the 24in wide white engine cowling band with green. The shade was a light apple green supplied from British sources.

Left, upper: *Caroline*, P-51D 44-13893 CS:E of the 370th Fighter Squadron, in the autumn of 1944. (T. P. Smith)

Left, lower: By the end of hostilities the elements had changed the green nose to a much lighter shade, which contrasts with the greens of the other Mustangs in this line-up at East Wretham. By this time Captain T. P. Smith's CS:E had also gained a canopy frame in the squadron blue. (T. P. Smith)

Above: The 368th Fighter Squadron's *Evelyn*, 44-11222 CV:I, on its landing approach. (T. P. Smith)

P-51B/C/D/K Mustangs, April 1944–September 1945. The spinner and adjacent 12in type identity nose markings were overpainted with green. Code letters were as used on P-47s, with size, colours and locations as standard for P-51s. There was little field-camouflaging of P-51s by the 359th Fighter Group, that carried out being dark green patching on wings and tailplane and along the top of the rear fuselage on P-51Ds. Parts of codes obscured by 'D-Day stripes' were reinstated on stripes in either black or white as appropriate. Darker shades of green were used for the Group marking from the summer of 1944 and by August the 368th Fighter Squadron was painting rudder trim tabs green as a squadron decoration. In November 1944, to obtain better long-range recognition, the green nose marking was extended back from the junction of the existing nose band and the anti-glare panel diagonally down to a point just aft of the exhaust manifold stack and then down to beneath the engine cowling at the leading edge of the wing root. The shade of green was generally a medium green but could vary, sometimes owing to fade. At the same time as the nose marking was extended, rudder colours were introduced. The 368th Fighter Squadron used yellow, the 369th red and the 370th dark blue. Tail numbers were not painted over in the 370th Fighter Squadron and rarely in the 369th. On 368th rudders the usual practice was to overpaint the tail number in yellow and then reinstate it in black. Type identity stripes were removed from November 1944 onwards. In the spring of 1945 the 368th embellished Mustang spinners with a tapering spiral of yellow.

Apart from their WW fin marking, OTU P-51s carried normal Group markings with individual identities mostly with bars. Numerals were not used.

361st Fighter Group

P-47D Thunderbolts, December 1943–May 1944. The aircraft carried the standard factory finish of Dark Olive Drab and Neutral Gray, with white type identity markings. Squadron codes, added in early January 1944, were B7 for the 374th Fighter Squadron, E2 for the 375th and E9 for the 376th, painted in the standard colour, size and locations for P-47s. In late March 1944 the Group overpainted the 24in wide white nose band with yellow. A few P-47Ds in bare metal finish and with black type identity markings, received prior to the Group's conversion to Mustangs, were given fuselage codes in black and the yellow nose band.

P-51B/C/D/K Mustangs, May 1944–September 1945. The majority of P-51B/C models received on conversion were in natural metal finish with black type identity bands. Only a dozen P-51Bs in factory camouflage of Dark Olive Drab and Neutral Gray are known to have been assigned at this time. The Group's yellow nose marking replaced the black

spinner and 12in wide cowling band. Code letters were as for the P-47s but 30in high. Field camouflaging of P-51s began in late May 1944 using dark green on the upper surfaces of wings, tailplane and fin and rudder. In most cases all the upper surfaces of the wings and horizontal tailplane, including elevators, were painted, while the fin and rudder were blotched round the edges, avoiding the tail number. On others only the inner or outer sections of the wing were camouflaged to break up the outline. The Group CO's P-51D had Insignia Blue patching instead of dark green and at least two other aircraft in the 361st were so adorned. It is believed that this was due to a temporary shortage of a suitable green rather than pilot fancy. Type identity stripes were removed from most Group aircraft during the summer of 1944 but this practice seems to have been overlooked on several aircraft at a later date. Generally, code letters were not obscured when 'D-Day stripes' were applied, and where they were they were reinstated in black or white as appropriate.

In order to avoid confusion with yellow-nosed 9th Air Force P-51s, in late July 1944 the Group's marking was extended back to a point just beyond the small perforated panel and then diagonally up to, slightly above and to the rear of the exhaust stack, before being taken back to the end of the engine bay. The anti-glare panel back to this point was overpainted with yellow. This new marking first appeared on the Group CO's aircraft, 44-13410 E2:C, and was applied to others during the first two weeks of August. From October 1944 the 375th Fighter Squadron extended the Group's yellow marking down the engine firewall to the end of the second long inspection panel below the exhaust stacks. In late October 1944 the 374th Fighter Squadron painted its Mustangs' rudders red, the 375th used medium blue and the 376th yellow. In most cases the tail number was left on an unpainted strip. In 1945 all the Group's P-51s also had the wing tips painted in the squadron colour. When more than 26 aircraft were assigned to a squadron the black bar used to distinguish duplicated individual aircraft letters was mostly carried below the letter. The 361st Fighter Group Mustangs were noted for a con-

Left: Manhandling a 500lb GP bomb before a well-stained 361st Fighter Group Mustang with the original Group marking. (USAF)

Top: The extended yellow nose marking on P-51D 44-13704 B7:H of the 374th Fighter Squadron. The extent of this Group marking was common to most aircraft in the 374th and 376th Fighter Squadrons. (J. D. Smith)

Above: The 375th Fighter Squadron's aircraft could be distinguished by that unit's practice of extending the rear of the Group marking below the exhaust stack, as seen on *Queen Jean* 42-106875 E2:D. (J. D. Smith)

Below: Mustangs of the 364th Fighter Group preparing for take-off at Honington, August 1944. The 385th Fighter Squadron aircraft in the foreground has red embellishments to distinguish it as a Flight Leader's aircraft. The squadron appears to have employed the same 18in high code letter stencils as previously used on its P-38s. (Mark Brown/AF Academy)

siderable degree of personal decoration, particular on rudder trimming tabs.

OTU aircraft used standard Group decor and apart from the black WW on fins carried no distinctive markings. Communications aircraft using the yellow Group nose marking were UC-61A Forwarder 43-14469, UC-78 Bobcat 42-32072 and AT-16 Harvard 43-12881. Two P-47Ds used for training post-war, 42-75228WW E2:L and 42-74744WW E9:Q, also had yellow cowlings.

364th Fighter Group

P-38J Lightnings, February–July 1944. The majority of the original combat aircraft were in factory-finish Dark Olive Drab and Neutral Gray, with a few in natural metal finish. Squadron codes were applied in white on camouflage and black on bare metal in the established locations and size for P-38s, that is, in 18in high characters, the squadron code on the rear section of fuselage booms and the individual aircraft letter on the radiator housing. Codes were N2 for the 383rd Fighter Squadron, 5Y for the 384th and 5E for the 385th. A white hyphen was used after the squadron code on some aircraft. Geometric devices for additional plane-in-Group recognition were painted on the outer sides of the upper sections of fins and rudders, approximately 30in at the widest points. The 383rd Fighter Squadron used a 'circle', the 384th a square and the 385th an equilateral triangle. The aircraft's individual letter was repeated on the inward-facing sides of the fins and rudders, approximately 36in high. The colours of these tail markings were white on camouflage and black on bare metal. On some aircraft the tail number was left on an unpainted strip, on others it was obscured and then reinstated in black or yel-

low. In late March 1944 Group identification markings were applied in the form of white propeller spinners and a 12in white band round the adjacent engine cowling. 'D-Day stripes' obscured all fuselage codes and, in common with other 8th Air Force P-38 units, these were not reinstated.

P-51D/K Mustangs, July 1944–September 1945. These aircraft were in natural metal finish with black type identity markings. Some were given dark green camouflage on the upper surfaces but only a few examples are known and these field applications ceased in September. Squadron codes were as for the P-38s, painted in black aft of the national insignia on both sides of the fuselage, the 384th and 385th using 18in or 20in high characters but the N2 of the 383rd being 30in high. The individual aircraft letter was not carried on the fuselage; instead, it was painted on the geometric tail devices, which were as used on the P-38s—that is, a disc for the 383rd, a square for the 384th and a triangle for the 385th—in black with white letters. The size of the triangle was 28in at its base and 36in in height, with 24in high letters; the square was 24in with an 18in high letter; and the circular device was 40in in diameter with a 30in high letter on the majority of

383rd Mustangs, with an alternative of 28in diameter with a 18in letter. Tail numbers were obscured by the large disc but the other sizes were above the number. For duplicated letters the bar was split either side of the letter, forming two small rectangular blocks.

As the identification marking of the 355th Fighter Group's P-51s was white a new Group marking had to be found for the 364th Fighter Group. The spinner was painted white and 12in of the adjacent engine cowling with alternating white and medium blue, 6in wide stripes parallel to the longitudinal axis of the aircraft. Some Flight leaders' P-51s in the 385th Fighter Squadron had red or red and black striped dorsal fins and rudder trim tabs.

OTU aircraft were identified by numerals painted on the tail symbols in white. These were in double figures, the 384th Fighter Squadron having 11, 12 and 14 and the 385th Fighter Squadron 21, 22 and 23. A camouflaged War Weary P-47D assigned for training post-war had the whole length of the cowling painted in the Group's white and blue markings. The 1st Scouting Force used P-51s with standard Group markings apart from individual letters not being on a geometric device background.

Left, upper: In contrast to the 18in high codes on the other two squadron's Mustangs, the 383rd Fighter Squadron's were 30in high. (Mark Brown/ AF Academy)

Left, lower: *Kraut Knocker*, 44-14423, was one of many 434th Fighter Squadron Mustangs that did not have the obscured part of the tail number reinstated on the red rudder. The fuselage codes are 18in high, through the use of the same stencils as cut for P-38 markings. (Robert Bromschwig)

Opposite, top: The 479th Fighter Group's Mustangs carried no nose markings as their means of recognition. The only bright colour on OTU P-51B 43-6779 J2:Y is the squadron's yellow rudder.

479th Fighter Group

P-38J Lightnings, May–September 1944. Approximately one-third of the original combat aircraft were in Dark Olive Drab and Neutral Gray factory finish. A few of the natural metal-finish aircraft were given field-applied camouflage of dark green to the upper surfaces of wings, tailplane and fuselage booms during June and July 1944. Squadron codes were L2 for the 434th Fighter Squadron, J2 for the 435th and 9B for the 436th. These were painted on the fuselage booms in the standard size, colour and positioning for P-38s. Geometric devices were painted on the outward-facing surfaces of fins and rudders, a 'circle' for the 434th, a triangle for the 435th and a square for the 436th. The maximum dimension was 30in for all three shapes. Colours were black on 'silver' finish and white on olive drab. The individual aircraft letter was repeated on inward-facing sides of the fins, 18in high in white, using the same stencils as for the fuselage codes. The Group marking was officially 'no colour', but this appears to have been interpreted as removing the camouflage paint from the spinners and 12in of the adjacent engine cowling. Fuselage codes were obscured by 'D-Day stripes' and not reinstated. When Colonel Zemke took command of the 479th Fighter Group in August 1944 he had the geometric tail markings removed and replaced by bright rudder colours, red for the 434th, yellow for the 435th and no colour for the 436th, a scheme similar to that in use in the 56th Fighter Group which he previously commanded. Several P-38s, passed to the 479th Fighter Group following the conversion of the 20th and 364th Fighter Groups to P-51s, retained these units' yellow and white cowling bands.

P-51D/K Mustangs, August 1944–September 1945. A shortage of Mustangs delayed the Group's conversion and the use of geometric devices on tails, though notified in early August, was not carried out. All original combat P-51s were in bare metal finish and all black type identity markings were removed on receipt. The same squadron code combinations as used on P-38s were applied to the Mustangs in the standard colour, size and positioning for the type. Duplicated letters carried a bar beneath them. Additionally, the rudders of 434th Fighter Squadron aircraft were painted red and the 435th's yellow, and the 436th adopted a black and white checkerboard of 12in squares. The 436th's marking was short-lived for in November 1944 all the squadron's rudders were painted black. Tail numbers were removed when rudders were painted. On some later replacements tail numbers were not overpainted and on others, in the 434th and 435th Fighter Squadrons, they were repainted in black over the red or yellow. In most cases the tail numbers were still removed completely from the fin.

OTU aircraft used the numerals 2, 3 and 4 for individual identities, in each squadron, but there were exceptions which were given letters. A two-seat conversion of P-51B 43-6865 J2:Q was painted overall yellow in the spring of 1945.

RECONNAISSANCE ORGANISATIONS

7th Photographic Group (R)

F-5A/B/C/E/F/G Lightnings, July 1943–October 1945. The original F-5As of the 13th Photographic Squadron at Mount Farm were finished in an overall light blue with a darker azure blue on the upper surfaces, dappled in many areas. It is believed that this was an intermediate scheme prior to the introduction of the so-called Synthetic Haze paint as the regular production finish for photographic reconnaissance aircraft. Later deliveries to Mount Farm were in Synthetic Haze, while resprays were usually in PRU Blue from British sources. Synthetic Haze was a darker shade than the cerulean blue with the slight green hue of PRU Blue. F-5E models received in the summer of 1944 in natural metal finish were resprayed with PRU Blue until approximately November 1944, when this was no longer considered necessary, and replacements were left 'silver'. Blue camouflage was eventually removed from all other F-5s. Few F-5As had a tail number and these were not generally seen until natural metal-finish aircraft were on hand. Where they were applied the colour was either yellow or black on the blue finishes. From the summer of 1943 the last three digits of the serial number were carried on the outward-facing sides of the F-5s' engines in white, 12in high. When F-5s operated in natural metal finish the engine cowling 'last three' were in black.

The 7th Photo Group F-5s were subject to the AEAF requirement for black and white stripes to be applied for operations in support of the cross-Channel invasion in June 1944. No unit markings were carried until the spring of 1944, when coloured spinners were used by the squadrons: the 13th Photo Squadron used red, the 22nd white or bare metal and the 27th dark blue. At first only the front section of the spinner was painted in the squadron colour while the rear part often carried a Flight colour. The air scoop panel on the outboard engine sides was also painted in a squadron colour on some aircraft. This panel, which was removed for regular maintenance, became the location point for the Group marking introduced early in 1945. This marking comprised a red stripe stretching from the spinner back to the leading edge of the wing, some 86in. The width of the stripe was as the scoop panel, 10in. In addition to the red stripe the propeller spinners were painted Insignia Blue as a further Group mark-

ing. At the same time as the Group marking was introduced the squadron colours were transferred to the tail. As with 8th Air Force fighter units, squadrons within the Group were distinguished by different coloured rudders. The 13th Photo Squadron used red, the 14th medium green, the 22nd white and the 27th dark blue.

In mid May 1945 squadron codes as listed in SD110 and CD302 were painted under the left wing, together with an individual letter. The characters, in black, were each 36in by 24in. The 13th Photo Squadron used ES, the 14th is believed to have used QU, the code for the 22nd is unknown and the 27th used G2.

Spitfire XIs, October 1943–April 1945. The scheme was the standard RAF finish of PRU Blue, with the US national insignia superimposed on the roundels which usually gave a disc of 32in diameter. When the aircraft were received, the RAF serial numbers were 4in high in Sky Grey characters on the rear fuselage. Sky Grey was very pale, almost an off-white. For clearer identification, from the spring of 1944 the serial number was repeated on the vertical tail. The two prefix letters were painted just above the top rudder hinge, one on the fin and one on the rudder, each about 6in high in white. The three digits of the number were painted in white below the letters but twice the size, 12in high. Usually two digits were on the fin and one on the rudder. During January 1944 the Spitfires were concentrated in the 14th Photo Squadron. The 7th Photo Group

Right, top: Synthetic Haze-finish F-5Es of the 13th Photographic Squadron taking off from Mount Farm, late summer 1944. (Robert Astrella)

Right, centre: F-5 Lightnings were operated in bare metal finish in the final months of the war when uniform Group and squadron colour markings were established. The Roundel Blue spinner and red cowling stripe was the 7th Photographic Group's marking and the red rudder that of the Group's 13th Photographic Squadron. The last three digits of the serial number were painted in black on the outward-facing sides of the lower engine cowling panels. (Robert Astrella)

Right, bottom: P-51K 44-11569 with the 13th Photographic Squadron's red rudder and 7th Group nose markings. No squadron or individual aircraft letters were carried on these Mustangs, which gave close escort to F-5 photographic sorties. (Robert Astrella)

Above: MB950, one of the first Spitfire PR.XIs received by the 7th Photographic Group late in 1943. The serial can be seen on the rear fuselage painted in light grey on the PRU Blue finish. (Robert Astrella)

Spitfires carried black and white 'D-Day stripes' from 5 June 1944 until ordered to be deleted. During the spring of 1944 the spinners of the Spitfires, which had hitherto remained in the normal finish of RAF Roundel Blue, were painted in Flight colours, yellow and white.

Early in 1945 Group and squadron markings were introduced. A 12in wide red stripe extended along the engine cowling from the spinner to the firewall, with the spinner itself in Roundel Blue or Insignia Blue. The squadron marking was a green rudder, a camouflage shade being used, probably the British Light Green. Serial numbers reinstated on the rudder green were white. During the early months of 1945 a few Spitfires had all PRU Blue paint removed and were operated in polished bare metal with the object of obtaining high speeds. The serial number characters on the fins of these aircraft were in black.

At least two and usually three Spitfire Vs were on hand in the 14th Photo Squadron for conversion training. These were finished in the standard RAF day fighter colours of Ocean Grey and Dark Green with Sky undersurfaces. As with the Mk XIs, the serial numbers were painted on the vertical tail in white and in some cases a 12–18in high call-letter was painted above this. In the early spring of 1944 the training aircraft were given red spinners and also had a WW suffix after the tail number. At least one Spitfire V, AR404, had all camouflage paint removed during the summer of 1944. All Spitfires were returned to the RAF by May 1945.

P-51D/K Mustangs, January–June 1945. In natural metal finish, these aircraft were distributed among all four squadrons and were given the same Group markings, a dark blue spinner and a 12in by 83in red stripe from spinner to the firewall, directly under the exhaust manifold. Rudder colours were red for the 13th Photo Squadron, medium green for the 14th, white for the 22nd and dark blue for the 27th. Apart from the standard tail number in black, no other lettering or numerals were carried until squadron code markings were painted under the left wing in May 1945.

Right, upper: A red-tailed Mosquito PR.XVI, NS515, preparing to take off. The white call-letter M on the fin is in a circular patch of PRU Blue, indicating a 653rd Bomb Squadron aircraft. (Albert Krassman)

Right, lower: An all-black finished Mosquito XVI of the 654th Bomb Squadron with red tail letter Q and red serial NS581. The photograph was taken in January 1945 before red spinners were introduced by this squadron. (Ben Shaver)

The only B-25C Mitchell in the 8th Air Force was operated by the 7th Photo Group, mostly as a communications aircraft although in August 1944 it flew night photographic sorties along the French Channel coast. *Miss Nashville* 42-53357, originally in Dark Olive Drab and Neutral Gray, was painted with PRU Blue and finally had all camouflage paint removed and was flown bare. Other communications aircraft operated by the Group included AT-23B Marauder 42-107481, AT-6D Texan 42-85066 ES:K and L-5 Sentinel 42-98998.

25th Bomb Group (R), originally 802nd Reconnaissance Group (P)

Mosquito PR.XVIs, April 1944–June 1945. These aircraft carried the standard PRU Blue finish overall with Roundel Blue spinners and black serial numbers. British roundels were painted out, but the placement of the US national insignia, AN-I-9b, bore no relation to the location of the roundels. On the wings the centre of the US insignia was approximately 72in from the tip. The overall diameter of the circular part of the marking was 40in. The same size national insignia was used on the fuselage and placed 96in from the centre of the wing root. The 8th Reconnaissance Weather Squadron, Light (P) was by June 1944 carrying an individual aircraft letter on the tail fins of its Mosquitos. Painted in white, 18in high, the letter was encompassed by an

outline circle of 30in diameter and approximately 3in 'thick'. The 8th Reconnaissance Squadron, Special (P) operated Mosquito PR.XVIs with similar markings except that the tail call-letter had no surrounding device. This unit was engaged in a variety of photographic tasks and a number of its aircraft had all undersurfaces painted black as well as the vertical tail and all but the spine of the fuselage. The rest of the aircraft remained in PRU Blue. A non-gloss black was used initially and later aircraft so painted had the gloss finish Jet ANA 622. 'D-Day stripes' were carried by the 802nd Reconnaissance Group during the required period.

In August 1944, following a number of attacks on American-operated Mosquitos over Germany by long-range fighters, the vertical tail surfaces were painted red. By this date the two Mosquito squadrons had been regularised as the 653rd and 654th Bomb Squadrons, and the red paintwork brought a change in tail markings. The outline circle of the 653rd Bomb Squadron was eliminated, leaving the call-letter on a 24in disc of PRU Blue. The 654th Bomb Squadron Mosquitos in day camouflage had the letter left on a square of PRU Blue, but later the letter was painted directly on to the red tail. However, the black-finished aircraft of the 654th did not receive the red paintwork and had either red or white call-letters on the fin. Within a month the requirement for warning red had been extended to the whole tail unit and the extremity of the fuselage from a point some 3 or 4in aft of the serial number. At some point during the spring of 1945 the 654th Bomb Squadron painted the propeller spinners of its Mosquitos red, the 653rd retaining the Roundel Blue spinners which was their standard finish. In mid-May 1945 white squadron codes and call-letters were painted under the left wing of 25th Bomb Group Mosquitos. The 653rd Bomb Squadron used WX and the 654th B? (the second letter has not been established).

B-26G Marauders, July 1944–March 1945. Used by the 654th Bomb Squadron for night photographic work, these Maruaders had the undersurfaces, vertical tail and all the fuselage apart from a top 'spine' sprayed with the black gloss reflective finish ANA 622 Jet. The remainder of the aircraft was Olive Drab. An 18in high yellow call-letter was painted on the fin below the tail number. The four B-26Gs used were 43-34226 T, 43-34205 Y, 43-34195 X, and 43-34193 W.

B-17F/G Fortresses, April–July 1944 and October 1944–August 1945. The 8th Air Force Heavy Weather Reconnaissance Flight and successor squadrons operated B-17s with normal factory-finish camouflage. An individual aircraft call-letter was painted on the fin below the tail number in yellow, usually 24in high. Most of these aircraft had been retired from combat units. When the 8th Reconnaissance Weather Squadron, Heavy, absorbed other flying weather units no unit markings were carried on the Fortresses or when the unit became the 652nd Bomb Squadron. The re-equipment of the squadron with B-17Gs in natural metal finish during the last months of 1944 also brought no unit markings other than radio call-letters on the fin in black. In mid-May 1945 the 652nd Bomb Squadron B-17s had their SD110 code of YN plus call-letter painted under the left wing.

B-24J Liberators, July 1944–November 1944. These aircraft were in natural metal finish and carried a black call-letter, 24in high, on the lower fins. No other unit markings are known to have been carried.

Communications aircraft included UC-64 43-5368 with YN:Z under the left wing post-VE-Day.

67th Observation later **Reconnaissance Group**

Spitfire VA/Bs, October 1942–October 1943. These aircraft had the standard RAF day fighter camouflage of Ocean Grey and Dark Green shading on uppersurfaces and Medium Sea Grey undersurfaces. The 'friendly fighter type' recognition markings were retained on these aircraft—an 18in wide rear fuselage band and propeller spinner in Sky, and a 4in wide yellow stripe along the outer portion of each wing leading edge. As most of the aircraft received had served with the 31st and 52nd Fighter Groups prior to their North African commitment, the USAAF cocarde was already displayed. On the fuselage this was centred on the position of the RAF roundel, 32in in diameter. Where not already applied, a 2in wide yellow concentric ring was added to the fuselage cocarde. Serial numbers were repeated on the tail fin on most aircraft in 3in black characters. The fuselage letters of the 31st and 52nd Fighter Group's squadrons were not immediately painted out. On several aircraft they were still in place when codes were issued for the Group's squadrons as ZM for the 12th Observation Squadron, AX for the 107th, VX for the 109th and DA for the 153rd. (The Group and squadrons were not designated Reconnaissance until late June 1943.) The letters were 24in high in Sky, with the squadron code forward of the cocarde on the left side of the fuselage and aft on the right. The 153rd Observation Squadron ceased operating Spitfires in March 1943.

When the extended national insignia was introduced in late June 1943 the squadron letters were painted forward of this marking on both sides of the fuselage and the individual aircraft letter aft. At this

Below: The 654th Bomb Squadron (R)'s B-26G 43-34226, finished in Jet 622 on the undersurfaces and vertical tail. (Elmo Sears)

RECONNAISSANCE ORGANISATIONS

time the Sky fuselage band was painted out on 109th Reconnaissance Squadron Spitfires but not on the aircraft of the other squadrons. Spinner colours, yellow and red respectively, appeared on 12th and 107th Reconnaissance Squadron Spitfires in the summer of 1943, but it is not known whether these were personal decorations or Group-approved. In any case, they were not to be seen by the autumn of that year.

Havoc I/IIs and A-20Bs, February–October 1943. A number of worn RAF Havoc aircraft were received by the 67th Observation Group for training purposes. The colour scheme was Dark Earth and Dark Green shading on the upper surfaces with either Sky equivalent or black undersurfaces. A-20B Havocs were received from February 1943 in Dark Olive Drab and Neutral Gray factory finish. On 1 May 1943 all Douglas DB-7 types were concentrated in the 153rd Reconnaissance Squadron, sixteen A-20Bs, thirteen Havoc Is and six Havoc IIs. The Havocs were gradually transferred. The squadron letters DA were painted on the fuselage, 24in high in Sky, positioned forward of the cocarde on both sides of the fuselage with the individual letter aft.

L-4B Cubs, October 1942–July 1943. These were in Dark Olive Drab and Neutral Gray. All four squadrons of the Group had L-4Bs assigned, usually eight per squadron. These were given squadron codes (ZM, AX, VX and DA) and individual letters, 24in high in Sky, with the squadron code forward of the cocarde. During the summer of 1943 most of the aircraft were transferred to other units for communications use and they often retained the code letters on the fuselage with the new operators.

1st Scouting Force, later **857th Bomb Squadron**

P-51D/K Mustangs, July 1944–May 1945. All aircraft were in natural metal finish. Aircraft of the 355th Fighter Group were used during its experimental period and these were distinguished by a black bar painted below the squadron letters. From August 1944, when established at Honington using aircraft of the 364th Fighter Group, six additional P-51Ds were received for Scouting Force use. These aircraft, assigned to the 385th Fighter Squadron, carried the unit's standard markings until distinctive markings for the 1st Scouting Force were introduced in September. A 3in red stripe was painted round both top and bottom edges of the vertical and horizontal tail surfaces. The 385th Fighter Squad-

ron triangle on the vertical tail was removed and a black 24in high individual aircraft letter was painted on the bare metal of the fin. Additionally the spinner was painted red, with the 364th Fighter Group blue and white nose band removed or overpainted white. Until early in 1945 a few Scouting Force P-51s retained the blue and white striped nose band although having the other Scouting Force markings; the reason for this is unknown.

In March 1945 the unit moved to Bassingbourn and was given squadron status as the 857th Bomb Squadron, the identity of a defunct 492nd Bomb Group unit. The code 9H, in 24in high black characters, replaced 5E on the rear fuselages of the Mustangs. Other markings remained unchanged. At least one P-51B was assigned to the unit for training purposes. Following VE-Day B-17s and other types were assigned to the squadron for general weather reconnaissance but as far as is known these did not carry any distinctive markings.

2nd Scouting Force

P-51D/K Mustangs, August 1944–May 1945. All aircraft, in natural metal finish, were distributed among the three fighter squadrons. Standard 355th Fighter Group markings were carried and the only distinguishing feature for Scouting Force aircraft was initially a black bar above or below the squadron code letters of WR, OS and YF. The bar was 42–48in long and 4in wide. When the three squadrons of the Group adopted squadron-colour nose bands, in late November 1944, the Scouting Force Mustangs retained the white nose band and unpainted rudders. By that time the bar was only being painted above the squadron letters so that it could be seen more easily. The 2nd Scouting Force never received squadron status before the end of hostilities.

3rd Scouting Force later **862nd Bomb Squadron**

P-51D/K Mustangs, August 1944–May 1945. Aircraft used were in natural metal finish and assigned to the three squadrons of the 55th Fighter Group. Current 55th Fighter Group and squadron markings were carried by Scouting Force Mustangs until the latter part of December 1944, when special markings were approved and introduced. They consisted of a red checkerboard rudder, the checks being 6in square and painted directly on to the bare metal, and a 4in wide red stripe down the fin leading edge, that is, approximately 2in on each side. These markings took a month to apply to all 3rd Scouting Force Mustangs. The checkerboard stencils appear to be the same as used for the Group's OTU aircraft. The unit was given squadron status as the 862nd Bomb Squadron in mid-February 1945 but there is no evidence that that unit's code was ever used on the Mustangs.

B-17G Fortresses, January–May 1945. Eight B-17Gs without armament, in natural metal finish, were assigned, distinguished by a green and yellow checkerboard rudder with checks 6in square. Individual aircraft radio call-letters were painted on the fuselage only, forward of the national insignia, in black, 36in high, using the letters A to H.

19th Photographic Charting later Reconnaissance Squadron

Temporarily attached to the 8th Air Force for logistic support in April 1945, this unit operated B-17G/F-9 Fortresses from Watton and Thurleigh on photographic mapping sorties. The thirteen aircraft carried the number 19 followed by a hyphen and an individual radio call-letter on the fin below the tail number. Painted in black, approximately 18in high, the letters were in the range A to N. In the summer of 1945 the SD110 code 7A, followed by an individual call-letter, was painted under the left wing.

SPECIAL DUTY UNITS

Carpetbaggers — 801st Bomb Group (P) — 492nd Bomb Group

B-24D/H/J/L Liberators, December 1943–July 1945. Original aircraft were in Dark Olive Drab and Neutral Gray factory finish but the undersurfaces were soon painted matt black. From early 1944 most aircraft receiving night camouflage had all vertical surfaces painted black with only the upper surfaces of the wing, tailplane and in some cases the top of the fuselage left in olive drab. A few B-24Ls received in the final months of hostilities were overall Jet. This black finish was also applied to other Liberators during the second half of 1944, but where these were in day camouflage the upper surfaces were not blackened. Although the designations of the squadrons were changed, the assigned aircraft remained. No unit markings are known to have been carried, and the only sizeable identity markings were the tail number and radio call-letter, the latter 24in high

painted in Identification Yellow. The tail number on modified B-24H/Js, which had previously served with a combat bomber unit, were positioned on the inward-facing sides of the fins after these had been painted black. The colour of the number was usually red but sometimes yellow. In mid-May 1945 the two remaining active units of the 492nd Bomb Group, the 856th and 858th Bomb Squadrons, carried the squadron codes 5Z and 9A under the left wing in yellow together with the aircraft's call-letter.

C-47A Skytrains, July 1944–April 1945. Four C-47s were operated by the 856th Bomb Squadron on clandestine operations and were given matt black undersurfaces, fuselage sides, fin and rudder. An individual aircraft letter, 24in high, was painted in yellow on the fin. The C-47s were 42-92840 Q, 42-93728 Z, 43-15177 V and 43-47981 M.

A-26C Invaders, January–May 1945. Five A-26Cs were received by the 856th Bomb Squadron for clandestine operations over Germany, painted overall in Jet gloss black and with the tail number and propeller warning line on the fuselage in red. An 18in high individual aircraft letter, positioned on the fin directly above the tail number, was also painted in red. The aircraft were 43-22500, 43-22524, 43-22513, 43-22610 and 43-22626 U.

Mosquito PR.XVI aircraft used on 492nd Bomb Group 'Red Stocking' sorties were 654th Bomb Squadron aircraft on detachment.

Night Leaflet Squadron 422nd later 858th subsequently 406th Bomb Squadron

B-17F/G Fortresses, September 1943–May 1945. Original B-17Fs were in Dark Olive Drab and Neutral Gray factory finish, being selected aircraft from the 422nd Bomb Squadron of the 305th Bomb Group. These aircraft had their undersurfaces overpainted matt black, the area covered being that originally in Neutral Gray with some intrusion over the fuselage olive drab. Normal 422nd Bomb Squadron unit markings were maintained—the 48in fuselage codes (JJ) and call-letters in light grey and the 28in high yellow call-letter on the tail. The Group Triangle G marking was also retained until the unit moved to Cheddington in June 1944 and was redesignated the 858th Bomb Squadron. The fuselage squadron letters were retained and continued to be used on some surviving aircraft until the end of hostilities. A few natural metal-finish B-17s, assigned

Above: Black beauty. With an all-over black finish, *Tondalayo*, B-17G 43-37517 T, was the CO's aircraft in the 406th Bomb Squadron. On 4 March 1945 it was shot down when entering a British AA barrage over Harwich. (USAAF)

in the spring of 1944, were given overall coats of black with a yellow tail call-letter. B-17 strength was gradually reduced by natural wastage from July 1944 but there were still six on hand at the end of the war in Europe. A few of the retained aircraft were at about this time given an overall matt black finish with the call-letter 36in high in yellow above the tail number. During the third week of May 1945 the squadron code J6 was painted together with the call-letter in 36in high yellow characters under the left wing.

B-24H/J/M Liberators, July 1944–July 1945. All aircraft received were given black undersurfaces and those in natural metal finish were painted black overall. The black was the standard RAF Night product on most aircraft until early 1945, when replacements were painted in high gloss Jet. An individual aircraft call-letter was carried on the fin above the tail number, 24in high in yellow. At or near the end of hostilities the squadron code J6 was painted 48in high on the rear fuselage, also in yellow. The code plus the call-letter were painted on the underside of the left wing from mid-May 1945, once again in yellow.

Radio Counter Measures Squadron 803rd (P) later 36th Bomb Squadron

B-17F/G Fortresses, January 1944–September 1944. These aircraft carried the Dark Olive Drab and Neutral Gray factory finish. Most had seen previous service and their paintwork was well worn. By August 1944 the squadron code R4 was painted 36in high on the fuselage forward of the national insignia in pale grey and the individual aircraft letter aft in the same colour. The individual letter also appeared on the fin in yellow, 24in high.

B-24H/J/M Liberators, June 1944–September 1945. Some six B-24Hs were received in Dark Olive Drab and Neutral Gray factory finish. Later aircraft were all in natural metal finish. The code R4 was carried on both sides of the fuselage aft of the waist gun position, 36in high. The individual aircraft letter, carried centrally on the tail fin, was 24in high and was usually placed below the tail number. The letters A to T were used with no exclusions. The colour both of codes and call-letter was light grey on camouflage and black on bare metal. All squadron aircraft were in bare metal finish by early 1945.

The 36th Bomb Squadron also operated four radar search P-38J Lightnings, 43-28479, 44-23156, 44-23501 and 44-23515. All were in natural metal finish with 18in black codes, the R4 carried on the boom radiator housing and the individual letter on the fin. One aircraft had the red cowling bar and red rudder of the 13th Photographic Squadron, its previous operator. P-51B 42-106775 R4:E in bare metal finish was also on the strength of the squadron at one time.

Air Sea Rescue Squadron 65th Fighter Wing Detachment B became 5th Emergency Rescue Squadron

P-47D Thunderbolts, May 1944–May 1945. The original complement of aircraft was in well-worn Dark Olive Drab and Neutral Gray finish as aircraft were obtained from seven different Fighter Groups and many were given a respray of Dark Green prior to receiving the new markings. The squadron code 5F was painted in white, 24in high, forward of the national insignia and the individual aircraft letter appeared aft on both sides of the fuselage. Individual letters were A to Y, with no exclusions. Only one aircraft was in natural metal finish, 42-25711 5F:D, which had black codes and tail numbers. Most aircraft of the original complement had the first digit of the tail number omitted when repainted for ASR service. Red, white and blue bands were painted round the engine cowling, the leading band red and each approximately 15in wide. An 18in wide yellow band was painted around each horizontal and ver-

tical tail unit, 25in from the tips. On the fin and rudder the band was above the tail number. The original instruction called for 18in chordwise bands round the wings but only one aircraft (5F:A 42-75855) is known to have been so painted. All other P-47Ds had $13^{1}/_{2}$ inches of each wing tip painted yellow on both surfaces. The letters WW were painted on the fin as a suffix to the tail number in yellow, $7^{1}/_{2}$ inches high, indicating the aircraft's War Weary status. All these markings were applied to the squadron's aircraft during May 1944. In June these aircraft carried 'D-Day stripes' during the required period and, where obscured, fuselage codes were reinstated in either black or white. No further natural metal-finish P-47Ds were assigned until after the unit became the 5th Emergency Rescue Squadron in January 1945.

Below: The CO of the 5th Emergency Rescue Squadron usually flew this P-47D, 42-75855 5F:A. It was the first Thunderbolt painted up in ASR colours at Boxted in May 1944 and had the yellow wing stripes which were only applied to one other aircraft before being discontinued. The residues of the stripe on the right wing can be seen on the leading edge and wheel cover. (Robert Astrella)

OA-10A Catalinas, January–June 1945. In overall matt white with a gloss white hull, these aircraft had black radio call tail numbers but no individual letters nor any unit markings. Several of the aircraft had personal decorations on the hull near the access panel. Nine OA-10s were specified as the squadron's complement of the type.

B-17G Fortress, March–May 1945. Six B-17Gs modified to carry an Airborne Lifeboat were War Weary aircraft from the 457th Bomb Group and the 406th Bomb Squadron. These aircraft carried the markings of their former assignments while operating with the 5th Emergency Rescue Squadron. Their identities were 42-31706 M, 42-38021 K and 43-37765 B, with red, yellow and white propeller bosses respectively. B-17Gs 42-38167 JJ:L, 42-37717 JJ:B and 42-39790 JJ:F were the Night Leaflet aircraft, having black undersides and retaining the fuselage letters from their first assignment to the 422nd Bomb Squadron of the 305th Bomb Group.

The 5th Emergency Rescue Squadron operated UC-64A Norseman 44-70289 for communications duties from November 1944 with a red, white and blue cowling. In May 1945 the aircraft had 5F-289 under the left wing in black.

TRANSPORT GROUPS

60th Troop Carrier Group

C-47 Skytrains and C-53 Skytroopers, June 1942–September 1942. These were finished in Dark Olive Drab and Neutral Gray with yellow tail numbers. An approximately 6in yellow surround was applied to the fuselage cocardes. Individual aircraft letters were painted on the rear fuselage, forward or aft of the cocarde and clear of door, in Sky, 24in high. No squadron markings were displayed.

62nd Troop Carrier Group

C-47 Skytrains and C-53 Skytroopers, September 1942. The finish was Dark Olive Drab and Neutral Gray, with yellow tail numbers. No other markings are known to have been carried.

64th Troop Carrier Group

C-47 Skytrains and C-53 Skytroopers, August–September 1942. Dark Olive Drab and Neutral Gray finish, with yellow tail numbers. An approximately 6in wide yellow surround was applied to the fuselage cocarde. Individual aircraft call-letters were painted on the fuselage, aft of the cocarde, in light grey, 18in high. No squadron markings are known to have been carried.

315th Troop Carrier Group

C-47 Skytrains and C-53 Skytroopers, December 1942–October 1943. Dark Olive Drab and Neutral Gray finish, with yellow tail numbers. Squadron code letters were painted 36in high in yellow forward of the cocarde on both sides of the fuselage, with the individual aircraft letter aft in similar size and colour. The codes were NM for the 34th Troop Carrier Squadron and UA for the 43rd Troop Carrier Squadron. The 34th, equipped with C-53s, had its thirteen aircraft lettered A to M. The 43rd's aircraft, C-47s, were lettered N to Z minus V. All but six of these aircraft were detached to operate in North Africa in the spring of 1943.

27th Air Transport Group

C-47 Skytrains, C-53 Skytroopers and various other types, February 1943–January 1944. The C-47s were in Dark Olive Drab and Neutral Gray finish and carried no distinctive unit markings until the formation of the 31st Air Transport Group in the 9th Air Force Air Service Command. To distinguish between the two Groups of C-47s, the 27th ATG had a small circular device approximately 12in high painted on the fin above the tail number. In January 1944 control of the 27th ATG passed to the Air Service Command of USSTAF. No unit markings were carried by other British and US types operated by the 27th ATG.

TRAINING AND EXPERIMENTAL ORGANISATIONS

495th Fighter Training Group

P-47C/D Thunderbolts, August 1943–January 1945. The provisional 2906th Observation Training Group was charged with P-47 operational training, and the two provisional squadrons, the 2908th and 2909th Single Engine Flying Training Squadrons, received worn P-47C/D models in Dark Olive Drab and Neutral Gray factory finish with the standard white type identity markings. SD110 code letter combinations were used and painted on in standard size, colour and positioning for P-47s, that is, 24in high, white and forward of the national marking. These codes were VM for the 2908th and DQ for the 2909th. A number of aircraft also carried the code LA, and it is speculated that the Group was issued three combinations by the Air Ministry through the assumption that three flying squadrons existed. When the Group was regularised as the 495th Fighter Training Group in December 1943 the 551st Fighter Training Squadron used VM and the 552nd Fighter Training Squadron used DQ, although those aircraft coded LA continued to be seen for some weeks. Practically all P-47s used by the 495th FTG had seen service in combat units and often retained the coloured nose markings. By June 1944 there were more than 70 P-47s on strength and for training purposes the Group's complement was arranged into four 'squadrons', A, B, C and D. A and B were 551st FTS aircraft and C and D 552nd. 'A Squadron' Thunderbolts had red engine cowlings and rudders, B yellow cowlings and rudders, C blue cowlings and rud-

Below: B-17E 41-2629 served with the 326th Bomb Squadron in the 1st Combat Crew Replacement Center at Bovingdon during the last quarter of 1942 and much of 1943. Like most other B-17Es used by this organisation, it continued to carry the 326th Bomb Squadron markings during later training activities. This was also one of the Fortresses given a disruptive pattern of brown over the original olive drab and painted in Sky equivalent on the undersurfaces. The code letters JW were also in Sky. (Robert Astrella)

ders and D white cowlings and rudders. Respective squadron codes and other markings were retained. When natural metal aircraft were received by the Group these had fuselage letters painted in black. No 'D-Day stripes' were applied by the 495th FTG but several aircraft received in the months following the cross-Channel invasion had the residue of these markings.

P-38H/J Lightnings, August–December 1943 and August–December 1944. In Dark Olive Drab and Neutral Gray factory finish, these aircraft were assigned to the 552nd Fighter Squadron and given the code DQ in 18in high white letters positioned on the boom radiator housings with the individual aircraft letter aft on the boom. When P-38s were again assigned to the 495th FTG they were placed in 'A Squadron' of the 551st FTS and carried VM codes positioned as on earlier P-38s. Their only additional markings were red spinners and rudders. A few aircraft were in natural metal finish and the letters on these were black.

The 495th Fighter Training Group also operated three Spitfire Vbs until October 1944 with the RAF serials BM523, BL550 and AD573. Their unit markings are not known.

496th Fighter Training Group

P-38H/J Lightnings, January–August 1944. Original P-38Hs were in Dark Olive Drab and Neutral Gray factory finish. When assigned to the 554th Fighter

Training Squadron they were given the code B9. This was painted in white, 18in high, on the rear fuselage booms, with the individual aircraft letter on the boom radiator housings.

There were a variety of coloured spinners and nose tips on 554th FTS P-38s from the spring of 1944 but it is not known if these were unit markings, personal decorations or paintwork inherited from previous operators. Natural metal-finish P-38Js received in the summer of 1944 had black boom letters. 'D-Day stripes' were not applied to 554th FTS P-38s.

P-51B/C Mustangs, January 1944–March 1945. The original worn complement of P-51Bs was in Dark Olive Drab and Neutral Gray factory finish. All Mustangs were operated by the 555th Fighter Training Squadron and they carried the code C7 in 24in high white characters forward of the national marking on both sides of the fuselage, the individual aircraft letter being aft. When 'silver' P-51B/Cs were received later in 1944 the codes were painted in black. Standard type identity bands were carried. 'D-Day stripes' were not applied to 555th FTS Mustangs.

A variety of coloured nose markings were to be seen on the Mustangs of this squadron but it is believed that most were inherited from former operators.

The 555th Fighter Training Squadron also had two Spitfire Vs, one until June and the other until October 1944. These were W3310 and W3815; the latter carried the C7 code and individual aircraft letter M in the same position, size and colour as the P-51s. Interestingly, this aircraft operated with the old cocarde national insignia on the fuselage and none on the wings. Both aircraft were finished in Ocean Grey and Dark Green shadow shading, with Medium Sea Grey undersurfaces, but although they had Sky spinners they did not have the 'friendly fighter' rear fuselage band and wing leading-edge stripes. The 496th Fighter Training Group also used Westland Lysanders and Miles Masters, which remained in British markings.

1st Replacement and Training Squadron

B-17E/F/G Fortresses, September 1942–September 1944. The flying training element of No 11 CCRC/1 CCRC operated for a considerable period without any special unit insignia. In the summer of 1944 some of the B-17s assigned carried the code letters BV but it is not known if this was an SD110 code or a marking derived from the BV for Bovingdon base.

2nd Replacement and Training Squadron

No unit markings are known for the B-17 and B-24 aircraft used by No 12 CCRC/2 CCRC. Available

Below: A 1st CCRC B-17G (right of photo), 43-38782 BV:N. It is not known if the letters BV were from SD110 or simply the BV code of Bovingdon where the aircraft was based. (Robert Astrella)

Above: The 3rd G&TT Flight line at East Wretham, spring 1945. The two P-47Ds, 42-8381 LJ:B and 42-7896 LJ:D, carry standard markings for their type, but the two A-35 Vengences, while also having the code LJ, still retain British nationality markings. The name on LJ:B is *Little One*. (T. P. Smith)

photographic evidence depicts aircraft in camouflage finish without unit codes.

3rd Replacement and Training Squadron
B-26B/C and AT-23 Marauders, August 1943–September 1944. The majority of these aircraft were in Dark Olive Drab and Neutral Gray factory finish. It is believed that the unit code, W9, was carried in standard size and either yellow or grey.

4th Replacement and Training Squadron
No unit markings are known for the few B-17s serving with this unit.

1st Gunnery and Tow Target Flight
No distinctive markings were carried until mid-1944, when yellow bands were introduced on A-35B Vengeances. Approximately 24in at the top of the vertical tail, the primary engine cowling, and the projecting 'knuckles' of the landing gear were painted Identification Yellow. Similar markings on engine cowlings and tail tips were used on the A-20B Havocs and AT-23B Marauders acquired at the end of 1944. The

A-35Bs, finished in Dark Green uppersurfaces and with a medium grey on undersurfaces, carried white 18in high individual aircraft letters on the rear fuselage. Their tail numbers were painted in black on the fin approximately 8in high. The British serial number was frequently retained on the rear fuselage.

2nd Gunnery and Tow Target Flight
A-20B Havocs inherited by this unit from the 153rd Liaison Squadron were used from October 1943 to April 1945, in Dark Olive Drab and Neutral Gray factory finish. A 36in white individual letter, A to F, was carried on the fin above the yellow tail number. The Flight also had AT-23, A-35 and P-47 models on its strength at times.

3rd Gunnery and Tow Target Flight
Vengeance and Lysander aircraft obtained from the RAF were operated by this Flight with British markings and roundels, although the 3rd G&TT Flight code letters were added. LJ:I was carried by a Lysander and LJ:E, LJ:G; LJ:H and LJ:J by Vengeances. The Flight usually had three or four P-47Ds on strength from the spring of 1944. These carried standard white type identity markings and unit code letters, the latter being positioned forward of the fuselage national insignia as required on P-47s. Known P-47 identities are LJ:A, LJ:B, LJ:D and LJ:K, all with a yellow WW prefix to their tail number.

4th Gunnery and Tow Target Flight

The unit marking used on Havocs and AT-23 Marauders of this unit is believed to have been the code ZS. On the A-23Bs the code was forward of the national insignia and grouped with the individual aircraft call-letter and separated by a hyphen. The size of the letters was approximately 48in high and in yellow on camouflage finish.

Air Technical Section, VIII Fighter Command

This unit operated Spitfire Vs, P-38F/Hs, P-47 C/Ds, P-51Bs, Mustang Xs and other types from Bovingdon. The SD110 code letters VQ were used on single-engine aircraft with the unit code forward of the national insignia on both sides of the aircraft in standard white 24in letters.

Operational Engineering Section—8th Technical Operations

This unit was formed in Febraury 1944 to embrace all experimental and test work at Bovingdon using all types of US combat aircraft. The SD110 code Q3 was used on fuselages in the size, shape and colour appropriate to the aircraft type. In May 1945, when identification markings had to be displayed under the left wing, the form used was 8TO with a hyphen and the individual aircraft call-letter rather than the Q3 code as on the fuselage; for example, P-47M Thunderbolt 44-21113 Q3:A carried 8TO-A under the left wing.

HEADQUARTERS FLIGHTS

A Flight, 8th Air Force Headquarters

The varied selection of types on hand had no other marking than individual aircraft call-letters. These letters were painted in yellow on camouflaged aircraft and black on 'silver', the size being either 18in or 24in high and the location the fin or rear fuselage. The following aircraft were on strength in September 1944: B-17G 42-39968 A, UC-78 43-32091 B, UC-45F 43-35928 D, P-51D 44-13730 E, UC-78 43-32102 H, AT-6D 41-34624 J, UC-61A 43-14485 K, A-20G 43-9944 L, AT-23A 42-95724 M, P-47D 42-75224 VM:O, P-38J 42-67402 Q, RDB-7B AL672 S, UC-61A 43-14603 T, P-40 41-35954 U and AT-7 42-2429 V.

1st Air Division HQ Flight

B-17s and a variety of communication types carried only standard markings, some with call-letters on the fin.

Below: P-47D 42-75151 was used by the HQ Flight of the 1st Combat Bomb Wing but still retained the code letters of its former operator, the 82nd Fighter Squadron. Given a red fin, horizontal stabilisers and wing tips like the Fortresses, it carried a white triangle device containing an inverted red triangle with a white figure 1 and the letters of the Wing's three Groups placed round this inner triangle. (Paul Chryst)

2nd Air Division HQ Flight

B-24s and a variety of communication types carried only standard markings until spring 1945, when the B-24s sported green rudders. In May 1945 these aircraft were seen with 2AD under the left wing followed by a hyphen and individual call-letter.

3rd Air Division HQ Flight

In the autumn of 1943 a Square Z marking was notified for this unit but the only aircraft known to have carried the device was B-17F 42-29780, which had all camouflage paint removed and operated as a communications aircraft in bare metal finish. The Square Z marking was a standard 48in-sided square but the Z was stylised, with rounded ends and corners so that it appeared more like a reversed S. In winter 1944 the Division gave notice of a black and yellow checkerboard on rudders as the marking for B-17s of this Flight. This decor was three squares wide and seven high, but no aircraft so painted are known. Instead, the 3rd Air Division HQ made use of the Scouting Force weather B-17s for its purposes.

65th Fighter Wing HQ Flight

From summer 1944 the HQ Flight adorned the engine cowlings of its aircraft with alternating stripes of white and red, white foremost then red/white/ red/white. The width varied on different aircraft types. On P-47s the propeller boss was white with a red spiral and on P-51s the spinner was white with a red spiral. Aircraft carrying these markings at various dates were P-47M 44-21124, P-47C 41-6259WW, P-47D 42-26059, P-47C 41-6528WW, P-51B 43-6528WW, P-51B 43-6542WW, UC-78 42-58515 and L-4B 43-656. All but the L-4B carried the letters JA on the fuselage. On the left side the J was forward of the national marking and the A to the rear, and on the right the J was aft and the A forward. It is believed that this was not an SD110 code but the initials of the wing's commanding officer, Jesse Auton, following the practice of an RAF Wing Leader. The letters were 24in high and in black on bare metal and white on camouflage. In mid May 1945 the letters were painted under the left wing with a number; for example, the two-seat P-47C 41-6259 carried JA-2.

66th Fighter Wing HQ Flight

The P-47 and P-51 aircraft of the HQ Flight were given a multi-coloured checkerboard from the autumn of 1944. Engine cowlings had diagonally varying rows of red, white, green, yellow and black squares, 8in on the P-47s and 6in on the P-51s. The P-51 spinners were striped longitudinally with the same five colours. The two P-51s with these markings were 44-13590 *Piccadilly Prince III* and 44-11660 *Rachel-H 2nd*. No fuselage letters were carried. A similar nose marking was carried by AT-6 42-84586. Two armament-stripped B-17s used in 1945 did not have these markings; one, 42-97736, carried 66FW-D under the left wing in the summer of 1945.

1st Combat Bomb Wing HQ Flight

By the end of hostilities aircraft of the HQ Flight were using a device on the fins that consisted of three small red triangles positioned to form a large equilateral triangle. Superimposed on the lower left red triangle was a black letter L, on the top triangle the letter A and on the bottom right W, these being the identification letters of the Wing's three Groups. The centre part of the device formed an inverted triangle which was painted white or left bare metal and had a black figure 1 thereon. An individual aircraft letter was painted below the triangle. Three aircraft sporting this device were L-4B Cub 43-648 and B-17Gs 44-8883 and 44-6014.

Other Combat Bomb Wings are not known to have any distinguishing markings on their HQ Flight aircraft. However, in May 1945 most painted the Wing number as a prefix to an individual aircraft call-letter under the left wing. An example is the 40th Combat Wing's C-78 Bobcat 43-32092, which carried 40-X.

GROUP AND SQUADRON INSIGNIA

The form of insignia used by US Army Air Forces combat units originated in the First World War when Air Service squadrons on the Western Front adopted emblems to distinguish the aircraft of one unit from those of another. The emblem was generally of a comic or light-hearted nature, far removed from the usual classic heraldry of military formations. The emblems, completely unofficial during hostilities, were in November 1919 approved as official squadron insignia and continued in use with the successor units during the immediate post-war period. It was not until September 1923 that rules concerning air unit insignia were promulgated by the US Army. These stated that the common caricature design was acceptable, and that new insignia need not be of classic or heraldic composition.

It was required to be in good taste and sufficiently simple to enable the device to be applied to an aircraft's fuselage by stencilling. The preferred squadron insignia was contained within a circular shape, and limited to between 2 and 3ft diameter on an aircraft, distinguishable at up to 150yds. There were a number of unacceptable features: the device must not include numerals, the letters US, Air Service insignia, the flag of the United States, Coats of Arms of the United States of any part of them, the complete coat of arms or motto of any state or country, emblems or mottoes of any other US Army organisation, outlines of geographical maps, military decorations or service ribbons. During the inter-war years unit insignia continued to be looked upon primarily as an aircraft embellishment but in the late 1930s, when camouflage became a priority, such colour markings were unsuitable.

Apart from being displayed on aircraft, a unit's official insignia could be found in appropriate base buildings, such as headquarters offices, ready rooms and certain personnel quarters. It was also permissible for officers to carry a rendering of the insignia in the form of a 'patch' on the left breast pockets of casual flying jackets, such as the well known A-2. These patches were either painted on leather or woven, but in both cases they tended to be practical interpretations of the approved insignia.

With the United States' entry into the Second World War came a need for secrecy on the disposition and identity of military units. Group and squadron emblems had to be removed from aircraft, particularly those going to combat theatres, although there were a few examples of bombers arriving still displaying their unit's insignia. Jacket patches were still allowed, provided the jackets were not worn on combat missions. The most common form was the woven representation, and several 8th Air Force organisations had these made up in the United Kingdom for their personnel.

The Heraldic Section of the Army Air Forces in Washington was responsible for unit insignia. A new unit was permitted to design its own insignia and submit it for approval to the Heraldic Section, or the services of some outside agency could be enlisted to produce the design to be submitted. The Heraldic Section artists would also create the insignia if requested and provided with the unit requirements. This last was the assured way of obtaining an officially approved insignia as many of the designs submitted by units themselves were not accepted for one reason or another. In many cases, once a Group and its squadrons were overseas and created their own insignia they were either unaware that it had to be sent to the Heraldic Section for official approval or they did not bother to do so. There was no command objection in theatres of war to the use of unit patches, whether approved or unapproved, on non-combat clothing, stationery or on base signs, as this was considered a boost to morale.

Although a unit may have made continual use of an unofficial insignia throughout its operational period, often no record of such can be found in USAF archives simply because it was never officially acknowledged or recorded. Also, many approved insignia were classified obsolete in the years following the Second World War when successor units designed what they considered devices more appropriate to their current status and mission. Despite its historical connection, the original insignia so displaced was apparently not considered worthy of recording.

The accompanying illustrations cover all 8th Air Force combat Group and squadron insignia, both official and unofficial, that the compiler has been able to trace. Some devices were in regular use throughout a unit's stay in England but others saw very little use, and this is noted in the listing below. Details are also given as to whether the insignia illustrated is official or unofficial and whether it represents the original design or a variant or is based on a jacket patch.

Approved Indicates that the insignia illustrated is that officially approved for the unit by the USAAF Heraldic Section.

Unapproved Indicates that the insignia illustrated was designed and used by a unit but either never submitted for official approval, or submitted and rejected but still used by that unit.

Replaced Indicates that the original insignia was for some reason no longer favoured by the unit and was replaced by another design.

Patch Indicates that the illustration is the reproduction of a woven or painted jacket patch based on the original design and used during service with the 8th Air Force.

Base art Indicates that the illustration is based on a rendering of the emblem as applied to notice boards, wall decoration, stationery or other artefacts at the unit's wartime station. The rendering usually varies in some respect from the original design.

Common Indicates that the emblem was used extensively by the unit as a jacket patch or a display sign at the unit's base.

Rare Indicates that the insignia was little used on patches or rarely displayed at the station.

None Indicates that there was no official recognised insignia or any known unofficial emblem used by the unit during the Second World War.

The illustrations do not cover those units which were transferred to the 9th or 12th Air Force.

BOMBER GROUPS AND SQUADRONS

34th BG	Approved. Common.
4th BS	Approved. Common.
7th BS	Approved. Common
18th BS	Approved. Common.
391st BS	Approved. Common.
44th BG	Approved. Rare.
44th BG	Unapproved. Common. With different colour nose for each squadron.
66th BS	None.
67th BS	Approved.
68th BS	None.
506th BS	None.
91st BG	Unapproved. Common.
322nd BS	Approved.
323rd BS	Approved.
324th BS	Approved. Patch. Variant.
401st BS	Approved. Patch. Variant.
92nd BG	Approved.
325th BS	Approved. Patch.
326th BS	Approved. Patch.
327th BS	Approved. Patch.
407th BS	Approved. Patch.
93rd BG	Unapproved.
328th BS	Unapproved. Patch. Replaced goblin with bomb in 1943.
329th BS	Unapproved. Patch.
330th BS	Unapproved. Patch. Replaced devil with bomb in 1944.
409th BS	Approved.
94th BG	Unapproved design of bombs in squadron colours as HQ sign. Unavailable.
331st BS	Approved.
332nd BS	Approved.
333rd BS	Unapproved. A later variant did not have the eagle.
410th BS	Approved.
95th BG	Approved. Common.
334th BS	Approved.
335th BS	Unavailable.
336th BS	Rare. Patch.
412th BS	Rare. Unavailable.
96th BG	Approved.
337th BS	Approved.
338th BS	Approved.
339th BS	Approved.
413th BS	Approved.
100th BG	Unapproved. Rare.
349th BS	Approved. Patch.
350th BS	Approved. Patch.
351st BS	Approved. Patch.

Above: : Unit emblems were frequently selected for the decoration on the back of A-2 flight jackets. The white nose of the 44th Bomb Group's Flying Eight Ball indicates the 68th Bomb Squadron.

418th BS	Approved. Patch.
303rd BG	Approved. Common. Base art.
358th BS	Unapproved. Patch. Common.
359th BS.	Unapproved. Patch. Common.
360th BS	Unapproved. Patch. Variant. Common.
427th BS	Unapproved. Patch. Variant. Common.
305th BG	Unapproved. Base art. Common. At least six variants.
364th BS	Approved. Base Art.
365th BS	Approved. Base art.
366th BS	Approved. Patch.
422nd BS	Approved. Patch.
306th BG	Approved. Rare.
367th BS	Approved. Common.
368th BS	Approved. Common.
369th BS	Approved. Common.
423rd BS	Approved. Common.
351st BG	Unapproved. Common.
508th BS	Unapproved.
509th BS	Approved.
510th BS	pproved.
511th BS	Unapproved. Ball emblem relates to first combat CO's surname.
379th BG	Unapproved.
524th BS	Approved. Patch.
525th BS	Approved. Patch.
526th BS	Approved. Patch.
527th BS	Approved. Patch.

381st BG	Unapproved.
532nd BS	Approved. Common.
533rd BS	Approved. Common.
534th BS	Approved. Base art. Common.
535th BS	Unapproved. Patch. Common.
384th BG	Unapproved. Common.
544th BS	Unapproved.
545th BS	Unapproved.
546th BS	Unapproved.
547th BS	Unapproved.
385th BG	Unapproved.
548th BS	Approved. Replaced approved emblem of B-17 with lightning strike, 1943.
549th BS	Unapproved. Common.
550th BS	Unapproved. Replaced approved porcupine with bomb emblem in 1943.
551st BS	Approved. Common.
388th BG	Unapproved. Common.
560th BS	Approved. Base art. Walt Disney original had pink bomb and extra clouds.
561st BS	Unapproved. Base art. Replaced by cartoon bug on bomb in 1944.
562nd BS	Approved.
563rd BS	Unapproved. Base art.
389th BG	Unapproved. Common.
564th BS	Unapproved. Rare. No patches known.
565th BS	Unapproved. Rare. No patches known.
566th BS	Unapproved. Rare. Another design featured Fightin' Sam; also rare.
567th BS	Unapproved. Rare. No patches known.
390th BG	Unapproved. Features Framlingham Castle.
568th BS	Approved.
569th BS	Approved.
570th BS	Approved.
571st BS	Unapproved.
392nd BG	Unapproved. Patch. Common.
576th BS	None.
577th BS	one.
578th BS	None.
579th BS	None.
398th BG	Unapproved.
600th BS	Approved.
601st BS	Approved.
602nd BS	Approved. Patch. Walt Disney original.

603rd BS	Approved. Patch. Walt Disney original.	785th BS	Unapproved. Rare.
		786th BS	Unapproved. Rare.
401st BG	None.	787th BS	Unapproved. Rare.
612th BS	Approved. Variant.	**467th BG**	Unapproved.
613th BS	Approved. Variant	788th BS	Approved. 859th BS emblem similar. 788th BS re-formed from 859th BS.
614th BS	Approved.		
615th BS	Approved. Variant.	789th BS	Approved.
445th BG	None.	790th BS	Approved.
700th BS	Approved. Patch.	791st BS	Approved.
701st BS	Approved. Patch.	**482nd BG**	None.
702nd BS	Approved. Patch.	812th BS	Approved.
703rd BS	Approved. Patch.	813th BS	Approved.
446th BG	Unapproved. Base art.	814th BS	Approved.
704th BS	Unapproved. Patch.	**486th BG**	None.
705th BS	Unapproved. Patch. Three versions.	832nd BS	Unapproved. Patch.
706th BS	Unapproved. Patch. Two versions.	833rd BS	Unapproved. Patch.
707th BS	Unapproved. Patch. Two versions.	834th BS	Unapproved. Patch.
447th BG	Unapproved.	835th BS	Unapproved. Patch.
708th BS	Approved.	**487th BG**	Unapproved. Very rare. Appears to have been ignored in UK service.
709th BS	Approved.		
710th BS	Approved.	836th BS	None.
711th BS	Approved.	837th BS	None.
448th BG	Unapproved.	838th BS	None.
712th BS	Unapproved.	839th BS	None.
713th BS	Approved.	**489th BG**	Unapproved. Base art. Common.
714th BS	Approved.	844th BS	None.
715th BS	Unapproved.	845th BS	None.
452nd BG	Unapproved. Common.	846th BS	None.
728th BS	Approved.	847th BS	None.
729th BS	Approved. Base art.	**490th BG**	Unapproved. Base art. Rare.
730th BS	Unapproved.	848th BS	None.
731st BS	Approved. Base art.	849th BS	None.
453rd BG	Unapproved. Patch. Two other designs known but isolated display.	850th BS	None.
		851st BS	None.
732nd BS	None.	**491st BG**	Unapproved. Common.
733rd BS	None.	852nd BS	Unapproved. Patch.
734th BS	None.	853rd BS	Unapproved. Patch.
735th BS	Base art. Carried on B-24s, 1945. Another emblem had animated bomb.	854th BS	Unapproved. Patch.
		855th BS	Unapproved. Patch.
457th BG	Unapproved. Common.	**492nd BG**	None.
748th BS	Approved.	856th BS	None.
749th BS	Approved.	857th BS	None.
750th BS	Unapproved. Originally approved for disbanded 317th BS, 88th BG.	858th BS	None.
		859th BS	Unapproved. Modified version later adopted as 788th BS emblem.
751st BS	Approved.		
458th BG	None.	**493rd BG**	Unapproved. Base art.
752nd BS	Approved. Patch.	860th BS	None.
753rd BS	Approved. Patch.	861st BS	None
754th BS	Approved. Base art.	862nd BS	None.
755th BS	Approved. Base art.	863rd BS	Approved. Inherited from 13th Anti-Submarine Squadron. Little used in UK.
466th BG	Unapproved.		
784th BS	Unapproved. Rare.		

FIGHTER GROUPS AND SQUADRONS

4th FG	Unofficial. This design became the approved emblem of the 334th FS post-war.
334th FS	None. Used RAF 71 Sqn emblem.
335th FS	None. Used RAF 121 Sqn emblem.
336th FS	None. Used RAF 133 Sqn emblem.
20th FG	Approved. Common.
55th FS	Approved. Common.
77th FS	Approved. Common.
79th FS	Approved. Common.
55th FG	Approved.
38th FS	Approved.
338th FS	Approved.
343rd FS	Unapproved. 1942 patch. Rare. Mustang device from autumn 1944.
56th FG	Approved. Common.
61st FS	Approved. Common.
62nd FS	Approved. Common.
63rd FS	Approved. Patch. Common. Replaced stylised P-38 emblem in 1942.
78th FG	Approved. Common.
82nd FS	Approved. Common.
83rd FS	Approved. Common.
84th FS	Approved. Common.
339th FG	None.
503rd FS	Unapproved.
504th FS	Unapproved.
595th FS	Unapproved.
352nd FG	None.
328th FS	Unapproved. Base art. Rare.
486th FS	Unapproved. Base art. Rare.
487th FS	Approved. Common.
353rd FG	Unapproved.
350th FS	Unapproved. Base art.
351st FS	Unapproved. Base art.
352nd FS	Unapproved. Base art.
355th FG	Approved. Common.
354th FS	Approved. Common.
357th FS	Approved. Common.
358th FS	Approved. Common.
356th FG	None.
359th FS	Unapproved. Base art.
360th FS	Approved.
361st FS	Unapproved. Base art.
357th FG	Unapproved.
362nd FS	Approved.
363rd FS	Approved. Patch.
364th FS	Approved. Patch.
359th FG	Unapproved. Base art.
368th FS	Approved. Common.
369th FS	Approved. Common.

370th FS	Approved. Common.
361st FG	Unapproved. Base art.
374th FS	Approved.
375th FS	Unapproved. Patch.
376th FS	Approved.
364th FG	None.
383rd FS	Approved. Base art. Common.
384th FS	Approved. Base art. Common.
385th FS	Approved. Base art. Common.
479th FG	Unapproved. Rare.
434th FS	Approved. Replaced by emblem featuring a Jack of Hearts, late 1944.
435th FS	Approved.
436th FS	Approved.

RECONNAISSANCE GROUPS AND SQUADRONS

7th PG	None.
13th PS	Approved. Patch. Original Walt Disney design.
14th PS	Approved. Base art.
22nd PS	Unapproved. Patch. Camera black in other renderings.
27th PS	Approved.
25th BG(R)	None.
652nd BS	Approved. Patch. Originally devised for 8th Weather Reconnaissance Squadron(P).
653rd BS	Approved. Patch.
654th BS	Approved. Patch.
1st SF	Unapproved.
2nd SF	Unapproved.
3rd SF	Unapproved.

INDEPENDENT SQUADRONS

5th ERS	Approved. Earlier 65th Det B emblem had RAF roundel background.
36th BS	Unapproved. Patch.
406th BS	Unapproved. Early approved emblem not applicable to 8thAF unit.

8th Air Force emblem First design originated in the UK and used in 1942–43. Second design originated with USAAF Heraldic Office, which did not approve original design. Issued as patch in 1944–45.

34 BG

4 BS/34 BG

7 BS/34 BG

18 BS/34 BG

391 BS/34 BG

44 BG (1)

44 BG (2)

67 BS/44 BG

91 BG

322BS/91BG

323 BS/91BG

324 BS/91 BG

401 BS/91 BG

92 BG

325 BS/92 BG

326 BS/92 BG

327 BS/92 BG

407 BS/92 BG

93 BG

328 BS/93 BG

329 BS/93 BG

330 BS/93 BG

409 BS/93 BG

331 BS/94 BG

332 BS/94 BG

333 BS/94 BG	410 BS/94 BG	95 BG	334 BS/95 BG	336 BS/95 BG
96 BG	337 BS/96 BG	338 BS/96 BG	339 BS/96 BG	413 BS/96 BG
100 BG	349 BS/100 BG	350 BS/100 BG	351 BS/100 BG	418 BS/100 BG
303 BG	358 BS/303 BG	359 BS/303 BG	360 BS/303 BG	427 BS/303 BG
305 BG	364 BS/305 BG	365 BS/305 BG	366 BS/305 BG	422 BS/305 BG

306 BG

367 BS/306 BG

368 BS/306 BG

369 BS/306 BG

423 BS/306 BG

351 BG

508 BS/351 BG

509 BS/351 BG

510 BS/351 BG

511 BS/351 BG

379 BG

524 BS/379 BG

525 BS/379 BG

526 BS/379 BG

527 BS/379 BG

381 BG

532 BS/381 BG

533 BS/381 BG

534 BS/381 BG

535 BS/381 BG

384 BG

544 BS/384 BG

545 BS/384 BG

546 BS/384 BG

547 BS/384 BG

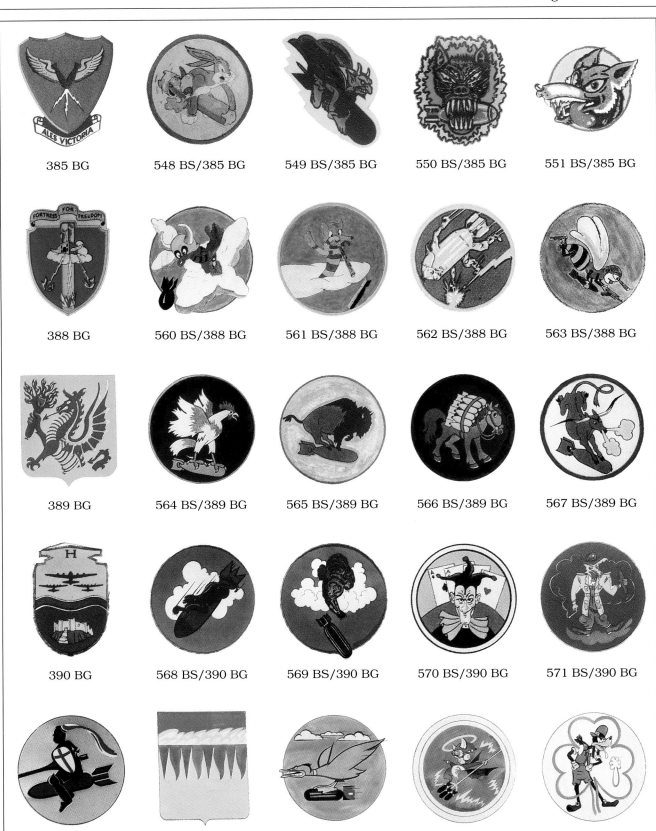

385 BG

548 BS/385 BG

549 BS/385 BG

550 BS/385 BG

551 BS/385 BG

388 BG

560 BS/388 BG

561 BS/388 BG

562 BS/388 BG

563 BS/388 BG

389 BG

564 BS/389 BG

565 BS/389 BG

566 BS/389 BG

567 BS/389 BG

390 BG

568 BS/390 BG

569 BS/390 BG

570 BS/390 BG

571 BS/390 BG

392 BG

398 BG

600 BS/398 BG

601 BS/398 BG

602 BS/398 BG

603 BS/398 BG   612 BS/401 BG   613 BS/401 BG   614 BS/401 BG   615 BS/401 BG

700BS/445 BG   701 BS/445 BG   702 BS/445 BG   703 BS/445 BG   446 BG

704 BS/446 BG   705 BS/446 BG   706 BS/446 BG   707 BS/446 BG   447 BG

708 BS/447 BG   709 BS/447 BG   710 BS/447 BG   711 BS/447 BG   448 BG

712 BS/448 BG   713 BS/448 BG   714 BS/448 BG   715 BS/448 BG   452 BG

728 BS/452 BG

729 BS/452 BG

730 BS/452 BG

731 BS/452 BG

453 BG

735 BS/453 BG

457 BG

748 BS/457 BG

749 BS/457 BG

750 BS/457 BG

751 BS/457 BG

752 BS/458 BG

753 BS/458 BG

754 BS/458 BG

755 BS/458 BG

466 BG

784 BS/466 BG

785 BS/466 BG

786 BS/466 BG

787 BS/466 BG

467 BG

788 BS/467 BG

789 BS/467 BG

790 BS/467 BG

791 BS/467 BG

812 BS/482 BG   813 BS/482 BG   814 BS/482 BG   832 BS/486 BG   833 BS/486 BG

834 BS/486 BG   835 BS/486 BG   487 BG   489 BG   490 BG

491 BG   852 BS/491 BG   853 BS/491 BG   854 BS/491 BG   855 BS/491 BG

859 BS/492 BG   493 BG   863 BS/493 BG

4 FG   20 FG   55 FS/20 FG   77 FS/20 FG   79 FS/20 FG

55 FG	38 FS/55 FG	338 FS/55 FG	343 FS/55 FG	56 FG
61 FS/56 FG	62 FS/56 FG	63 FS/56 FG	78 FG	82 FS/78 FG
83 FS/78 FG	84 FS/78 FG	503 FS/339 FG	504 FS/339 FG	505 FS/339 FG
328 FS/352 FG	486 FS/352 FG	487 FS/352 FG	353 FG	350 FS/353 FG
351 FS/353 FG	352 FS/353 FG	355 FG	354 FS/355 FG	357 FS/355 FG

358 FS/355 FG   359 FS/356 FG   360 FS/356 FG   361 FS/356 FG   357 FG

362 FS/357 FG   363 FS/357 FG   364 FS/357 FG   359 FG   368 FS/359 FG

369 FS/359 FG   370 FS/359 FG   361 FG   374 FS/361 FG   375 FS/361 FG

376 FS/361 FG   383 FS/364 FG   384 FS/364 FG   385 FS/364 FG   479 FG

434 FS/479 FG (1)   434 FS/479 FG (2)   435 FS/479 FG   436 FS/479 FG

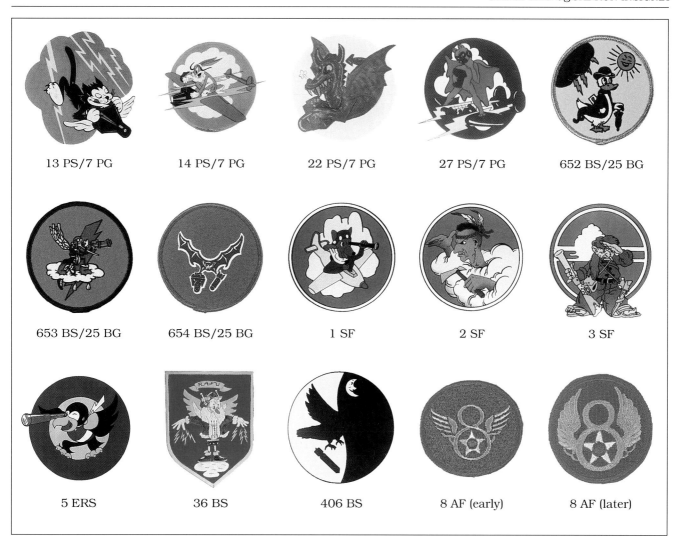

13 PS/7 PG   14 PS/7 PG   22 PS/7 PG   27 PS/7 PG   652 BS/25 BG

653 BS/25 BG   654 BS/25 BG   1 SF   2 SF   3 SF

5 ERS   36 BS   406 BS   8 AF (early)   8 AF (later)

Right: Squadron emblems were often displayed at the entrance to airfield domestic sites. Here Major Byron Trent, CO of the 333rd Bomb Squadron, poses beside a revised version of the unit's insignia near the Orderly Room hut, spring 1945. (Byron Trent)

INDEX